Urban Social Work

An Introduction to Policy and Practice in the Cities

Norma Kolko Phillips

Lehman College
City University of New York

Shulamith Lala Ashenberg Straussner

Ehrekranz School of Social Work
New York University

Allyn and Bacon

Boston • London • Toronto • Sydney • Tokyo • Singapore

Editor in Chief: *Karen Hanson*
Series Editor: *Patricia Quinlin*
Editorial Assistant: *Annemarie Kennedy*
Senior Marketing Manager: *Brad Parkins*
Editorial Production Administrator: *Bryan Woodhouse*
Editorial-Production Service: *Chestnut Hill Enterprises*
Composition and Prepress Buyer: *Linda Cox*
Manufacturing Buyer: *Suzanne Lareau*
Cover Administrator: *Kristina Mose-Libon*
Electronic Composition: *Publishers' Design and Production Services, Inc.*

Copyright © 2002 by Allyn and Bacon
A Pearson Education Company
75 Arlington Street
Boston, MA 02116

Internet: www.ablongman.com

Between the time Website information is gathered and then published, it is not unusual for some sites to have closed. Also, the transcription of URLs can result in unintended typographical errors. The publisher would appreciate notification where these occur so that they may be corrected in subsequent editions.

Library of Congress Cataloging-in-Publication Data

Phillips, Norma Kolko.
    Urban social work : an introduction to policy and practice in the cities / Norma Kolko Phillips, Shulamith Lala Ashenberg Straussner
        p.   cm
    Includes bibliographical references and index.
    ISBN 0-205-29019-1
    1. Social service. 2. Sociology, Urban. I. Straussner, Shulamith Lala Ashenberg.
II. Title.
HV40 .P48 2002
361.3′2′091724—dc21

                                                                2001046357

Printed in the United States of America
10 9 8 7 6 5 4 3 2 1   RRD   06 05 04 03 02 01

CONTENTS

PREFACE

The broad scope of social work practice in the cities presents a challenge for social work students and teachers alike. Historically, the social work profession grew out of the problems of the cities, and today, juxtaposed against the enormous wealth that is so evident in urban areas, once again we see an increased concentration of urban poverty and the problems that it brings.

It is puzzling that, in spite of the urban settings where so much of social work practice takes place, social work in the cities has not been the central theme for books that introduce students to the profession. Consequently, some students begin field-work, and later work in urban agencies, without adequate preparation for the kinds of complex situations that they are likely to encounter.

In the effort to better prepare students for social work practice in complex urban settings, we have focused on an understanding of the interrelationships among social problems, social welfare policies, and the delivery of services to clients through social agencies and organizations. To this end, we have revisited the systems perspective, applying it specifically to generalist social work practice. While preserving the basic concepts of the model of micro, mezzo, and macro practice, we have reframed the model in terms of *client, agency, and policy practice* (CAPP). All of the components of this model—client, agency, and policy—are viewed as equally important, thereby avoiding the hierarchy that is implied in micro, mezzo, and macro level systems.

In the CAPP framework, *client practice* includes direct services to, or on behalf of, individuals, families, groups, and also communities. Community work is considered "client practice" when the goal is to meet specific needs of a specific community.

Agency practice includes the social worker's roles within the agency, as well as the development and implementation of services.

Policy practice includes policy analysis, advocacy, and political social work, which encompasses participation in the political system, whether on the level of voting or hold-ing public office. Policy practice can also include community involvement when the goals of community work involve policy changes that affect the broader society. At this point, we move from client to policy practice, and the goal of the work moves from *case to cause*.

It should also be noted that research and evaluation are integrated within client, agency, and policy practice, and are important aspects of the CAPP framework.

This book is divided into three sections. In the first section, students are intro-duced to the profession, to the nature of the cities and urban social problems, and to the functions of social services and the structure of the service delivery system.

The second section focuses on the urban roots of social work and on social work in the cities today. Themes such as the role of government in providing for social ser-vices, eligibility requirements for services, and the nature of services that are available, are viewed as they developed historically and as they impact our social welfare system today. The final chapter in this section serves as a bridge between policy and practice, relating current policies to client situations. Highlighted are issues of poverty, sub-stance abuse, and health care.

The third section is devoted to social work practice in urban settings. Values and ethics, the foundation knowledge—including a chapter on diversity—and the skills needed for client, agency, and policy practice are presented.

Numerous vignettes are used throughout the book to illustrate practice issues. Students are encouraged to think critically, explore their own views, and consider the impact of social, economic and political forces affecting the lives of their clients.

We are very grateful for the support, comments, and suggestions from many people who have provided valuable help along the way, particularly to Professors Graciela Castex, Sharon Freedberg, Richard Holody, Patricia Kolb, and Carl Mazza of the Lehman College Social Work Program; Professors Madeline Moran, Randolph Ortiz, and the late Michael Duffy of the Sociology Program at Lehman College; and to Professors Dina Rosenfeld and Marjorie Rock, the members of the Practice and Human Behavior faculty, and Deans Thomas Meenaghan and Jeane Anastas at the Ehrenkranz School of Social Work, New York University. We appreciate the generosity of spirit and time shown by Professors Susan Voge, Janet Munch, and Eugene Laper of the Lehman College Library, the help from Aly Brennaman and Philip and Sho Kolko in coordinating some of the West Coast photographs, and assistance from Adam Straussner with the graphics and from David Phillips with layout. We also appreciate the support that Judy Fifer, Patricia Quinlin, Annemarie Kennedy, and Bryan Woodhouse at Allyn and Bacon have provided during the process.

That teaching and learning is one and the same process is clearer to us than ever. We know this from our experiences with our students, and also from working together as coauthors. We are of course grateful to our friends, and to our families—Joel, Adam, Sarina, and David—for their support and patience.

Norma Kolko Phillips
S. Lala Ashenberg Straussner
January, 2001

SECTION ONE

Understanding Social Work and Social Services in the Cities

Introduction

This section provides an introduction to the profession of social work, and includes a discussion of social work in the cities and an overview of the structure and functions of social welfare and social services in today's society.

Chapter 1 discusses the broad scope of social work as a profession and the educational requirements to become a social work practitioner. Some of the key features of the profession are introduced, including a brief discussion of systems theory and the application of the client, agency, and policy practice model.

Chapter 2 focuses on the cities, which historically is where the social work profession got its start and where the majority of social workers still practice today. Some of the special requirements for social workers practicing in urban communities are identified, including an understanding of the impact that city life can have on people, a knowledge of particular communities and their unique resources, and a sensitivity to diversity when working with multicultural populations. A summary of the fields of social work practice illustrates the broad range of services that are likely to be available to clients in urban communities.

The complex nature of social welfare, including its roles and functions in society, is discussed in Chapter 3. The nature and provision of social services in both the public and private sectors are described, as well as sources of help for all groups in society, not just for the poor. This chapter also identifies the values and assumptions underlying the various approaches to social welfare and their impact on the daily life of all people in urban communities.

CHAPTER

1 The Profession of Social Work

Social Workers and students demonstrate for reduced child welfare caseloads. National Association of Social Workers, Maryland Chapter, 2000

Most people who are interested in social work as a career have the desire to "help" others and want to be part of a helping profession. Helping people as a professional social worker, however, means more than listening to their problems, developing new programs for the needy, or lobbying for social reform. Becoming a social worker means joining a profession that is over 100 years old and sharing in the profession's knowledge, skills, and values.

This chapter provides an introduction to the profession of social work as it is practiced in urban communities. That is where the full range of social problems and needs have always been evident; that is where the profession got its start and where it continues to thrive today.

As students begin studying about social work and social welfare, it is important that they become familiar with some of the characteristics of social work that make it a unique profession. It is also important that students are knowledgeable about the scope of the course of study required for professional practice, and the various levels of educational preparation that are available. The following topics are addressed in this chapter:

- Definition and purpose of social work
- Characteristics of professions
- Introduction to some of the special aspects of the social work profession
- Three components of social work practice: direct services, development and implementation of programs and services, and social action
- Education for the profession
- Opportunities for employment
- Choosing social work as a career

What Social Workers Do

Social work is a helping profession with a history of responding to a wide range of social problems. Through the years, the profession has responded to human needs by:

- Providing direct services to individuals, families, groups, and communities
- Developing and delivering effective social welfare programs and services in agencies and organizations
- Advocating for social justice and the improvement of social conditions

Social workers provide services to every age group from newborns to the elderly. They help people who experience every kind of social and personal problem such as homelessness, marital problems, child abuse, or job stress. However, the scope of the social work profession goes far beyond providing direct help to an individual or a family, or perhaps a small group or a community. Often less visible, but certainly as important, is the mission of the profession to work toward social justice in the interests of people whose voices are least heard, such as the poor, children who are neglected or abused, or people who are oppressed. Social workers also work as agency administrators and supervisors to ensure the quality of services that are delivered and to develop new social service programs. In addition, social workers work as policy analysts, political lobbyists and advocates, educators, and as social researchers. The range of professional activities that social work professionals are engaged in is illustrated by the following examples:

- Eileen Carter was exhausted after standing in a crowded bus that had been stuck in Boston's Friday afternoon rush-hour traffic. When she got home, her husband flew into a rage, not only because she was late, but also because she had forgotten to bring home his usual six-pack of beer. He threatened to hit her, but instead he stormed out of the apartment, fuming. Scared and worried, Eileen immediately called the emergency number of the social worker at the Employee Assistance Program at her company. Suzanne Davis, the social worker, first listened as Eileen described how her husband hit her once in the past and how, in spite of her fear right now, she still loved him and didn't know what to do. The social worker then went on to support Eileen's right to protect herself and gave her the address of a shelter for abused women. She also suggested that they meet Monday morning in order to discuss what Eileen wants to do and to give her information about other resources in the community that could be helpful, such as Al-Anon, a women's support group, and an intervention program for families of alcohol-dependent individuals.

■ Lydia Olivera, a social worker who directs a large shelter for the homeless in Los Angeles, has been concerned about the inability of many shelter residents to maintain the jobs provided to them by the city's Welfare-to-Work program. She discussed this problem with the social worker at the shelter, Arthur Wu, who offered to develop a job-readiness program for the residents before they began working. He thought this would help prepare them for the jobs they would be doing, and also give them some "people skills" that they would need to get along with their supervisors and co-workers.

■ Representatives of the social work profession in Baltimore were invited to testify during the State Assembly hearings to address the quality of child welfare services in the state of Maryland. They advocated for funding for a bill that had been passed by the state legislature two years earlier. The bill would result in fewer clients for case-workers and for additional funding for new staff. Funding for these changes would "make it possible to properly protect Maryland's neglected and abused children" ("Caseload reduction is sought in Maryland," 2000, p. 5). After their testimony, these social workers joined their colleagues and social work students in a demonstration out-side the statehouse to publicize this issue.

Points to Ponder

During 1999, there were 813,000 social workers employed in the United States (Bureau of Labor Statistics, 2000).

The Purpose of Social Work

The purpose of the social work profession has been clearly described by the National Association of Social Workers (NASW), which, as its name implies, is the professional association for social workers in the United States. According to NASW:

> The primary mission of the social work profession is to enhance human well-being and help meet the basic human needs of all people, with particular attention to the needs and empowerment of people who are vulnerable, oppressed, and living in poverty. A historic and defining feature of social work is the profession's focus on individual well-being in a social context and the well-being of society. Fundamental to social work is attention to the environmental forces that create, contribute to, and address problems in living.
>
> Social workers promote social justice and social change with and on behalf of clients. (The term 'clients' is used inclusively to refer to individuals, families, groups, organizations, and communities. Social workers are sensitive to cultural and ethnic diversity and strive to end discrimination, oppression, poverty, and other forms of social

injustice. These activities may be in the form of direct practice, community organizing, supervision, consultation, administration, advocacy, social and political action, policy development and implementation, education, and research and evaluation. Social workers seek to enhance the capacity of people to address their own needs. Social workers also seek to promote the responsiveness of organizations, communities, and other social institutions to individuals' needs and social problems (NASW, 1996, p.1).

As a profession, social work has a commitment to address social problems such as oppression, poverty, and the full range of human pain and suffering. While not limited to urban areas, social problems are often widespread in cities.

Through the years, the social work profession has moved back and forth between a focus on direct services to clients and social reform. When social workers shift their focus from a particular issue affecting a client to a broad social concern that affects many people, this change is referred to as moving from "case to cause." The need for social workers to work toward social change and greater social justice—to work for a cause—is apparent in urban communities of all sizes.

Points to Ponder

"The importance of social work practice in urban areas has historical, current and future significance. The profession's origins are deeply rooted in urban areas across the United States, and the founders of the profession developed and advanced practice with urban areas as a focus. . . . the future of the profession will rest on how well social work can address urban issues" (Delgado, 2000, p. 6.)

Characteristics of Professions

All professions have a standard that includes a body of knowledge, a range of skills that enable the professional to carry out the mission of that profession, and an ethical or value-based guide for professional actions. We expect all professionals to meet certain standards. For example, we assume that when we go to the dentist, he or she has the *knowledge* needed to work effectively, and knows what to look for to make an accurate diagnosis. We take for granted that the dentist has good *skills*, especially when using the drill or extracting our wisdom tooth. We trust that the dentist conforms to professional *values*—that his or her behavior is ethical, and that he or she has not lied about the need for treatment, or charged for work that was not done. Furthermore, we expect the dentist to respect our privacy—to not turn to the next patient and reveal that we have a lot of cavities because we don't floss. This is the value of *confidentiality* that is shared by all helping professions, including social work.

All professions have standards for professional behavior and educational requirements to prepare for the profession. National professional organizations monitor those standards and promote the values and interests of the profession. Practitioners in various professions also are monitored by, and accountable to, a state regulatory agency through a system of licensing or certification. The issue of licensing and certification of social workers will be discussed later in this chapter.

An Introduction to Some Special Characteristics of the Social Work Profession

Social work, too, is based on a *body of knowledge*, on *skills* that enable social workers to practice effectively, and on *values* that guide professional behavior. These values are reflected in the *Social Work Code of Ethics*, which is formulated by the National Association of Social Workers.

Although the three components of the social work profession—values, knowledge, and skills—will be discussed at length later in this book, it is useful to begin thinking about some of the characteristics that, in combination with each other, contribute to the uniqueness of this profession.

An Interdisciplinary Knowledge Base: The Foundation of Social Work Knowledge

In order to be an effective social worker, the individual needs a broad understanding of human nature and the society in which we live. To prepare students for this work, the social work curriculum is built on a *liberal arts perspective*, and includes content from such disciplines as sociology, psychology, biology, economics, and political science. In addition, an understanding of the knowledge base of the profession requires some background in such fields as history, ethnic and cultural studies, gender studies, cultural and medical anthropology, and the humanities.

Social work education uses accumulated knowledge from these diverse academic disciplines that, taken together, provide the intellectual underpinnings of the profession. For example, by incorporating elements from biology, psychology, and sociology, social workers bring together an interdisciplinary knowledge base that is then integrated into the *biopsychosocial perspective*. This perspective forms the framework for social work assessment that will be discussed in Chapter 9.

Focus on the Client-Worker Relationship: A Key Social Work Skill

Social work is unique among the helping professions because it uses the *relationship* between the social worker and the client as its main tool for helping. Social workers providing direct services do not turn to concrete tools to provide help, as do other helping professions. For example, a social worker does not write prescriptions for medicine as a psychiatrist might; a social worker does not take temperatures as a nurse might; nor does a social worker evaluate psychological tests as a psychologist might. Rather, the social worker uses his or her skills to build a *professional relationship* with the client. It is within the context of this relationship that the social worker provides help, identifying and building on the strengths of people and communities.

The widely diverse nature of urban populations, which represent many different lifestyles and values, as well as racial, ethnic, cultural, and religious identities, requires that social workers be open to learning about their clients and that they respond sensitively to their unique needs. In addition, they need to be able to recognize and encourage their clients' aspirations and their strengths that can help them to achieve their goals. This is referred to as the *strengths perspective*.

Points to Ponder

According to Saleebey (1997), "To really practice from a strengths perspective demands a different way of seeing clients, their environments, and their current situation. Rather than focusing on problems . . . mobilize clients' strengths (talents, knowledge, capacities, resources) in the service of achieving their goals and visions . . ." (pp. 3–4).

Emphasis on Client Self-Determination: A Basic Social Work Value

Another important characteristic of the social work profession is its emphasis on *client self-determination*. This characteristic is particularly important when we think about how we "help" people. Students sometimes think about help as giving advice or telling someone how to act. However, we all know how easy it is to give advice. We also know that such well-meaning advice, whether from family members or friends, is not always useful. Many times people close to us cannot be objective in their understanding of our needs and feelings, particularly when they have a vested interest in how we feel and act. Generally, by the time people seek the help of a social worker, they already have received advice and guidance from family members or peers; advice that they did not find to be particularly helpful or adequate.

Social work practice is based on the recognition that each person is an individual who has his or her own values and needs, and is built on respect for the uniqueness of each individual. Rather than imposing their own values and goals on their clients, social workers help their clients figure out what the *clients'* goals are, and how these goals can be accomplished. It is a core social work principle that clients are helped to take actions based on *the client's own value system and life goals*, and not the social worker's. For example, a social worker working with a pregnant woman who is considering an abortion may have a deep religious belief that abortion is a "sin"; a belief that conflicts with those held by the client. This challenge to client self-determination can also be seen in the case of Eileen Carter, which was discussed earlier. Although personally Suzanne Davis thought that Eileen would be better off if she left her husband, in her role as a professional she could not impose her values on the client. Social workers must support a client's self-determination as long as that client is not actively endangering him- or herself or planning to hurt another person.

In order to carry out the mandate of client self-determination, the social worker must develop *self-awareness*. It is only through such self-awareness that the worker is able to separate his or her personal values from professional values. Only by becoming aware of the conflict between their personal and professional values and separating them from their professional responses are social workers able to be effective in helping their clients. Learning about the values that form the foundation of the social work profession, developing self-awareness, gaining professional knowledge, and developing practice skills are processes that continue long after one has received a social work degree. These will be discussed in greater detail in later chapters.

Systems Theory and Its Application to Social Work

Systems theory, part of the knowledge base for social work practice, focuses our attention on the interrelatedness of clients, the environment, and society. Brill (1998) defines a system as "a whole made up of interrelated and interdependent parts. The parts exist in a state of balance, and when change takes place within one, there is compensatory change within the others" (p. 63). The three different levels of systems are referred to as the micro (small), mezzo (medium), and macro (large) systems, all of which interact with each other.

The approach to systems theory described in this book focuses on:

- *Client practice* (micro level)
- *Agency practice* (mezzo level)
- *Policy practice* (macro level)

While this framework supports the core concepts of systems theory, it specifically applies them to social work practice.

Three Components of Social Work: Client, Agency, and Policy Practice

Throughout its history in the United States, the practice of social work has included work with clients, work in organizations or social service agencies, and work on policy issues relating to social welfare. These three components of social work practice—client, agency, and policy—can be viewed from the perspective of systems theory.

- *Client practice*, also known as micro system intervention, refers to the provision of direct services to, or on behalf of, clients, including services to individuals, families, groups, and communities.
- *Agency practice*, also referred to as mezzo system intervention, includes the development and implementation of programs and services, as well as supervision and administration of social agencies.

■ *Policy practice*, or macro level intervention, refers to policy analysis and advocacy for just social welfare policies.

Client Practice: Providing Direct Services to, or on Behalf of, Individuals, Couples, Families, Groups, and Communities

Client practice includes all direct services that are provided to, or on behalf of, clients. As previously noted, the National Association of Social Workers includes in its definition of "clients" not only individuals and families, but also groups and communities. Examples of client services might include counseling a young woman in Santa Fe who was recently diagnosed with breast cancer, helping a couple in Seattle adopt a child, organizing a trip to a free concert in the park for a group of isolated older adults in New York City, or helping a group of tenants in Washington, DC establish a safety patrol.

When working in the cities, social workers work with clients from many different cultures. In order to be effective in helping diverse groups of people living in the cities address the issues and problems that they face, social workers must gain an understanding of the relationship between peoples' behavior and the environments in which they live and work. They need to have an understanding of their clients' values, which may be related to their ethnic cultures, and develop good practice skills. In addition, social workers need to become knowledgeable about the wide array of services and resources that can be used to help their clients achieve their goals.

Agency Practice: Developing and Implementing Programs and Services within Social Service Agencies and Organizations

Social work agencies and institutions reflect the mission and standards of the social work profession and serve as vehicles for the delivery of direct services to people. It is within these agencies that social service programs are implemented or carried out. It is the nature of the implementation of programs in agencies that ultimately determines *how* social services are to be offered (Chambers & Stadum, 1991).

All social workers employed by agencies and organizations, as well as social work students in field placements, are involved in agency practice. It is therefore important that all social workers become familiar with their role in the agency setting and with the roles and responsibilities of other staff members. Agency practice may include program administration, supervision, program evaluation, development of program policies and services, fund-raising, grant writing, public relations, and networking with professionals in other institutions and with public officials. In order to successfully perform their functions as supervisors and administrators, social workers must also be knowledgeable about the requirements of numerous regulatory and funding organizations, and about the bureaucratic nature of the many large organizations typically found in cities. In addition, they need to acquire the special skills necessary to affect change within such organizations.

Many social workers practice in institutions such as hospitals or schools whose main function is not the provision of social services. These institutions serve as *host* agencies for social work. In many host agencies, social workers work along with other professionals as part of a team that provides a variety of professional services to people.

Points to Ponder

Over 70 percent of social workers who are members of NASW work with clients in direct service. Close to 16 percent work in administration, over five percent are supervisors, and four percent are teachers (Gibelman & Schervish, 1997).

Policy Practice: Influencing Social Welfare Policies

Most social workers participate in activities related to policy practice at least some of the time. While the job of some social workers is to analyze the impact of current social welfare policies on all governmental levels, many social workers are active participants in the political change process. Social work professional organizations, social service agencies, individual social workers, and community groups use social action techniques, such as advocacy and lobbying, in order to influence social welfare policies, as was seen in the activities of the social workers in Baltimore described previously. Social workers work as coalition builders, coordinating the efforts of various groups and agencies to advocate for a particular cause that has an impact on the broad society. As noted earlier in this chapter, when the goal of social work intervention shifts from direct practice aimed at the concerns of a particular client, such as a family or a community, to policy concerns impacting the broader society, this shift is called moving from *case to cause*.

Policy practice requires knowledge of policy analysis, policy development, and policy advocacy, which may include social action. Social workers also may need to use legal advocacy to help protect or establish specific legal rights for clients and for the profession.

Social workers often help to mobilize their clients to become involved in the political arena. In addition, social workers have many opportunities to become politically active in urban communities; in fact, more and more social workers choose to run for political office.

Points to Ponder

In 1999, four social workers were members of the United States Congress. Following the 2000 election, this number increased to six, with two social workers in the Senate and four in the House of Representatives (O'Neill, 1999; <www.naswdc.org> accessed December 8, 2000).

The Interrelatedness of Client, Agency, and Policy Practice

Social workers are often involved with client, agency, and policy practice simultaneously. For example, Bill Rivera, a social worker on a pediatric unit in a large city hospital, is providing social work services to families with terminally ill children. In planning to start a family support group, he found that only a few of the parents were able to attend such a group during the week. Based on his conversations with many parents, he concluded that if this kind of a group were to be scheduled on the weekend, many more families would attend. Therefore, as part of his agency practice, he is advocating with the hospital administration to expand its program and establish a weekend family support group. In addition, Bill Rivera is also active in policy practice. Through his work with the families of ill children at the hospital, he has become aware that many of the families lack medical insurance, thereby limiting their ability to obtain the help they need. He has joined with his colleagues at the local chapter of the National Association of Social Workers to establish a coalition of health and social service organizations to advocate for health-care reform.

In order to recognize unmet needs in communities and work effectively toward creating and maximizing services, it is important that social workers have a thorough understanding of how client, agency, and policy practice are interrelated. The knowledge, skills, and values needed for client, agency, and policy practice will be discussed in greater detail in later chapters.

Points to Ponder

No matter what the values or intentions of a social welfare policy are (macro level), and how carefully an agency administers the program (mezzo level), the real impact of the service rests with the social worker who is working with the client (micro level). Popple and Leighninger (2001) give the following example: "If Congress passes a law stating that individuals are entitled to a certain benefit (macrolevel policy) and state and local agencies develop regulations and procedures for delivering the benefit (mezzolevel policy) but the social workers charged with delivering the benefit do not support the policy and so obstruct the process such that few people actually receive the benefit, what actually is the policy? The policy is that people do not get the benefit" (p. 32).

Education for the Profession

To fully understand what is involved in preparing for the social work profession, it is important to appreciate the comprehensive nature of the education needed to obtain a degree in social work.

Points to Ponder

In 1997, 12,949 students graduated with a baccalaureate degree in Social Work, and 15,058 received an MSW degree. During 1998, there were 42,443 baccalaureate students and 23,759 master's degree students attending schools of social work in the United States (Beaucar, 1999; Statistics from the Division of Standards and Accreditation, 1999).

Baccalaureate and Master's Social Work Programs

Some students decide to pursue a career in social work while they are undergraduates and select social work as their major. These baccalaureate students earn either a Bachelor of Arts (BA) with a major in social work, a Bachelor of Science (BS) with a major in social work, or a Bachelor of Social Work (BSW) degree. All these baccalaureate degrees are considered to be equivalent in terms of employment or admission to graduate school.

The baccalaureate degree with a major in social work from a social work program accredited by the Council on Social Work Education (CSWE) is recognized by both NASW and CSWE as the requirement for entry-level professional practice. Students who have earned their bachelor's degree in social work may decide to work in a social service agency, or go on to study for a master's degree in social work (MSW).

Unlike many other graduate programs that require an undergraduate degree in the same discipline, it is not necessary to have an undergraduate major in social work in order to apply to an MSW program. Many people make the decision to study social work after they have completed a bachelor's degree in another field. It is also not unusual for individuals to work for years in a variety of other fields before deciding to go back to school to study social work.

The MSW is required for some social work agency jobs and, in combination with other requirements that vary from state to state, is also essential in order to work as an independent practitioner providing clinical services. The typical master's level program takes two years of full-time study. However, many graduate schools offer part-time options, some of which allow students to take up to five years to complete the program.

Points to Ponder

As of 1999, there were 417 baccalaureate programs in social work and 131 MSW programs in the United States and Puerto Rico that were fully accredited by the Council on Social Work Education. An additional 33 baccalaureate and 20 MSW programs were preparing for accreditation (Lennon, 1999).

The Social Work Curriculum

The Council on Social Work Education (1997a,b) requires that the social work curriculum in both baccalaureate and master's level programs include content in the following:

- Social work values and ethics
- Human diversity
- Social and economic justice
- Populations at risk
- Human behavior and the social environment
- Social welfare policy and services
- Social work practice
- Social research
- Fieldwork practicum

Baccalaureate social work programs provide the professional foundation necessary for entry-level generalist social work practice. Education for generalist practice prepares students for client, agency, and policy practice (micro, mezzo, and macro level social work practice). A typical master's level program provides both a first year generalist foundation and a second year specialization. Education for specialization provides students with the extensive knowledge needed to work in a particular practice area, such as working with older adults, abused children, crime victims, agency administration, political advocacy, research, and in many others fields of practice such as those listed at the end of Chapter 2.

Points to Ponder

The Council on Social Work Education has described the differences between education for the BSW and for the MSW:

"The baccalaureate level prepares students for generalist social work practice, and the master's level prepares students for advanced social work practice in an area of concentration. These levels of education differ from each other in the depth, breadth, and specificity of knowledge and skill that students are expected to synthesize and apply in practice.

Both levels of social work education must provide professional foundation curriculum that contains the common body of the profession's knowledge, values, and skill. This common base is transferable among settings, population groups, and problem areas" (CSWE, 1997a).

Fieldwork

In addition to classroom study, students in both baccalaureate and master's degree social work programs learn through fieldwork, which is an internship in a social agency or organization. Fieldwork in urban communities is designed to provide social work students with the opportunity to address challenging social issues through client, agency, and policy practice (at the micro, mezzo, and macro levels). The internship is supervised by a fieldwork instructor who has an MSW degree, experience working as a social worker, and special preparation to supervise students. Fieldwork provides the student with:

- Carefully supervised hands-on experience with clients
- The opportunity to learn the workings of social service agencies
- Experience working within communities
- Familiarity with social welfare policies as they impact the social worker's day-to-day practice with clients
- Knowledge about the processes of policy formulation and change

The minimum requirement for fieldwork is 400 hours for baccalaureate students and 900 hours for master's-level students. However, many programs establish more extensive requirements. A typical undergraduate social work program includes two full days a week in a social agency for one year, while a typical graduate program includes three full days of fieldwork for two years. Some schools offer special programs that make it possible for students who are already employed in a social work agency to do their internships there.

The MSW with Advanced Standing

Graduates of baccalaureate social work programs that are accredited by the Council on Social Work Education may apply to a master's program for advanced standing and may receive up to one year of credit toward their MSW. Baccalaureate social work programs prepare students as generalist social workers, and most MSW programs devote their first year to teaching generalist social work, with the second year focused on a specialization. Advanced standing takes into account that the first year of the MSW is similar to the baccalaureate curriculum.

Not all MSW programs offer advanced standing, and not all graduates of baccalaureate programs are granted advanced standing. Decisions regarding the inclusion of advanced standing and the criteria for admission of students with advanced standing are determined by each graduate program. The Council on Social Work Education has established a five-year limit after receiving the bachelor's degree in Social Work for students to be granted advanced standing in an MSW program.

Post-Master's Programs for Social Workers

Although the MSW is considered the terminal degree for professional practice, a growing number of social workers continue their education in a variety of post-master's programs. These programs address specific areas of practice, such as administration, supervision, gerontology, or substance abuse treatment. Other social workers return to study for a doctorate in social work, earning either a DSW (Doctor of Social Welfare) or a Ph.D. (Doctor of Philosophy) degree. While the education for both doctoral degrees is usually the same, it is up to a university or a state regulatory agency to decide which degree is offered. A doctoral degree is useful for college teaching, research, and policy analysis, as well as high-level administration and practice positions.

Points to Ponder

In 1998, there were 2,102 students enrolled in doctoral programs in Social Work in the United States. However, only 286 social workers received doctoral degrees the previous year (Beaucar, 1999; Lennon, 1999).

Professional Credentials: Certification and Licensing

Most states offer certification or licensing for social workers, although the type of credential varies from state to state. Credentials serve to ensure that people identifying themselves as social workers have met state requirements in education, experience, and supervision. Credentialing provides protection for the public, who are consumers of services. Credentials are particularly important for social work because historically the term "social worker" has been used by many people who have not had the benefit of education for the profession.

NASW also offers its members opportunities for several credentials. The most commonly held credential is membership in the Academy of Certified Social Workers (ACSW), which is available to members of NASW who have (1) the MSW degree from a program that is accredited by the Council on Social Work Education, (2) two years of supervised post-master's experience, and (3) passed a written exam. NASW certification of baccalaureate social workers through the Academy of Certified Baccalaureate Social Workers (ACBSW) was started in 1991. However, only a small number of baccalaureate social workers sought this certification and it was terminated in 1995.

Professional Organizations

Professional organizations serve the functions of establishing standards of professional behavior and monitoring its members' compliance to those standards. In addition, such organizations promote the values and interests of the profession, and provide forums for the collegial exchange of ideas and for networking.

The major professional organization for social workers is the National Association of Social Workers. This organization was formed in 1955 when several organizations representing specific fields of practice merged with the American Association of Social Workers to form one inclusive organization to represent the values and interests of the profession. Today, in addition to the national organization in Washington, DC, each state has one or more local NASW chapters.

Points to Ponder

NASW has 155,000 members in 54 chapters in all 50 states, Puerto Rico, and the Virgin Islands, plus an International chapter <www.naswcd.org>.

One of the most important activities of NASW is the formulation of the Code of Ethics, which serves as the reference point for professional behavior. NASW also publishes several journals, including *Social Work*, and a monthly newsletter. In addition, it publishes professional books and maintains a library holding materials related to the history of the profession. Local NASW chapters publish their own newsletters that include local job listings and educational opportunities, as well as local news related to the profession. Annual conferences and other educational programs are held by the various chapters, as well as the national organization, to encourage sharing of new knowledge among members. Further, NASW participates in political advocacy to promote legislation representing the values and goals of the profession. Recently, NASW has established "Specialty Sections" for social workers with special interests, including Aging; Alcohol, Tobacco, and other Drugs; Private Practice; and School Social Work. These sections serve as a vehicle for connecting social workers with similar interests throughout the country.

While NASW attempts to respond to the interests of all social workers, there are numerous other social work organizations that are directed toward special interest groups and groups based on ethnic identification. Among the various organizations are: the Association for the Advancement of Social Work with Groups, the Society of Clinical Social Workers, the National Association of Black Social Workers, the Association for Women in Social Work, the Social Welfare Action Alliance (formerly known as the Bertha Reynolds Society), the Social Work History Group, and the National Network for Social Work Managers. Some of these groups also publish journals and newsletters, and have Internet list-serves and chat rooms. In addition, many social workers become members of other professional organizations, such as the American Public Health Association, the American Public Welfare Association, the Employee Assistance Professionals Association, the Gerontological Society of America, and the American Orthopsychiatric Association.

Opportunities for Employment

The range of job opportunities for social workers is especially broad in the cities. There are many job opportunities for baccalaureate social workers in fields such as child welfare, gerontology, health care, substance abuse treatment, and homelessness. These jobs may be with public agencies or in agencies in the private sector. Social workers with a master's degree generally have a wider range of employment options with greater opportunities for advancement and higher salaries.

Choosing Social Work as a Career

Whether holding a baccalaureate, master's, or doctorate in social work, most social workers find this profession intellectually engaging and emotionally enriching, particularly when working in the stimulating urban environment. Moreover, many students who decide to pursue other career paths find that the skills learned through social work education can be carried over to other professions. These skills include:

- Increased self-awareness
- Interviewing skills and communication
- Skills in assessment of, and intervention with, individuals, families, groups, and communities
- Skills in assessment of organizational dynamics and in affecting organizational change
- Understanding the profound economic and political impact on society and on individuals
- Skills in social action and social change
- Social research skills

Conclusion

Individuals select a career for a variety of reasons, including personal values, life experiences, skills, and interests. For some, the career path toward social work is clear from an early age; others arrive at it after pursuing other vocational interests or having certain life experiences. How each person arrives at the decision to study social work reflects the personal story of that individual.

Regardless of how an individual arrives at the decision to explore social work, it is important that all students understand the characteristics of the social work profession and the scope of the educational requirements for professional practice. These will help students recognize both the opportunities and limitations of the profession and begin to assess the "match" of the profession to their own career goals.

Those social workers who choose to practice in the cities can find many opportunities for rewarding professional experiences. They will work with clients representing many cultures and lifestyles, and will confront a wide range of social problems and numerous sources of help. The next chapter will examine some of the social problems of the cities, the social services and programs that have developed in response to the needs of urban communities, and the complex network of social services organized into fields of practice.

REFERENCES

Beaucar, K. O. (1999, July). Class of '99 graduates into 21st century. *NASW News, 44*(7), 5.

Brill, N. I. (1998). *Working with people: The helping process* (6th ed.). New York: Longman.

Caseload reduction is sought in Maryland. (2000, April). NASW *News, 45*(4), 5.

Chambers, C. A. & Stadum, B. (1991). An exploration of new themes in the study of American philanthropy arising from archival research. *Essays on philanthropy, 3*. Indianapolis, IN: Indiana. University Center on Philanthropy.

Council on Social Work Education. (1997a). Curriculum Policy Statement for baccalaureate degree programs in social work education, Section B5.2. Section B.50, Purpose and structure of baccalaureate social work education.

Council on Social Work Education. (1997b). Curriculum Policy Statement for Master's degree programs in social work education, Section M6.0.

Delgado, M. (2000). *Community social work practice in an urban context*. New York: Oxford University Press.

Gibelman, M. & Schervish, P. H. (1997). *Who we are: A second look*. Washington, DC: NASW Press.

Lennon, T. (1999). *Statistics of social work education: 1998*. Alexandria, VA: Council on Social Work Education.

National Association of Social Workers. (1996). *Code of ethics*. Washington, DC: Author.

O'Neill, J. V. (1999, July). The Capitol in their sight. *NASW News, 44*(7), 1.

Popple, P. R. & Leighninger, L. (2001). *The policy-based profession: An introduction to social welfare policy analysis for social workers*. Needham Heights, MA: Allyn and Bacon.

Statistics from the Division of Standards and Accreditation. (1999, Fall). *Social Work Education Reporter*.

2 Human Behavior in the Urban Environment— The Response of Social Work

Remembering and grieving a friend in New York City, 1999. Photo by Norma Phillips

The diversity of populations in the cities, the broad range of social problems frequently found there, and the scope of resources that may be available in some cities, all contribute to make working in urban communities particularly interesting and personally rewarding. At the same time, the many types of social problems and their severity can pose immense challenges to social workers practicing in the cities.

In order to assist their clients, social workers need to have an understanding of the complexities of urban environments. They need to be sensitive to the situations commonly found in the cities and to be knowledgeable about the nature of urban life and the range of impact that the urban environment can have on people. Social workers need to be able to work with clients from many different cultures, be able to recognize their strengths, and help them to mobilize these strengths in the interest of fulfilling their life goals. Social workers also need to be aware of the different services that can be helpful to their clients, be able to identify which services are unavailable, and advocate for a more responsive social welfare system.

This chapter discusses:

- Changes in urban populations
- A psychosocial approach to understanding urban communities
- The pervasiveness and high visibility of urban social problems
- Social work practice in the cities
- The fields of social work practice commonly found in urban areas

Changes in Urban Populations

As more people choose to live in urban areas, more and more parts of the United States are becoming urbanized. For example, the western part of the United States, which historically had been known for its "wide open spaces," has become the most urbanized region of the country, with 86 percent of its population living in the cities (Egan, 1996).

In the United States as a whole, the percentage of the population living in urban areas almost doubled between 1900 and 1990, as seen in the following chart:

Change in Urban Population in the U.S.

Year	Percentage of Population Living in Urban Areas
1900	39.6
1930	56.1
1960	69.9
1990	75.2

(U.S. Census Bureau, 1995)

The trend toward urbanization has affected the entire country, and as of 1990, only four states had less than 50 percent of their population living in urban areas. These were: Mississippi, 47 percent; Maine, 45 percent; West Virginia, 36 percent; and Vermont, 32 percent. The highest percentages of residents living in urban areas are found in: Washington, DC, which is 100 percent urban, California, which is 93 percent urban, New Jersey and Hawaii, both of which have 89 percent of their residents living in urban communities, and Nevada, which is 88 percent urban (U.S. Census Bureau, 1998).

The growth of urban populations is happening not just in the United States, but is a worldwide phenomenon. In fact, the increase in the number of cities in the developing countries is even greater than in the U.S. (United Nations Children's Fund, 1996). It is estimated that by the year 2007, for the first time, over half of the world's population will be living in urban areas (Palen, 1997).

Points to Ponder

Urban residents include groups that are not traditionally associated with city life. For example, over 70 percent of the 1.9 million Native Americans live in urban settings today. This came about largely as the result of Relocation Act initiated in the mid-1950s. However, unlike some other migrant groups, Native Americans tend to be scattered in the cities, and therefore may not have the social supports or the political power that can develop when population groups cluster together (Marden, Meyer & Engel, 1992; Walters, 1999).

A Psychosocial Approach to Understanding Urban Communities

Urban communities are defined differently by different disciplines, and are viewed according to the interests of each discipline. For example:

■ Demographers look at communities by the size of their population. According to this model, an "urban area" is defined as comprising a central place which, together with its adjacent densely settled surroundings, contains a population of at least 50,000 people (U.S. Census Bureau, 1995).

■ Sociologists view urban communities from the perspective of their impact on social dynamics such as geographical segregation, social isolation, and marginalization of particular groups.

■ Cultural anthropologists are interested in describing and understanding urban culture.

■ Economists look at income, productivity, and job opportunities in urban areas as compared to nonurban areas.

■ Mental health professionals such as social workers, psychologists, and psychiatrists focus on the dynamic relationship between the urban environment and its residents. They consider the social and psychological functioning of people and the impact of people on their environment. They also are concerned with services that are, or need to be, available to meet the social and emotional needs of urban residents.

According to Marsella (1998), urbanization is both a *process* and a *product* that includes parameters related to:

Population, such as location, age, gender, race, social class, migratory status, distribution of population groups, and residential mobility

Economy, such as the kinds of industries that exist, productivity, wage levels, and transportation systems

Environment, such as density and noise levels, rates of air and water pollution, natural resources, and location

Culture and psychosocial lifestyle, including the quality of life, health and social pathologies, and values

Political situation, such as distribution of power, corruption, and social justice (p. 625).

In summary, "urbanization ultimately represents a convergence of specific population, environmental, economic, cultural, and political forces with their psychosocial consequences" (Marsella, 1998, p. 625). Although this definition includes some aspects of urbanization that will remain outside the focus of this book, it integrates the various perspectives on urban life and points out the psychosocial issues that are relevant to social work practice, as discussed below.

The Impact of City Life

Philosophers and social scientists throughout the centuries have wondered about and studied the impact of city life on people. Plato considered urban life to be malevolent, and 18th and 19th century philosophers "associated cities with decay, depravity and distress" (Marsella, 1998, p. 624). Yet, urban life can provide numerous opportunities, including "seemingly endless options for money, opportunity, freedom, excitement, diversity, intellectual stimulation, improved public utilities and services, transportation facilities, accessibility to health care services, and multiculturalism" (Marsella, 1998, p. 624).

Much of the discussion concerning urban communities has focused on the consequences of city size, density, and diversity for people living in urban areas. Sociologists from Georg Simmel (1905/1969), to Robert Ezra Park (1916), and Louis Wirth (1938), representing the *determinist* theory of the cities, identified largely negative social and psychological effects of urban life. For example, Simmel (1905) suggested, "The psychological basis of the metropolitan type of individuality consists in the intensification of nervous stimulation which results from the swift and uninterrupted change of inner and outer stimuli" (quoted in Fischer, 1984, p. 28). This phenomenon was later described by Stanley Milgram (1970) as "psychic overload," resulting from what some people experience as an onslaught of sensory stimuli in the cities, including "sights, sounds, smells, actions of others, their demand and interferences" (Fischer, 1984, p. 29).

Louis Wirth (1938) furthered Simmel's thinking in his writings on alienation and urban stress. Wirth suggested that the *size*, *density*, and *heterogeneous* nature of the cities requires adaptations that may result in interpersonal estrangement, social isolation, and lack of social supports, which may contribute to physical and mental illness.

From the perspective of social structure, Wirth saw that the size, density, and heterogeneity of the cities resulted in the development of numerous different neighborhoods, each representing different lifestyles with different values and beliefs. The fragmentation in peoples' lives, as they may work, live, study, and socialize in different neighborhoods, leads to a loosening of relationships and to increased "anomie," which Fischer (1984), drawing on the work of Max Weber, defines as "a social condition in which the norms—the rules and conventions of proper and permissible behavior—are feeble. Because people do not agree about the norms, they tend to challenge or ignore them" (p. 31). Consequently, in order to maintain social order, bureaucratic rules and procedures, such as those involving police interventions, are established, while social intimacy is diminished.

Other sociologists, representing the *compositional* theory of the cities, maintain that since urbanites live the majority of everyday life in a particular location, the features of the large urban environment do not necessarily impact negatively on their personality or social organization. Rather, the city is seen as a "mosaic of social worlds" composed of "intimate social circles based on kinship, ethnicity, neighborhood, occupation, lifestyle, or similar social attributes" (Fischer, 1984, p. 32). These separate social worlds, also referred to as urban "enclaves" (Abrahamson, 1996), offer cohesiveness and protection to their members. While the size of urban communities has limited impact on the individual, what is important is the richness of opportunities they may offer, for example, in employment or education. Likewise, the type of employment or educational opportunities found in urban communities will have an influence on the composition of their population, impacting characteristics such as age, gender, educational levels, and income levels of their residents.

Fischer (1975) offered yet another theory, the *subcultural* theory, which attempts to synthesize some of the themes of the determinist and compositional theories. He sees the impact of population density on urbanites in a more positive light, and suggests that rather than destroying social groups, urbanism strengthens groups by offering people opportunities to form specialized subgroups, which represent various identities and individualized interests. Additionally, large cities produce new subcultures: "Urbanism has unique consequences, including the production of 'deviance,' not because it destroys social worlds—as determinism argues—but because it creates them" (Fischer, 1984, p. 36).

Although these theorists approach the experience of urban life from different perspectives, they all acknowledge that cities present complex patterns of social living. For many urban residents, the stimulation and diversity of the cities present rich opportunities for intellectual, social, and emotional growth. For others, the same stimulation and diversity are experienced as highly stressful, leading to both personal problems and problems for the society. It is not surprising, then, that historically it was in the cities that many social problems first became widely apparent, and that this is where efforts were made to find ways of responding to them.

Factors Contributing to the Pervasiveness and High Visibility of Social Problems in Urban Areas

The topic of social problems of the cities is a highly complex one, and numerous theories related to their causes and ways of solving them have been suggested. The discussion that follows attempts to highlight just a few of the circumstances that can contribute to urban social problems (Phillips, 1997). These dynamics need to be considered by social workers practicing in the cities. They include:

- The high frequency of occurrence of social problems in urban areas
- Widespread discrimination and institutional oppression
- Migration of people unprepared for urban life
- Inadequate resources to address social problems
- High levels of social and psychological stress

First, though, it is important to caution against stereotyping cities as the seat of all social problems. It must be recognized that similar issues exist in all settings, not just urban communities. While each setting has its own characteristics, and the scope, visibility, and the impact of social problems may differ, no community today is immune from them (Phillips, 1997).

The High Frequency of Occurrence of Social Problems

Problems such as poverty, discrimination, overcrowded housing, crime and violence, homelessness, high rates of school dropouts, substance abuse, and HIV/AIDS, exist in communities of all sizes. However, they occur with greater frequency and therefore are more visible in the cities. For example, foster care for children is most frequently seen in the cities. "In New York State . . . two-thirds of the children in care are from New York City, though the city is home to less than half of the state's residents" (Holody, 1997, p. 135).

Points to Ponder

Poverty in the U.S. has become an increasingly urban problem. While half of the poor in the U.S. lived in rural areas in the 1960s, today this number has been reduced to 22 percent. In contrast, almost twice as many, 43 percent, of the poor live in the cities (*Out of Sight, Out of Mind*, 2000).

Social problems are most visible in "inner-city" areas—those parts of the cities that were historically referred to as urban ghettos and which are characterized by "overcrowded and deteriorated housing, high infant mortality, crime, and disease" (Clark, 1989, p. 11).

When social problems occur with such frequency that they affect many people within a particular neighborhood, they tend to have a demoralizing impact on the entire community. For example, a decrease in employment opportunities in inner-city areas can lead to the deterioration and demoralization of neighborhoods. In a study of the rates of employment among black men in three inner-city neighborhoods in Chicago between 1950 to 1990, William Julius Wilson, Professor of Social Policy at Harvard University, found that 69 percent of black men over the age of 14 were working in 1950, and that just a slightly smaller proportion, 64 percent, were employed in 1960. However, by 1990, only 37 percent of men 16 years old and over living in the same communities were employed during a typical week. Wilson (1998) points out that, "The disappearance of work has had devastating effects not only on individuals and families, but on the social life of neighborhoods as well . . . (such as) crime, family dissolution, welfare, low levels of social organization . . ." (pp. 89–90). The loss of a middle class presence in inner city areas has also meant that there is little to counterbalance the demoralizing effects of social problems, such as joblessness, on the community (Wilson, 1987). In fact, it has been hypothesized that communities develop a greater tolerance for deviant behavior when there is an absence of role models for prosocial behavior (Black & Krishnakumar, 1998).

Other problems that are more visible in the cities are crime and violence. These problems are highly visible not only because of their frequency, but also because of the attention they draw from the media. Although people in the largest cities are almost three times as vulnerable to crime as people in rural areas (U.S. Department of Justice, 1996), the focus of so much attention on urban violence serves not only to warn, but also to exacerbate peoples' fears. This fear leads some people to "perceive the need to carry weapons for self-protection, thereby increasing the likelihood of their becoming involved in further violence as either victims or perpetrators" (Straussner & Straussner, 1997, p. 63).

Widespread Discrimination and Institutional Oppression

Discriminatory behavior is particularly common in the cities because of the heterogeneous nature of their populations. Many groups of people are targets of discrimination, whether based on race, ethnicity, culture, age, gender, religion, sexual orientation, disability, poverty, or language spoken. While historically various immigrant groups such as the Irish, the Jews, the Italians, the Chinese, and the Japanese have experienced discrimination in the United States, the most persistent discrimination today is experienced by Native Americans; blacks, including African-Americans, people from the Caribbean, and people from Africa; Latinos; Asians; and people of Middle Eastern backgrounds. Hate crimes, such as gay bashing and assaults that are driven by perceived differences in race, religion, ethnicity, and culture, are all too common in urban areas.

Points to Ponder

Hate crimes are aimed at numerous population groups. For example, an incident in Chicago on Independence Day in 1999 included an attack on three different groups: "A white gunman cruised the streets of Chicago . . . shooting from a car at a dozen people, all of them black, Jewish, or Asian. An African-American man, a former basketball coach at Northwestern University, was killed, and six Orthodox Jews walking home from Sabbath prayers were injured . . . The shooting began . . . in Rogers Park . . . known as one of the most racially diverse neighborhoods in the country . . ." ("Former Coach Shot . . . ," 1999, p. 12).

Another form of discrimination can be seen in urban public schools. Since the exodus of the middle class from the cities to the suburbs began in the 1940s, fewer middle-income children have been left in the urban public school system. With the loss of children from this economic group, and with children from many upper income families going to private schools, the public school systems in the cities have become largely economically segregated (Black & Krishnakumar, 1998), resulting in *de facto* racial segregation.

In addition, many urban schools are underfunded. The consequences of this are vividly pointed out by the Children's Defense Fund (1999): "Is it fair that poor children in the poorest neighborhoods have the poorest schools, the poorest prepared teachers, the poorest equipment, the poorest school buildings, libraries, and laboratories, the fewest computers, counselors, school nurses, and enrichment programs, and the lowest expectations by teachers and a public that blame them for achieving poorly on the tests for which we have not prepared them? Philadelphia's public school children receive $45,000 less a classroom than children in the surrounding suburban school districts" (p. xiii).

Points to Ponder

Jonathan Kozol, in his groundbreaking book, *Savage Inequalities* (1991), documents the extent and effects of racial segregation and underfunding on urban public schools. Based on 1989 figures, he found that on average, only $5,265 was spent for each child educated in a Chicago high school, compared to $9,371 spent for each child in the well-to-do Chicago suburbs.

Migration of People Unprepared for Urban Life

With their promise of freedom and opportunity, the cities have always been magnets for both the adventurous and the desperate. Most people move to urban areas in search of better opportunities for work or for education, either for themselves or their families, and for many, the cities have served and continue to serve as gateways to success.

However, some who migrate to urban areas, whether from other parts of the United States or from other countries, are faced with unemployment, underemployment, discrimination, poor housing, and language barriers. Those without familial and social supports to help them make the transition to the new culture and to city life are at greater risk for poverty, social isolation, and personal and family problems.

One group that has traditionally been drawn to the cities is adolescent runaways. Although it is difficult to arrive at an accurate count, in 1994 there were an estimated 1.3 million runaways in the United States. Many runaways arrive in the cities with a range of social, health, and emotional problems that may include depression, histories of physical or sexual abuse, and suicidal behavior. Unprepared for independent living

Points to Ponder

During the middle of the 1800s, millions of people from rural areas in Ireland immigrated to cities in the United States. The majority of these immigrants "rarely if ever entered a city in the old country until they were on their way to the port of embarkation. . . . The simple, innocent countryman . . . became the denizen of a city, for which he was unqualified by training, by habit, and by association" (Maguire, 1868/1969, pp. 215–216, 219).

and desperate for a means of subsistence and for companionship, many turn to prostitution and drugs, and are at high risk for HIV/AIDS (Weiner & Pollack, 1997).

Inadequate Resources or Lack of Willingness to Address Social Problems

Some cities do not have the financial resources to provide services that would assist people in maximizing their potential, while other cities may have the resources, but do not choose to provide services, particularly for the poor. Consequently, there may be a lack of affordable, good-quality housing, or a lack of adequate police protection, schools, or recreational facilities. For example, preschool children and their parents are underserved in many urban communities. The high cost of living in the cities drives up salaries, and this, in combination with high rents, keeps the cost of child care particularly high. In fact, in many cities, the average cost per year to keep a four-year-old child in a day care center is much more than the cost of public college tuition, which benefits from government subsidies. The following ten cities have the most expensive child care costs, compared to the costs of college tuition at a public college:

	Cost of Day Care	College Tuition
Dane County, Wisconsin	$6,240	$2,747
Honolulu	6,188	2,298
Seattle	6,136	2,982
Alameda County, California	6,032	2,731
Anchorage	5,784	2,552
Kansas City and Johnson County	5,200	2,223
Wake County, North Carolina	5,068	1,841
Atlanta	4,992	2,244
Omaha	4,940	2,269
Reno/Washoe County	4,420	1,814

(Children's Defense Fund, 1999, p. 56.)

High Levels of Psychological Stress

Some studies have supported Wirth's (1938) claim that aspects of the urban environment can have adverse psychological effects. For example, it has been found that environmental stressors such as noise, dirty streets, and abandoned buildings can contribute to psychological problems (Lazarus, 1966). Risk factors associated with child abuse and neglect also have been linked to conditions of urban environments, particularly in impoverished inner-city communities. These risk factors include "housing density, geographic mobility, single parent status, or the abuse of substances such as 'crack' cocaine and alcohol" (Guterman, 1997, p. 114). Another study found that there is a greater incidence of problems such as delinquency, aggression, behavior problems, and mental illness in children living in the cities than in children living in rural areas (Black & Krishnakumar, 1998).

Social Work Practice in the Cities

Given the complexities of urban communities, social workers practicing in the cities will need to deal with many challenging situations. In order to be effective in providing help to urban clients, social workers need to intervene through client, agency, and policy practice.

Client practice involves:
- Viewing clients within the context of their culture and social environment
- Identifying clients' strengths and coping capacities
- Finding resources that could enable clients to function more productively, including informal support networks that are formed in specific neighborhoods
- Taking an active role in identifying the unmet needs of the communities in which they are working
- Advocating for resources not yet developed to meet the needs of individuals, families, groups, and communities
- Identifying environmental obstacles affecting the goals and daily activities of clients, such as limited access to public transportation for disabled individuals, or fear of violence that keeps people homebound
- Making effective referrals of clients to other agencies

Agency practice involves:
- Maximizing agency services on behalf of clients, such as recruiting and hiring social workers whose ethnocultural backgrounds are similar to the clients
- Developing effective programs to meet the changing needs of clients
- Evaluating the agency's programs and practices
- Accessing information about services of other agencies and networking with other professionals

Policy practice involves:
- Analyzing the impact of existing social welfare policies and programs on individuals, families, groups, communities, organizations, and the society
- Understanding the process of political change
- Using social action strategies, such as advocacy, including lobbying and letter-writing campaigns, mass media, and current technology to inform and influence the development of policies

Issues Related to Multiculturalism

Given the diversity of people living in urban communities, social workers need to be able to work with people who have a wide range of values, customs, lifestyles, and languages. However, many people move away from the values and customs of their culture, developing personal styles and coping skills that may be atypical of their cultural group. Therefore, while it is important to learn about various cultures and use this knowledge when it is appropriate, social workers need to focus on learning about their particular clients, without stereotyping individuals or groups.

Points to Ponder

According to the 1990 census, only 3 percent of people in the United States under the age of 18 were born outside the U.S. However, 80 percent of immigrant children and adolescents were living in cities. The following cities had a particularly high percentage of young people born outside the United States:

Los Angeles	21%
San Francisco	19%
Miami (Dade County)	18%
New York City	12%
Houston	10%

("The Numbers Game," 1993)

It is also important that social workers view their clients within the context of the clients' social environment. For example, a social worker may not be able to communicate easily with a client because of a language difference. However, that same client may live in an area where almost everyone speaks the same language, and may not consider communication to be a problem in his or her day-to-day life.

When working in a setting that provides services to clients from many cultures, the social worker must pay special attention to:

- Personal experiences of clients who have encountered discrimination, including the impact of those experiences and clients' responses
- Knowledge about various cultures, including attitudes toward issues such as gender roles, physical discipline of children, caring for older adults, and utilizing health, mental health, and social services
- The extent to which the client subscribes to, or differs from, the values and attitudes of his or her cultural group
- Strategies for dealing with situations that are useful for the particular client, such as religious beliefs and attitudes toward spiritual healing

- The complex array of environmental supports specific to particular cultures, communities, and individuals; these may include informal personal networks, peer support groups, and cultural and religious groups
- The social worker's own cultural biases and personal values that may interfere with his or her ability to be helpful to clients; if this self-awareness is not developed, it is likely that biases will negatively influence the social worker's ability to be helpful to clients

Points to Ponder

"We are not culture-free or value-free as individuals. Yet, as members of the helping professions, we mistakenly think that we can handle ourselves in ways that nullify our own biases . . . Before we can develop services that are appropriate for clients from ethnic groups, we as helping professionals must develop our awareness of our own ethnic heritages and cultural fabrics. Work on self-awareness is a continuous and ongoing process" (McAdoo, 1999, p. 320).

Fields of Practice

At the same time that complex social situations exist in the cities, a wide variety of services to meet the needs of people tend to be available in urban areas. The range and the quantity of social service agencies and organizations one frequently finds in urban communities can confound even the most seasoned social workers, much less students and clients. In order to better understand how agencies relate to each other, it is useful to organize them into categories based on the populations they serve and the kinds of services they provide. These categories are known as *fields of practice*, also called *practice areas*.

Services in any practice area can be offered by the public sector and by voluntary and for-profit agencies in the private sector. They may also be offered by other organizations, such as labor unions, employers, fraternal groups, or self-help groups. For example, mental health counseling can be provided by a federal Veterans' Administration hospital, by an outpatient clinic of a city hospital, by a voluntary family service agency, by a private clinician, or by a labor union. Some services have specific eligibility requirements. For example, the use of a city clinic may be restricted to those who live in a certain *catchment*, or geographic area, while services offered by labor unions can be used only by their members and their families.

The services that agencies offer depend on the *mission*, or *function* of each agency. For example, a child welfare agency is not likely to provide housing services to homeless women, even though some of the mothers of the children receiving their care may be homeless.

Some services may be more available than others in a given community. For instance, due to lack of funding or community objections, an urban community may not have any facilities for substance-abusing individuals with AIDS, while such services may be more readily available in the next city.

The availability of services provided by the public sector is determined by local, state, or federal government policies, and by the funding that is made available for these programs. Similarly, the extent to which voluntary agencies provide a given service is determined not only by their function, but also by the amount of money that they receive from contributions, grants, or from the government. At times, funding is earmarked for a particular service or program. For example, a voluntary agency that receives special funding for cultural programs for clients cannot use any of this money for another service, even though this same agency lacks funding for counseling services for rape victims.

Fields of Practice Commonly Found in Urban Areas

The most common fields of practice in urban communities include:

- *Adolescent Pregnancy and Adolescent Parenthood*, including prenatal, health, nutritional, and counseling services for adolescent mothers and fathers, and services for their children
- *Agency Administration*, including development and implementation of agency programs and policies
- *AIDS and HIV*, including prevention and intervention programs, HIV testing and counseling services, and programs for babies born HIV-positive and for AIDS orphans (the children of parents who have died of AIDS)
- *Case Management*, including arranging and coordinating services and assisting clients in using the various services
- *Child Abuse and Neglect*, including prevention and intervention services such as parenting classes, and provision of homemaking services
- *Child Welfare*, including adoption, foster care and kinship foster care, day care, and after-school programs
- *Criminal Justice*, including juvenile justice, probation, parole, drug courts and other diversion programs, and forensic treatment and rehabilitation programs
- *Delinquency Prevention and Intervention*, including school-based programs, after-school sports programs, counseling, summer recreation programs, and specialized activities sponsored by the police or the criminal justice system
- *Domestic Violence*, including counseling services for battered women and men, specialized programs for batterers, and shelters for battered women and their children
- *Education*, including special education services for children with special needs and services for their families
- *Elder Abuse*, including protective and counseling services to older adults in their homes, in agency programs, or in institutions
- *Employee Assistance Programs (EAPs) and Union-Sponsored Member Assistance Programs (MAPs)*, including brief treatment and referral services for personal and

work-related issues, as well as financial and legal assistance for workers and their families

- *Family Planning*, including pregnancy prevention, abortion, and fertility services
- *Gay, Lesbian, Bisexual, and Transgendered Persons' Services*, including peer support, professional counseling, and advocacy programs
- *Genetic Counseling*, including services to expectant parents and to people with a history of genetically transmitted disorders in their families
- *Health*, including inpatient and community-based services, and specialized prevention programs for children and adults
- *Homelessness*, including shelters and other housing, and an array of counseling, educational, vocational and recreational services
- *Housing*, including advocacy for, and provision of, adequate and accessible low-income and subsidized housing
- *Hunger*, including the establishment of food programs and the distribution of food to various populations including children, families, and the elderly
- *Immigration*, including informational, supportive, and advocacy services to documented and undocumented immigrants
- *Income Maintenance*, including financial support programs for needy individuals and families, welfare-to-work programs, and financial support programs of the Social Security Act, such as Supplemental Security Income (SSI), retirement benefits, survivors' insurance, and disability insurance
- *International Social Work*, involving the sharing of experiences, problems, and approaches to client, agency, and policy practice in various countries. This may take place through consultation, teaching, professional conferences, Internet communication and publication
- *Legal Services*, including legal representation for the poor, landlord–tenant disputes, immigration, and issues related to divorce and child custody
- *Mediation Counseling*, including couples, divorce, and peer group mediation and conflict resolution services
- *Mental Health*, including inpatient and community-based treatment services, discharge planning, supportive housing, employment services, and support services for families
- *Mentally Challenged*, including supervised housing, counseling, educational, vocational, transportation, and rehabilitation services, and supportive services for families
- *Occupational Social Work*, including employment and career counseling, job displacement services, relocation assistance, pre- and postretirement counseling, consumer services, wellness programs, and corporate philanthropy
- *Older Adults*, including recreation, food, transportation, residential, supportive, and custodial programs, as well as counseling and informational services to families
- *Physically Challenged*, including housing, counseling, educational, vocational, transportation, and rehabilitation services, and supportive services for families
- *Political Advocacy*, including organized and individual efforts to impact social welfare legislation on the federal, state, or local level; organizing and helping clients

to engage in political advocacy; and the social action efforts of the National Association of Social Workers and other professional social work organizations

- *Political Social Work*, including running for political office or accepting a political appointment
- *Recreation*, including sports, health, and leisure programs, and other services for children, adolescents, adults, and the elderly
- *Research*, including outcome studies, program evaluation, and research of social problems, policy assessment, and practice approaches
- *Substance Abuse*, including an array of preventive and interventive services for alcohol and drug abusers and their families, and services for those with co-occurring disorders, such as mentally ill substance abusers (MICA)
- *Victims' Services*, including counseling, financial, housing and other services for victims of violent crimes, domestic violence, and rape; services for survivors of accidents, fires, and natural disasters; services for victims' families
- *Vocational Rehabilitation*, including assessment of vocational readiness and intervention with emotional problems interfering with vocational training
- *Welfare-to-Work*, including provision of vocational counseling and help with obtaining and maintaining work, as well as analyzing the impact of the policies related to this approach

Overlapping Fields of Practice

In spite of efforts to categorize fields of practice, many programs fall into gray areas and it is difficult to decide to which field of practice they belong. For example, should adoption be considered part of Child Welfare or a separate field of practice? Should there be one field of practice called Domestic Violence, or should there be separate ones for child abuse, spousal abuse, and elder abuse? The answers to these questions are less important than the understanding that the service delivery system is complex and sometimes confusing, with many fields of practice overlapping.

How we conceptualize the practice areas changes over time in response to changes in the political and social environment, as well as changing needs of clients. For example, Welfare-to-Work is a new field of practice reflecting the changing policies related to welfare reform. It is shaped by policies related to other fields of practice, such as income maintenance and vocational rehabilitation, and establishes new connections between these traditionally separate fields of practice.

The Need for Comprehensive and Coordinated Social Services

The often fragmented nature of social services becomes apparent when we attempt to help individuals and families forge links with the complex network of benefits and services that they need in order to function optimally. For example, Yolanda Brightstar, a hospital social worker working with Mrs. Anna Aiello, an elderly widow being discharged after a long hospital stay due to a broken hip and pneumonia, helps her obtain a referral for Meals-on-Wheels, the Visiting Nurse Service, and legal assistance for an eviction notice that was received during her hospital stay. While obtaining these services necessitated numerous phone calls and a lot of paperwork, their coordination was not that difficult.

At times, however, the efforts to coordinate services become highly complex and frustrating due to the fragmentation of existing services. For example, Martin Owens, a 32-year-old man with a history of violence, mental illness, and alcohol and cocaine abuse, requires the involvement of services connected to at least three different fields of practice: mental health, substance abuse, and criminal justice. In addition, he requires help with such services and benefits as housing, vocational rehabilitation, legal services, and income maintenance. The need for coordination of complex cases has resulted in the development of the relatively new field of practice known as *case management*.

Conclusion

This chapter highlighted some of the complexities inherent in working in urban areas, and outlined the range of social services that are generally found in the cities. The level of services available in different urban communities is uneven, and can range from sparsity to a highly-developed system of services that respond to the complex needs of people living in the cities.

In the following chapter, students are introduced to important concepts that shape our current social welfare system and social work practice in urban communities. These include the functions of social work and social welfare in society, the underlying values represented by social work programs and services, and the structure of social service programs, organizations, and agencies.

REFERENCES

Abrahamson, M. (1996). *Urban enclaves: Identity and place in America*. New York: St. Martin's Press.

Black, M. M. & Krishnakumar, A. (1998, June). Children in low-income, urban settings. *American Psychologist 53*(6), 635–646.

Children's Defense Fund. (1999). *The state of America's children yearbook: A report from the Children's Defense Fund*. Boston: Beacon.

Clark, K. B. (1965/1989). *Dark ghetto: Dilemmas of social power* (2d ed.). Hanover, NH: Wesleyan University Press.

Egan, T. (1996, December 29). Urban sprawl strains western states. *New York Times*. National, pp. 1, 20.

Fischer, C. S. (1975). Toward a subcultural theory of urbanization. *American Journal of Sociology 80*, 1319–1341.

Fischer, C. S. (1984). *The urban experience* (2d ed.). San Diego, CA: Harcourt Brace Jovanovich.

Former coach shot to death near Chicago; others injured. (1999, July 4). *New York Times*, A12.

Guterman, N. (1997). Parental violence towards children. In N. K. Phillips & S. L. A. Straussner (Eds.),

Children in the urban environment (pp. 113–134). Springfield, IL: Thomas.

Holody, R. Children in out-of-home placements. In Phillips, N. K., & L. A. Straussner (Eds.). *Children in the Urban Environment* (pp. 135–153). Springfield, IL: Thomas.

Kozol, J. (1991). *Savage inequalities*. New York: Crown.

Lazarus, R. S. (1966). *Psychological stress and the coping process*. New York: McGraw-Hill.

Maguire, J. F. (1868/1969). *The Irish in America*. London: Longman, Green, and Co. Reprinted in *The American immigration collection*. New York: Arno Press and *The New York Times*.

Marden. C. E., Meyer, G., & Engel, M. H. (1992). *Minorities in American society* (6th ed.). New York: HarperCollins.

Marsella, A. J. (1998, June). Urbanization, mental health, and social deviancy. *American Psychologist 53*(6), 624–634.

McAdoo, H. P. (1999). Family ethnicity: Challenges for the 21st century. In H. P. McAdoo (Ed.),

Family ethnicity: Strength in diversity (pp. 319–320). Thousand Oaks, CA: Sage.

Milgram, S. (1970). The experience of living in cities. *Science 167*, 1461–1468.

Palen, J. J. (1997). Urbanization. In R. K. Vogel (Ed.), *Handbook of research on urban politics and policy in the United States* (pp. 31–41). Westport, CT: Greenwood Press.

Park, R. E. (1916). The city: Suggestions for investigation of human behavior in the urban environment. Reprinted in R. Sennett (Ed.), *Classic essays on the culture of cities* (pp. 91–130). New York: Appleton-Century-Crofts, 1969.

Phillips, N. K. (1997). Growing up in the urban environment. In N. K. Phillips & S. L. A. Straussner (Eds.), *Children in the urban environment* (pp. 5–24). Springfield, IL: Thomas.

Simmel, G. (1905/1969). The metropolis and mental life. Reprinted in R. Sennett (Ed.), *Classic essays on the culture of cities* (pp. 47–60). New York: Appleton-Century-Crofts.

Straussner, J. & Straussner, S. L. A. (1997). Impact of community and school violence on children. In N. K. Phillips & S. L. A. Straussner (Eds.), *Children in the urban environment* (pp. 61–77). Springfield, IL: Thomas.

The Numbers Game. (1993, Fall). *Time Magazine*, Special Issue, 14–15.

United Nations Children's Fund. (1996). *The progress of nations*. NY: Oxford University Press.

U.S. Bureau of the Census. (1995). Urban and rural population: 1900 to 1990.

U.S. Bureau of the Census. (1998). Urban and rural population, 1960 to 1990, and by State, 1990.

U.S. Department of Commerce. (1998, September 24). Internet Report, CB98-175. Income and Poverty Information.

U.S. Department of Justice. (1996, October 13). Internet Report, Crime Rate.

Walters, K. L. (1999). Urban American Indian identity, attitudes and acculturation styles. *Journal of Human Behavior in the Social Environment, 2*, 163–178.

Weiner, A. & Pollack, D. (1997). Urban runaway youth: Sex, drugs and HIV. In N. K. Phillips & S. L. A. Straussner (Eds.), *Children in the urban environment* (pp. 209–226). Springfield, IL: Thomas.

Wilson, W. J. (1998). Jobless ghettos: The impact of the disappearance of work in segregated neighborhoods. In L. A. Daniels (Ed.), *The state of black America 1998* (pp. 89–108). Washington, DC: National Urban League.

Wilson, W. J. (1987). *The truly disadvantaged: The inner city, the underclass, and public policy*. Chicago: University of Chicago Press.

Wirth, L. (1938). Urbanism as a way of life. *American Journal of Sociology 44*, 3–24.

CHAPTER

3 From Social Welfare To Social Services: Functions and Structure

Feeding the hungry in Portland, Oregon, 2000. Photo by Adrian Gaut

It is important that all social workers have a good understanding of the scope, nature, and objectives of the broad social welfare system, and of the role that social work agencies play in that system. This chapter identifies the values and assumptions underlying our current welfare system. It also addresses some of the complex and controversial issues related to distribution of public welfare, such as economic and social injustices that derive from benefits provided to corporations and to the middle and upper classes, and the segregation of public benefits for the poor into stigmatized programs.

Other issues addressed in this chapter are:

- Various forms of welfare, including fiscal, occupational, and social welfare
- Values and functions of social welfare, including humanitarianism and helping people in need, and equality of opportunities for people
- Structure of social services, including the public, private non-profit, and private for-profit organizations

What Is Social Welfare?

Social welfare can be defined as the tangible and specific responses of a society to the needs and wants of its people, and the mechanisms that are in place to improve the quality of life. In addition to programs that are designed to provide services to people, the social welfare system includes policies that determine what benefits will be available and to whom, and the nature of agencies and institutions through which services are delivered. In some cases, the function of policies may be to mitigate between people and the social problems in the environment that adversely affect them, or to prevent damaging effects of potentially adverse situations, such as the Food Stamp program that prevents hunger in cases of unemployment or low-income earnings. In other cases, policies are not directed at particular social problems, but lead to the establishment of services needed by everyone, such as public education for children.

Although much of the work of social workers is directed toward helping the poor, social welfare includes benefits and programs that help people in all socioeconomic groups. However, in order to understand *social welfare*, it is important first to clarify how we think about *welfare*.

Various Forms of Welfare

The use of the term *welfare* generally elicits visions of poor people receiving help from government programs such as public assistance or food stamps. However, this limited view does not include the many other forms of welfare that are built into our society. Richard Titmuss (1963), a well known British economist, has suggested that *all* people, not just the poor, are provided with welfare benefits. In fact, the United States today provides what sometimes are extravagant welfare programs, not for the poor, but for the wealthy, for the employed, for corporations, for farmers, and for other groups.

Titmuss (1963) identified three different forms of welfare:

- Fiscal welfare
- Occupational welfare
- Social welfare

It is useful to examine this broad view of welfare in order to gain a more realistic understanding of the roles that government and society take in providing economic benefits for all people.

Fiscal Welfare

Fiscal welfare is a product of tax laws, and provides economic benefits for people through the tax system. Such benefits may result from tax laws at the federal, state, or local levels of government. For example, the federal income tax was originally intended as a *progressive tax* designed so that people with higher incomes would pay a higher percentage of their money earned in taxes. The purpose of the progressive tax was to redistribute the wealth of the society more equally. However, over the years the tax laws in the United States have changed. Today, many people with a great deal of money benefit from tax loopholes that provide vehicles to reduce the amount of taxes they must pay. For example, people who own one or more houses can deduct the interest on their home mortgages as well as their real estate taxes, while people who rent their apartments or houses are unable to use their rent as a tax deduction. In this way the tax system continues to benefit the wealthier members of society.

Points to Ponder

The U.S. has the largest gap between the rich and the poor among 18 industrialized nations, and currently within the U.S. there is greater inequality in income between the "haves" and the "have-nots" than there has been in the past fifty years (Miringoff & Miringoff, 1999).

Another example of fiscal welfare is state or city sales tax, which is a *regressive tax*. A regressive tax requires that everyone pays the same percentage in taxes, regardless of how much money the person has. This tax also benefits the richest segment of society. For example, Melinda Hamid, a student whose family is wealthy, pays $60.00 for a college textbook. The sales tax in her state and city is eight percent, and consequently she pays an additional $4.80 in tax. Unlike Melinda, her fellow student, Rob Sanders, is struggling financially, but he also has to pay the same $4.80 in tax when purchasing his copy of the book. We can therefore see how regressive taxes favor people who have larger incomes, while they place greater burdens on those with less money.

Fiscal welfare has also been used for the benefit of other socioeconomic groups. Through the provision of such programs as Earned Income Tax Credits for low-wage working families, tax benefits are given to working people whose earnings fall below a designated amount. This has been referred to as "America's single biggest anti-poverty program" ("America's Unfinished Agenda," 2000, p. 26). Other forms of fiscal welfare include income tax deductions for child care for working parents, and deductions for college tuition for families whose income is below a designated amount.

Points to Ponder

The federal Tax Relief Act of 1997 introduced the Hope Scholarship and Lifetime Learning tax credits. These two new programs provide tax relief of up to $1,500 for college students whose families' income is below $50,000 for single, and $100,000 for married taxpayers.

Occupational Welfare

Occupational welfare is designed to benefit people through their employment. This form of welfare may include what are often referred to as "fringe benefits." It may include employers' contributions toward medical insurance for their employees and the employees' families, contributions by employers to retirement plans, sick pay, paid vacation time, personal leave, and other benefits that many people receive through their workplace. For example, people working for large corporations or the newer dot.com companies may also receive stock options.

For some people, occupational welfare benefits are quite extensive and may include adoption subsidies, child care, membership in a country club, moving expenses, assistance in purchasing a home, and tuition benefits for themselves and their family members. Today, many large corporations and government institutions also provide Employee Assistance Programs, which provide short-term counseling and referral services to employees and their families at no cost to the employees. Generally, fringe benefits are more extensive for people who earn the most, such as administrators and executives.

Social Welfare

Social welfare includes both services to the poor and services that benefit all income groups. Following are just a few of the familiar social welfare programs and services that are provided for the poor in many urban areas through our present system of social welfare:

- The unemployed and the working poor whose wages are too low to meet their basic needs may turn to income maintenance, Medicaid, and the Food Stamp Program.
- Families unable to afford the high rents in the cities may live in subsidized public housing.
- Working parents who cannot afford private child care may turn to publicly funded child care programs, including day care, after-school programs, and summer camp programs.
- Substance abusers may seek help from publicly funded rehabilitation programs.

On the other hand, social welfare is not limited to benefits for the poor alone. Consider, for example, the following benefits and programs:

- Public education, including not only elementary and high school education, but also public higher education such as state and city colleges and universities
- Special programs at public libraries and museums
- Public parks and recreational facilities
- Cultural programs, such as free concerts and other public performances
- Medicare, which is available to all people at age 65 years

Other Forms of Government Welfare

In addition to the benefits that all economic groups receive through fiscal, occupational, or social welfare, the government provides other forms of economic relief. These programs may be targeted at helping specific groups of people, or they may help businesses, or even other countries. While sometimes termed subsidies, these are, in fact, government-sponsored welfare programs. For example, federal aid is provided to:

- People in areas experiencing natural disasters such as hurricanes, floods, or earthquakes
- Farmers
- Banks in times of economic crisis
- Other countries during times of economic or political crises

In addition, financial benefits are given by the federal, state, and local governments to corporations in what has been termed *corporate welfare* (Abramovitz, 1983; Huff & Johnson, 1993). This type of welfare may take the form of outright subsidies, grants, real estate, low-interest loans, services, or tax breaks. According to Barlett & Steele (1998), the federal government alone gives $125 billion annually to corporations in tax breaks and subsidies for numerous projects. These can include, for example, the purchase of crop insurance for tobacco farmers, shipbuilding, and inexpensive electricity for casinos. It also includes relief for corporations from paying federal excise tax on airline tickets, as well as the surcharge on airline tickets that everyone else pays when traveling. Revenues from these sources are used to pay air-traffic control costs. This tax and surcharge relief alone, which benefits corporate executives even when they use company planes for pleasure trips, cost taxpayers about $3 billion during the 1990s.

One must question why, among all the groups receiving welfare in its various forms—the middle class and the wealthy, banks, farmers, corporations, and even foreign governments—it is only the poor who are stigmatized, or made to feel like a failure, when they apply for or receive social welfare benefits.

Points to Ponder

The Chief Executive Officer of AlliedSignal is quoted as complaining about " 'hundreds of thousands of able-bodied people who stay on welfare for years at a time.' " Yet, "over the past five years, the company earned more than $4 billion. . . . During that same period of soaring profits, Allied collected more than $150 million in state and federal corporate welfare . . . Allied gets export subsidies, loans and guarantees overseas, breaks on real estate taxes, federal research contracts and incentives to build new offices" (Barlett & Steele, 1998, p. 84).

Values and Functions of Social Welfare

Social welfare supports particular values, and at the same time it serves several functions. The value of *humanitarianism* supports the function of helping people in need, while the value of *equality of opportunity* supports the development of programs directed toward groups that have a history of oppression in society. These, however, are complex issues that can be viewed from several perspectives.

The Value of Humanitarianism—Helping People in Need

Humanitarianism, also referred to as compassion, is a religion-based value reflecting the concerns that people may have for each other. For centuries, humanitarian concerns have motivated individuals and groups to provide aid to others.

Humanitarian aid may be provided voluntarily by individuals, as well as through organized groups, such as public or voluntary organizations, religious institutions, or neighborhood or self-help groups. In addition to contributing money to organizations, humanitarian efforts common in today's urban communities are seen in the following examples:

- In Oakland, a Catholic church sponsors a shelter for the homeless.
- A high school junior in Tampa volunteers to read to the elderly in a nursing home.
- A police precinct collects toys for hospitalized children in New Orleans.
- In Cincinnati, a community theater group collects cans of food for distribution to a food pantry.
- Social work students at a college in Minneapolis collect winter coats for mentally ill individuals living in supportive housing.
- In Chicago, a retired school teacher volunteers to be a "buddy" to a young man with AIDS.

For some people, giving derives from the personal wish to help others, or it may have religious significance. For others, what looks like humanitarianism may reflect other values, such as looking for a tax deduction, approval from others, or obtaining community service credit for school. It is clear that motivations for giving are personal and are not always obvious.

The Value of Equality of Opportunity— Development of Programs for Oppressed Groups

In the interest of achieving greater equality of opportunity in the society, many social welfare programs are created to improve the life circumstances and options for low-income, or other oppressed groups. For example, many cities and states have excellent publicly-supported colleges and universities with low tuition for their residents. These may include law, medical, and business schools, and, of course, undergraduate social work programs and graduate schools of social work. Such subsidized educational institutions offer opportunities for learning and career development for many people who may otherwise be unable to go to school. At the same time, these educational programs benefit their communities and society as a whole by developing an educated labor force.

Other public social welfare programs provide opportunities for a more productive and higher quality of life for millions of people. Among these are:

- Health insurance programs, such as Medicaid, Medicare, and the Children's Health Insurance Program (CHIP)
- Nutrition programs, such as Food Stamps for the financially eligible, and the Women's, Infants' and Children's Program (WIC), which offers nutrition counseling and food for financially eligible pregnant women and young children at risk for medical problems
- Recreation, housing, and nutrition programs for low-income older adults, such as senior day centers, senior housing, and Meals-on-Wheels, all of which serve to improve the quality of life for many urban residents

While the creation of these programs clearly opens up many opportunities for improved health care, education, social mobility, and quality of life, one can readily see how the reduction of such programs serves to limit opportunities for large groups of people (Piven & Cloward, 1971).

The Structure of Social Services

Social services are provided through two broad categories, called sectors. Each sector is guided by policies determined by its sources of funding and accountability. The sectors are:

- The public sector, which includes all the agencies and organizations funded and administered by federal, state, and/or local governments
- The private sector, which includes voluntary, nonprofit agencies as well as private, for-profit organizations

Public Sector Benefits and Programs

Social welfare benefits and social services in the public sector are created and governed by laws and regulations at the federal, state, and local levels of government. The fact that a social service is called public does not necessarily mean that anyone who wants to use it can do so. For example, while anyone can use a public library, not everyone is eligible to receive public assistance. Rather, it means that the money to fund public services comes from the government through tax monies. Policies guiding public social services, such as who is eligible to receive the services, what the services should consist of, and even who can be employed to administer or provide such services, all are determined by law and public regulations.

In attempting to understand the public sector of social welfare, it is useful to separate social welfare benefits and services into two groups: those based on the *institutional model*, also called the *universal model* of social welfare, and those based on the *residual model*, also called the *selective model* of social welfare (Kahn, 1979; Wilensky & Lebeaux, 1965).

The Institutional Model

The institutional model is based on the belief that people have the right to have their basic needs met, and that the government has an obligation to meet those needs. Based on a commitment to "social justice," individuals are eligible to obtain benefits and services regardless of their income and without stigma.

Although people must apply for many of the institutional benefits, eligibility is based on conditions that are universally accepted in our society, such as age, employment status, or medical condition. Public education is an example of an institutional benefit. All children within a specified age range are entitled to a free public education, regardless of how much money their families have. Unemployment insurance is another example of an institutional benefit, as is Medicare, Part A, which is a universally-provided health benefit for those over 65 years of age.

The period of eligibility for various institutional benefits differs. Some benefits, such as Medicare, are ongoing for the remainder of the person's lifetime, while others, such as unemployment insurance, are time-limited.

As more people in the middle class experience a common need, it is more likely that policies and programs will be developed to address it through an institutional benefit. This can be seen today, for example, in the recognition of the need for a government-sponsored program to help pay for prescription medicine for older adults.

The Institutional Model and the Welfare State

Although there are many different definitions of a *welfare state*, in this book it is defined as a nation that provides most social welfare services based on the institutional model. For example, England, Canada, and Sweden have traditionally been considered welfare states. Although a growing number of welfare states are experiencing financial problems and are cutting back on some of their benefits (Lyall, 1999), in those countries the government still assumes the major responsibility for health care for everyone, for

Points to Ponder

In the Netherlands, the government provides paid maternity leave for a period that ranges from 16 to 68 weeks at 100 percent of the mother's salary; in Britain, all mothers receive 18 weeks government-paid maternity leave at 90 percent of the mother's salary; even in tiny Lichtenstein, the government provides 12 weeks leave at 80 percent of the mother's salary (Olson, 1999).

children's allowances for families with children under a specified age, for extended unemployment insurance, and for maternity and paternity leave. The institutional benefits in the United States are much more limited.

The Residual Model

The residual model of public welfare is based on the belief that individuals and their family members have the responsibility for meeting their own basic needs (Moroney & Krysik, 1998). This belief is based on the following assumptions:

- Opportunities for work exist for all people
- All people are able to earn enough money to support themselves if they want to
- If people are unable to support themselves and their families, it is their own fault

Therefore, society provides social welfare benefits only in cases of extreme need, serving the purpose of a *social safety net*. Whereas benefits under the institutional model are based on a commitment to social justice, as described above, benefits under the residual model are based on the notion of public charity. The benefits provided are as minimal as possible and for as brief a time as possible. Among the most common residual benefits are public assistance, Medicaid, food programs, and public housing programs.

Residual benefits are *means-tested*. Before applicants for assistance can receive services, they must provide proof that their income and assets fall below a particular amount—an amount that is defined by law. This amount differs for various benefits, and may vary from state to state, or even from city to city. For example, both the eligibility requirements for public assistance and the level of benefits provided are determined by each state, and vary from one state to the next.

Variations in the benefits offered are based on several factors such as:

- The differences in the cost of living in various cities
- The financial resources of a given community
- Differing attitudes toward the poor and toward the role of government in ensuring the quality of life for all people (Groskind, 1994)

Applying for residual benefits is generally stigmatizing. In many instances, the application process is a demeaning experience, regardless of the reason that the person needs the benefits. In addition to proving financial need through the means test, applicants for residual benefits must meet other eligibility requirements, which might include age, residence, physical diagnosis, and immigration status.

Challenges to the Assumptions Underlying the Residual Model

Economic and social conditions, including *economic causes of poverty* and the consequences of *institutional oppression*, are important factors contributing to the inability of people to support themselves and their families. These factors challenge the assumption that individuals are fully responsible for their poverty.

ECONOMIC CAUSES OF POVERTY

Often ignored in the discussion of poverty are societal causes of financial need, such as:

- Low wages, particularly the minimum wage
- High cost of medical insurance, which affects low-wage earners the most because their medical insurance generally is not a fringe benefit paid by their employers
- Involuntary unemployment and underemployment resulting from economic recessions and depressions, downsizing of corporations, movement of industries to other countries where wages are much lower, or the seasonal nature of jobs such as construction and recreation-related employment
- Inadequate duration and rates of unemployment insurance
- High cost of living because of inflation
- High rents, particularly in and near large cities

Points to Ponder

According to the U.S. Department of Housing and Urban Development, there was a five percent decrease in affordable rental units nationwide from 1991 to 1997. Then-Housing Secretary Andrew M. Cuomo stated in September 1999, "The sad truth is that more and more people working at low-wage jobs, as well as older Americans living on fixed incomes, are being priced out of the housing market as rents rise" (Stout, 1999, p. A14).

Due to the inadequate protections against poverty built into the social system in the United States, in times of economic crises, many people have no choice but to turn to the safety net of residual social services for their survival.

Points to Ponder

In San Jose, California, some people working full time are homeless because of the high rents in the area. "... 34 percent of the estimated 20,000 homeless people in Santa Clara County in 1999 had full-time jobs. ... And those figures fail to count the growing number of families doubled up in single apartments, or paying $400 a month to live in a garage or to sleep on a stranger's living-room floor. And it is not the minimum-wage earner who is scrambling to survive here. More teachers, police officers, firefighters, commissioned salespeople—all people who make more than $50,000 a year and would be comfortably middle-class in many other places—are seeking the services of area homeless shelters" (Nieves, 2000, p. 20).

INSTITUTIONAL OPPRESSION AS A CAUSE OF POVERTY

Poverty can also be a consequence of the ongoing experience of discrimination and institutional oppression. Although many forms of discrimination are illegal, they often occur in subtle, and sometimes covert or hidden ways. Discrimination that is covert, but also is pervasive and incorporated within the fabric of society, is called *institutional oppression.*

As a consequence of institutional oppression, many people are deprived of opportunities that might open doors to economic mobility. The ongoing experience of discrimination and oppression can negatively impact peoples' self-image and their goals for the future. This dynamic is reflected in the following observation regarding the discrepancy of school performance between black and nonblack students in a middle-income neighborhood in Evanston, Illinois. According to the author, "some students and parents say that teachers and guidance counselors, white or black . . . have lower expectations of African-American students and that this may ultimately translate into self-fulfilling prophecies of mediocrity" (Belluck, 1999, p. 15).

Given the pervasiveness of institutional oppression, it is important that social workers be alert to the impact that this may have for their individual clients and for society as a whole (Keefe, 1978), and that they work for social justice, advocating for the elimination of oppressive practices.

Costs and Benefits of Services Representing the Institutional and Residual Models

Social welfare benefits and services can be evaluated in terms of both economic and social costs and benefits. According to Jansson (1999), the most efficient services are those that "will most benefit consumers at the lowest cost" (p. 212). How a service benefits clients can be described in many ways. For example, one might look at the benefit of providing housing for a homeless family in a shelter, or one can look at quality of life issues, in which case the shelter will be found to be an unacceptable place for children to live. Improving the quality of life for clients also has an impact on the quality of life of the community.

Those who favor fewer public-sector benefits support the residual model of programs and services, which appears to be cheaper, at least in the short run. Others recognize that, even aside from humanitarian concerns, a more developed social welfare system, represented by the institutional model of programs and services, is more likely to prevent problems that, in the long run, can result in greater economic cost for the community.

In many instances, what looks like a costly benefit or program ultimately proves to be both beneficial and less costly for the community. For example, providing free vaccinations for babies and young children protects both the individual child and the community. Services such as prenatal care and parenting classes for teen parents, early intervention for developmentally delayed preschoolers, after-school programs for children of working parents, and home care for older adults are just some of the programs that can ultimately prevent or reduce the severity of problems, save money, and improve society. Other programs, such as affordable tuition at city and state universities, or vocational training for ex-offenders, prepare people to become more productive and earn higher salaries, in turn bringing money back to the government through taxes paid. In addition to saving money for society in the long run, programs that improve the quality of life for clients are also likely to prevent family breakdown and provide greater opportunities for people.

Points to Ponder

According to research carried out by the Community Service Society in New York City, it costs less to pay for permanent housing for homeless people than to house them in temporary shelters. Annual costs of maintaining a person in permanent housing is $12,500, while it costs $20,000 a year to keep a person in a homeless shelter (Gershenson, 1999).

The Private Sector

The private sector of social welfare includes two separate and very different types of organizations. First are the voluntary, nonprofit agencies, which began to emerge in the United States in the latter half of the 1800s, as will be described in Chapter 5. The second type of private sector organizations are private, for-profit agencies. Such for-profit agencies are a recent development.

Voluntary Nonprofit Organizations

Some people assume that an organization or agency is designated voluntary because social workers volunteer their services instead of being paid. Although this was true when the first social service agencies were formed, it certainly is not the case today, as social workers who work in voluntary agencies earn their living there. Rather, when we discuss voluntary nonprofit agencies and organizations, the word *voluntary* refers to the funding of the agencies. All voluntary agencies are funded, at least in part, by voluntary contributions, including contributions from individuals and from private foundations. We are all familiar with fund-raising drives of voluntary nonprofit organizations such as the American Red Cross. Today, almost all voluntary agencies have *mixed funding sources*, including funding from public sources, such as Medicaid, Medicare, or federal, state, or local grants, as well as receiving a portion of their funds from voluntary sources.

Many public sector agencies contract with voluntary agencies and pay them to carry out services generally associated with the public sector, as frequently occurs in providing foster care for children. In such cases, "The voluntary agency offers services as a substitute for government" (Demone, 1998, p. 233).

Voluntary agencies are nonprofit (also called not-for-profit) because they are not privately owned by individuals or stockholders who can profit from the money coming into the agency. Rather, after paying their expenses, including salaries, the income of the agency is used for the benefit of the agency. Agencies that are nonprofit also have tax advantages. For example, they are not required to pay income tax, real estate tax, or sales tax.

It is important for clients and also social workers to consider the values and accountability of voluntary nonprofit organizations. There is a tendency on the part of many people drawn to the social work profession to make the assumption that all nonprofit agencies are "good" because they offer help to people, and that they reflect humanitarian values. However, the fact that an organization has a voluntary nonprofit designation tells us nothing about its values or practices. The way in which one defines "good" is based on each individual's values. Different agencies represent a wide range of values, some of which may be objectionable to some people. Therefore it is essential that social workers become familiar with the values, goals, methods of working, standards, and accountability that guide particular agencies before referring clients or seeking employment there. For example:

- The goal of a hospice setting is to make patients comfortable during the last stages of terminal illness, but not to prolong the patient's life.
- Some agencies will help pregnant women with various services, but will not support a plan for abortion, even if it is the woman's choice.
- Some agencies maintain policies against hiring or providing services to gays and lesbians.
- Some agencies hire only people who have had particular personal experiences, such as recovery from substance abuse.

Policies that guide voluntary agencies are determined by the boards of directors and executives of the agencies. The board of an agency is responsible for hiring the executive director and the administrators, who in turn hire other staff members. Agency executives and administrators are then accountable to the board of directors. Although clients and social workers sometimes are represented on boards of directors, in most agencies the board is made up of philanthropists who contribute money to the agency. Although some board members may have little in common with the clients of the agency, others may be personally involved with the clients' circumstances, either through their own or their family members' experiences. For example, Lelani Donahue, a social work supervisor in a high school in Honolulu, was recently invited to become a member of the board of directors of the local chapter of the Alzheimer's Society. Her father died of Alzheimer's disease a year ago, and she had been volunteering for this organization two evenings a week, answering their telephone hot line and training other volunteers.

Voluntary agencies that accept public funding are accountable to the government, as well as to their board of directors. Such agencies must meet certain standards for service, including compliance with the policies of nondiscrimination. If a voluntary agency chooses not to accept government money it may have more latitude with regard to the hiring of staff members and the clients it serves.

Although almost all agencies provide services to people regardless of their religion, it is useful in understanding the policies and traditions of religiously-affiliated agencies to recognize their origins and present connections to religious institutions. Agencies within the voluntary nonprofit sector can be identified either as *sectarian*, connected to a specific religion, or *nonsectarian*, which are secular.

Sectarian Agencies

Giving help to people in need has traditionally been seen as a religious function, and many of today's social work agencies got their start under religious auspices. Agencies that are religiously affiliated are known as *sectarian* agencies. Such agencies receive funding from particular religious organizations and their services generally represent the values and traditions associated with those religions. For example, Catholic agencies usually do not offer abortion counseling, and Jewish agencies may be closed for a Jewish holiday even if few of their current clients are Jewish.

If a religiously-affiliated agency receives any funding from government sources, as most do today, it must provide services to all people, regardless of their religious identification or beliefs. However, such funding does not affect the kinds of services offered by the agency. In some instances clients may not be aware of the religious affiliation of an agency. It is especially important that social workers and clients alike be made aware of the religious affiliation of sectarian agencies because of the impact this may have on the services offered.

Nonsectarian Agencies

Nonsectarian agencies are those voluntary agencies that are not religiously affiliated. Similar to the sectarian agencies, they are funded by voluntary contributions, and the policies of the agency are determined by a board of directors. Nonsectarian agencies generally have mixed funding, receiving part of their funds from voluntary contributions and some from the government. Once they accept public funding, they are also subject to government laws and regulations.

Private For-Profit Organizations

In keeping with the trend toward privatization of many public services, the privatization of social services in the United States has escalated during the last decade (Demone, 1998). Just like a business, such organizations are owned by an individual or group, or by a group of stockholders. They are run as businesses with the goal of earning profits for the owners or shareholders.

Although for many years some social workers had worked in private practice, recently numerous for-profit services have emerged, expanding the scope of social work from its traditional structure of working within public and voluntary social agencies. Today, for-profit programs can be found in a variety of fields of practice:

- In child welfare, as more and more day care centers operating as for-profit businesses are located in private industry and in institutions, such as hospitals and colleges
- In recreation, as more private recreation programs are introduced, particularly in urban areas
- In substance abuse services, where many for-profit rehabilitation programs exist
- In services to older adults, as more and more private nursing homes, extended care, and residential facilities are built
- In health and mental health services, as treatment services are privatized and many private managed care facilities exist
- In corrections, as services in prisons are turned over to for-profit companies

As this trend continues, we can expect to see more and more clients obtaining services through such organizations and more and more social workers employed by them. For instance, in the Delaware correctional system, a private medical services contractor provides services for inmates with chronic mental illness and retardation, and to prisoners who are dually diagnosed with mental illness and substance abuse (Peters & Hills, 1993).

Although private, for-profit organizations may fill the gap in areas where public or voluntary services are lacking, they also raise concerns regarding accountability and ethical practices. These concerns can result from the potential conflict between profit making and providing needed services.

Points to Ponder

More than 50 percent of social workers who obtained their MSW in 1997 were employed in non-profit settings. Another 25 percent worked in public settings, and 18 percent worked in for-profit organizations (Beaucar, 1999).

Social Services under Other Auspices

In addition to services provided by the public and private sectors, numerous social services are also offered through other auspices, or sponsorship:

- Religious institutions such as churches, temples, mosques, or synagogues
- Labor unions
- Employers
- The military
- Fraternal organizations
- Self-help groups
- Corporations

Points to Ponder

Utility companies have been hiring social workers to work with customers who are behind in payment of their utility bills. Their goal is to help people deal with personal and economic problems that interfere with them keeping up with their payments. This can include helping the person apply for government assistance and other benefits. For example, since 1994, Baltimore Gas and Electric has had a staff of 15 people, including several social workers, who work directly with their customers. They provide services to about 3,000 low-income families each year (Yardley, 1999).

Conclusion

This chapter has identified contradictions within the welfare system in the United States, pointing to the generally-held assumption that public welfare is for the poor, while in fact huge benefits are offered by the government to other groups of people through the occupational and fiscal welfare systems. At the same time that social welfare services for the poor have been provided in the form of segregated residual programs that are punitive and highly stigmatized, the occupational and fiscal welfare programs that reach the middle and upper classes are viewed as a benefit that people, organizations, and businesses are entitled to receive.

However, the public sector is not the only source of social services. As seen in this chapter, many services are also delivered through the private sector, including voluntary nonprofit and private for-profit organizations. In addition, there are various social services delivered through other auspices such as labor unions, religious institutions, fraternal organizations, and self-help groups. These public and private sector social services and programs combine to form the existing social welfare system.

Part 2 presents a brief summary of the development of urban social welfare, beginning with the introduction of social welfare in England, and then traces the growth of public and voluntary social welfare programs, first in the American colonies and later in the United States. It is those historical processes that have led to the development of our current social services. The Section concludes with a discussion of contemporary urban problems and social welfare policies and their link to social work practice today.

REFERENCES

Abramovitz, M. (1983). Everyone is on welfare. *Social Work, 28*, 440–445.

America's unfinished agenda. (2000, May 20). *The Economist, 24*, 26.

Barlett, D. L. & Steele, J. B. (1998, November 16). Fantasy islands and other perfectly legal ways that big companies manage to avoid billions in federal taxes. *Time Magazine*, 79–93.

Belluck, P. (1999, July 4). Reason is sought for lag by blacks in school effort: Sensitive issue debated. *New York Times*, pp. 1, 15.

Children's Defense Fund. (1999). *The state of America's children, Yearbook 1999*. Boston: Beacon.

Demone, Jr., H. W. (1998). The political future of privatization. In M. Gibelman & H. W. Demone, Jr. (Eds.), *The privatization of human services*, Vol. 1 (pp. 205–244). New York: Springer.

Gershenson, A. (1999, January 24). Donors visit the recipients of their generosity. *New York Times*, Metro Section, p. 34.

Groskind, F. (1994). Ideological influences on public support for assistance to poor families. *Social Work, 39*, 81–89.

Huff, D. D. & Johnson, D. A. (1993). Phantom welfare: Public relief for corporate America. *Social Work, 38*, 311–316.

Jansson, B. (1999). *Becoming an effective policy advocate* (3d ed.). Pacific Grove, CA: Brooks/Cole.

Kahn, A. J. (1979). *Social policy and social services* (2d ed.). New York: Random House.

Keefe, T. (1978). The economic context of empathy. *Social Work, 23*, 460–465.

Lyall, S. (1999, April 18). Britain's prescription for health care takes a seat. *New York Times*, International, p. 3.

Moroney, R. & Krysik, J. (1998). *Social policy and social work: Critical essays on the welfare state*, (2d ed.). Hawthorne, New York: Aldine de Gruyter.

Miringoff, M. & Miringoff, M. L. (1999). *The social health of the nation: How America is really doing*. New York: Oxford.

Nieves, E. (2000, February 20). Many in Silicon Valley cannot afford housing, even at $50,000 a year. *New York Times*, National, p. 20.

Olson, E. (1999, June 13). Swiss will decide if motherhood warrants salary protection. *New York Times*, p. 11.

Peters, R. H. & Hills, H. A. (1993). Inmates with co-occurring substance abuse and mental health disorders. In H. J. Steadman & J. J. Cocozza (Eds.), *Mental illness in American prisons* (pp. 159–212). Seattle: National Coalition for the Mentally Ill in the Criminal Justice System.

Piven, F. F. & Cloward, R. (1971). *Regulating the poor*. New York: Vintage.

Stout, D. (1999, September 24). Odds worsen in hunt for low-income rentals. *New York Times*, p. A14.

Titmuss, R. (1963). *Essays on the welfare state*, (2d ed.). Boston: Beacon.

Trattner, W. (1999). *From Poor Law to welfare state*, (6th ed.). New York: Free Press.

Wilensky, H. & Lebeaux, C. (1965). *Industrial society and social welfare*. New York: Free Press.

Yardley, J. (1999, January 17). The gas company as social worker. *New York Times*, pp. 35, 39.

SECTION TWO

Overview of the Development of Urban Social Welfare

Introduction

The development of social welfare policies and programs is a dynamic, ongoing process that is guided by changing social and economic conditions. If we are to understand the functions along with the limitations and possibilities of our social welfare system today, and if we are to recognize the impact that it has on social work practice, we must see how this system has been and continues to be shaped by social and economic conditions.

Although one can go much further back in history and explore both ancient and religious origins of concepts such as charity, philanthropy, and social justice, this book will begin by looking at these concepts as they emerged in England between the 14th and 17th centuries. As will be seen in Chapter 4, that was the system of social welfare that was brought by the English settlers to the American colonies, and that same system continued to influence the later development of social welfare in the United States. In fact, critical elements of our present social welfare system can still be traced to laws passed in England more than 650 years ago.

Chapter 5 is concerned with the early development of social welfare in the United States. Events such as the Industrial Revolution, the abolition of slavery, and the growth of cities following massive waves of migration and immigration led to the emergence of social work as a profession and to the growth of the voluntary sector.

The beginning of the public sector on the federal level during the Great Depression is traced in Chapter 6. This chapter also focuses on the growth of the public sector through the 1960s and up to the Clinton presidency. The simultaneous growth of social work is described.

Chapter 7 discusses some of the critical urban social problems that we are facing today and focuses on the policies that have been developed in response to them. The impact of these policies on clients and on the practice of social work is illustrated. This chapter serves as a bridge from the policy section to the practice section that follows.

CHAPTER

4 Origins of the Social Welfare System in England and the American Colonies

People working on the waterfront in salem, Massachusetts, 1771. Library of Congress/etching by Balthasar Friedrich Leizelt

One might wonder what our current approach to poverty and social welfare has to do with English laws passed over 650 years ago. But, as will be seen, some of the attitudes that were reflected in those laws continue today, influencing how we as a society respond to people experiencing a wide range of social problems. As Karl de Schweinitz, a noted historian of the welfare system in England, wrote in 1943, ". . . to understand our own past, we must look to England. There is our inheritance. For more than six hundred years, English statesmen and other English leaders have been writing in statute and literature the record of their attempts to deal with insecurity and human need. Everything that we have addressed to this end derives from their experience or has been influenced by it" (p. v).

Even this brief exploration of the emergence of the social welfare system in England will suggest the powerful and lasting forces it has exerted on social welfare in the United States, particularly on the institutional and residual models of our "modern" public welfare system. This chapter will address:

- The breakdown of feudalism and beginning of industrialization in England during the 14th century, and the insecurity brought about by social, economic, religious, and demographic changes
- The beginnings of the involvement of the English government with the social welfare needs of its people, and the development of a series of laws culminating in the English Poor Law of 1601
- The carry-over of principles of the English Poor Law of 1601 to the poor laws formed in the American colonies
- Issues related to social justice and oppression that persisted in the American colonies despite the colonial poor laws

The Beginnings of Industrialization and the Growth of Cities in England

Looking back to the mid-1300s in England, we see that several processes were taking place that contributed to the growth of industrialization and urban centers.

Breakdown of the Feudal System in England

The feudal system, which had existed for more than 300 years, was in the process of drawing to a close. Under the feudal system, political and economic power was held by wealthy land owners, while most of the population were agricultural workers living as serfs on feudal manors. Under this arrangement, both the economic and social needs of the serfs were met by the lords of the manor (Trattner, 1999). Consequently, when the feudal system came to an end, it brought about basic economic, social, and demographic changes that reshaped how and where people lived, the kind of work they did, the nature of family life, and the nature of the society. One pivotal change that was brought about was the movement of people to the cities, where new social and economic problems emerged, including poverty, homelessness, begging, and thievery.

Several developments served as catalysts to the ending of the feudal system. These developments included the changeover from an agrarian to an urban-based, industrialized economy, the introduction of the enclosure movement, and the ravages of the bubonic plague (Trattner, 1999).

Impact of Industrialization and the Enclosure Movement

Driving the changeover from feudalism to an industrialized economy was the introduction of the woolens industry in England. This industry had developed in many European countries, and in 1331, King Edward III encouraged weavers from Holland to migrate to England. There they joined Flemish weavers already in England, and a highly profitable woolens manufacturing industry was born. Within forty years, England was ready to begin exporting woolen cloth (de Schweinitz, 1943). In order to supply wool for this new and successful business, existing farmland was converted into pastures for sheep grazing. As pastures had to be enclosed to confine the sheep, the changeover in the use of land came to be known as the "enclosure movement."

Points to Ponder

A popular proverb of the time was, "Enclosures make fat beasts and lean poor people." The fat beasts referred to the prosperous landlords, and the lean poor people referred to the serfs who lost their land on the manors (Rice & Grafton, 1994).

While the enclosure of land made it possible to supply raw materials needed for the new woolens industry, the ongoing transfer of land from farming to grazing also contributed to the eventual breakdown of the medieval economy. Serfs whose families had been established in the manorial system for many generations were forced to leave their homes, their work, and the social structure that supported their way of life. While the serfs gained their freedom, at the same time they lost the protection of the lords and barons who had provided them with some measure of economic and social security. Left without this security, the former serfs had to search for ways of providing for their own needs.

Points to Ponder

"In return for imposing a strong measure of constraint on individual freedom, feudalism . . . provided a form of social insurance against the exigencies of life" (Trattner, 1999, p. 4).

Labor Shortages in the Cities Following the Bubonic Plague

The bubonic plague, a disease which was carried by fleas living on rats, spread rapidly across Europe between 1347 and 1350, killing 25,000,000 people—one quarter of the population of Europe. It was called the "bubonic" plague because of the buboes, or swellings, that it caused in the lymph nodes of the groin or armpit. It was also known as the black plague, or the black death, getting its name from the infected black sores that preceded the swellings. Death could occur within days. The plague reached England in 1348, and was followed by two more epidemics that also affected the next generation. By 1400 the population of England was reduced by almost 50 percent (de Schweinitz, 1943; Tierney, 1959).

The plague affected all parts of England, creating labor shortages throughout the country. However, as the animals carrying the disease thrived in warm, dry places, the highest mortality rate was among people living in crowded urban dwellings (Mollat, 1986). This loss created severe shortages of labor in the cities.

With their shortage of labor, the cities in England attracted the unemployed. Agricultural workers left their villages in search of greater economic opportunities and a promise for a better future in the cities. According to Tierney (1959), "There was never a time when so many men had such strong incentives to wander away from their towns and villages to try to better their condition, and the roads became filled with vagrants looking for work or for loot or lured by promises of fabulously high wages" (pp. 111–112).

Social and Economic Insecurity in England

In addition to the ongoing breakdown of the feudal system, the beginnings of industrialization, and the shortage of labor brought about by the plague, other social, economic, religious, and demographic shifts were occurring in England, which also contributed to the insecurities that characterized this time.

Social Changes: The Relocation of Soldiers Returning from War

In addition to the serfs who were searching for new homes and work, social instability was worsened during the century following the outbreak of the bubonic plague as soldiers returning home from the Hundred Years' War attempted to relocate. This war between France and England was fought intermittently between 1337 and 1453, and thousands of English soldiers were discharged after every military campaign. Rather than return to life in their villages, many soldiers took to the road, joining "the bands of vagabonds, half-beggars, half-bandits, who were beginning to infest the countryside" (Tierney, 1959, p. 112).

Economic Changes: The Introduction of a Wage-Based Economy

By the end of the 15th century, a wage-based economy had taken hold in England, and, for the first time, the former serfs became dependent on their wages for all of their economic needs. No longer living within the confines of the feudal manor and raising their own food, they were now faced with new challenges, such as finding a place to live, finding work, paying rent, and buying food. The necessity of finding ways to provide for their own and their families' economic and social needs drove many people into the cities searching for employment.

Religious Changes: The Loss of Charitable Aid through the Catholic Church

Changes within the existing Catholic Church led to the further erosion of the traditional sources of help for people in need. In England during the 16th century, there was no separation of church and state, and the church was a public institution (Trattner, 1999). A compulsory tax was paid by parishioners for the care of the poor in church institutions, such as local parishes and monasteries. In addition, it was common for the well-to-do to leave endowments for the poor, to be administered by the parish priest (Tierney, 1959).

Although corruption in the Catholic Church during the early 1500s interfered with its charitable efforts (Tierney, 1959), to some extent the Catholic Church continued to grant help to those in need. Help was given to individuals in their homes, as well as in institutions. Care to needy groups, such as the elderly, orphans, lepers, travelers, and the destitute was provided in monasteries and in hospitals run by religious orders. However, as a result of the Protestant Reformation in England in 1536, the monasteries were dismantled, and the charitable efforts of the Catholic Church in England came to an end (Tierney, 1959). Consequently, this void had to be replaced by secular means.

Demographic Changes: The Rise of Cities

The number of people residing in the cities in England during the 1300s was small, as compared with the total population of the country. In spite of the relatively small population, these cities were the centers for the emerging industrialization.

Points to Ponder

Most of the population of 2,500,000 in England at the close of the 14th century were still agricultural workers. The population of London in the year 1377 was only 35,000. Other cities, such as York, had close to 11,000 residents, and Bristol had only 9,500 (de Schweinitz, 1943, p. 4).

Displaced agricultural workers, returning soldiers, and the sick and needy who had been cared for in the monasteries and hospitals drifted toward the cities in search of housing and employment. Some were incapable of working, while others lacked the skills necessary for independent living. Desperation drove many to stealing and begging; vagrancy was common (Mollat, 1986).

In London, as in many port cities in Europe, the poor lived in a district near the waterfront. There the rents were lowest, but social problems were widespread. Life was particularly difficult for unmarried women or poor widowed women trying to support themselves and their children. Wages for work as laundresses and seamstresses, which were the most common positions available for women in the cities, were very low; consequently some women turned to prostitution.

Given the increasing social and economic problems and the lack of resources available to the needy, it was left to the government to step in and deal with the increasing poverty and social upheaval (Trattner, 1999).

New Problems Need New Solutions: Government Involvement with the Economic and Social Needs of People

The growing number of people in the cities in England, together with the increase in social problems that developed there, highlighted the question of who would step in to provide support and a social structure for people who were in desperate circumstances.

In addition, personal, social, and economic problems that are inevitable in an industrial economy had arisen, and no provisions were in place to respond to them. For example:

- There was no income for people who were unemployed.
- There was no income for people who were sick or who had had an accident.
- There was no support for children whose parents were unable to work or who had died.
- There was no income for the elderly when they could no longer work.

Beginning in the middle of the 14th century, the government in England stepped in to control the social disturbances that had developed as a result of the breakdown of the feudal system. Through the passage of a series of laws, efforts were made by the government to address such conditions as unemployment, poverty, stealing, begging, and roaming from place to place. As England continued along the path toward further industrialization, more attention was paid to economic causes of poverty, and the government assumed a greater role in responding to the needs of the poor.

Points to Ponder

"England was beginning to experience the economic complications arising from industrial developments. Manufacture had spread until a depression could throw all the members of a family and, indeed, the people of a whole neighborhood out of work. . . . From this moment forward, casual employment, underemployment, intermittent employment, seasonal employment, cyclical employment would be the portion of the worker. At the same time, an industrial civilization would be baffled by the problem of how to provide him with an equivalent of the provision against sickness, old age, and the other personal exigencies which, however inadequate, had been the corollary of his serfdom. These were the circumstances under which . . . poverty became a concern of government. Out of the efforts to solve this problem came a long and varied series of measures and establishments; the latest of which is our present system of social security" (de Schweinitz, 1943, pp. 11, 13).

Efforts of the government to respond to the growing poverty and social disorder were started in England with the passage of the *Statute of Laborers* in 1349. Over the next 250 years, a system of public sector social welfare was formulated, culminating in the *English Poor Law of 1601*. These laws spelled out a system of government-sponsored help for the needy in England.

Similar laws, intended to regulate wages, prices, mobility of workers, unemployment, begging, and relief, were passed around the same time in other European countries, including France, Spain, Portugal, Belgium (then Flanders), Holland, Germany, Switzerland, Italy, and Poland (de Schweinitz, 1943; Mollat, 1986). The laws passed in England, however, stood out: "The system was more complete and methodical, as a result of which it helped to establish principles that influenced the life of the poor for a long time to come" (Mollat, 1986, p. 202). These were the laws that served as a model for the colonies in America, and later for the United States.

The Statute of Laborers of 1349

The first of a series of laws was the Statute of Laborers, introduced in England in 1349. This law was aimed at protecting the interests of employers by controlling wages and controlling the supply of labor, while at the same time restoring social order.

The law mandated that a maximum wage be set in order to restore wages to the level they had been prior to the plague. In addition, workers were prohibited from changing employment. Consequently, people were forced to accept any work and any wage that was offered. The law also limited vagrancy by imposing travel restrictions on the unemployed and on the old and the sick. Further, it made it illegal for employable people to beg and receive charity (Mollat, 1986; Trattner, 1999).

The Act of 1531 and the Law of 1536

The Act of 1531 established, for the first time, two categories of needy people, separating those who could work and those who could not. This law gave local officials the power to identify people in need of help, to register them, and to assign them to particular areas in which they could beg. De Schweinitz (1943) points to the significance of this law: "Compared with present systems of aid for those in need, this may seem like no provision at all. Actually it represented the beginning of definite assumption by government of responsibility for the care of persons in economic distress. In arranging to certify eligibility for begging and in defining areas in which the individual might beg, England had gone a considerable distance toward the administration of relief" (p. 21).

Five years later the Law of 1536 expanded the principles of the Act of 1531. On the one hand, this law continued to mandate severe treatment for those who presumably could work but would not. De Schweinitz (1943) quotes from the law to illustrate the harshness of the punishments: "Any . . . sturdy vagabonds, and valiant beggars . . . upon due examinations and proof of the continuance of his said loitering, wandering and idleness, or vagabondage, shall . . . not only [be] whipped again . . . but also shall have the upper part of the gristle of his right ear clean cut off . . . [If] having the upper part of the right ear cut off . . . and . . . found guilty . . . of continual loitering and idleness, then every such sturdy vagabond and valiant beggar . . . shall have judgment to suffer pains and execution of death as a felon and as enemies of the Commonwealth" (p. 22).

Despite its harshness, this law offered a significant contribution to the development of social welfare policies by introducing the provision of financial relief for those who were not able to work. This approach to helping the needy replaced the permission to beg, which was provided for in the Act of 1531. Money to be used for the care of the poor was to be collected by government and church officials through voluntary contributions. Providing financial aid for needy people unable to work became a key component of subsequent social welfare legislation.

The English Poor Law of 1601

The English Poor Law of 1601, also known as the Elizabethan Poor Law, is generally identified as marking the beginning of public-sector social welfare in England. This law actually was a consolidation of numerous previous laws addressing the treatment of the poor that had been developed subsequent to the Statute of Laborers. The English Poor Law of 1601 included many important features, some of which still impact public social welfare as we know it today. Major features of the Poor Law of 1601 included:

▪ The principle that the government has the responsibility to meet the needs of some of the poor, and that some of the needy have a legal right to assistance. In order to decide who should be helped by the government, three categories of the needy were identified: the *worthy poor*, the *unworthy poor*, and *children*.

The worthy poor, also called the impotent poor, consisted of those unemployed individuals who were not able to support themselves and their families because of serious illness or handicap or because they were too old to work. These people were considered worthy of receiving help. Worthy poor adults were given help, either by financial assistance in their own homes, which was called "outdoor relief," or in institutions such as almshouses, referred to as "indoor relief."

The unworthy poor were also called the able-bodied poor. These individuals were considered unworthy of receiving help because they were seen as being employable if only they were not "lazy," "sinful," or somehow unwilling to work. Conditions that may have affected their ability to work but that were not easily recognized, such as medical or mental illness, were not taken into account. Their poverty was seen as a moral, rather than an economic, issue. Because the unworthy poor were blamed for their own poverty, they also were held responsible for alleviating it. Therefore, the able-bodied poor were given work and those who did not work were punished by being placed in a house of correction, or by being whipped, stoned, and sometimes even put to death.

Care for needy, dependent children became a public responsibility. Help was given in the form of placing children with families of tradesmen as apprentices. The family providing the apprenticeship was not paid, but the children were expected to work for the tradesman during the period of the apprenticeship. The expectation was that the children would eventually become self-supporting.

▪ Responsibility for support spanned three generations. Financially-able adults were held responsible for their children and grandchildren, and financially-able children were responsible for their parents and grandparents.

▪ Authority over the implementation of the Poor Law was given to the local community even though the legislation was national. Assistance was financed by a special local tax to be paid by every household and administered by the local government.

■ The law was implemented by "overseers of the poor," who were appointed in local communities, either by the church or by the county. Their function was to identify the needs of the poor and provide help, as well as to collect taxes from employed residents (Trattner, 1999).

Points to Ponder

Tawney (1926) has said of the English Poor Law, "In England, after three generations in which the attempt was made to stamp out vagrancy by police measures of hideous brutality, the momentous admission was made that its cause was economic distress, not merely personal idleness, and that the whip had no terrors for the man who must either tramp or starve" (p. 262).

Amendment to the Poor Law: The Law of Settlement and Removal of 1662

There were no important changes to the Poor Law for over fifty years. Then, in 1662, the Poor Law was amended to include the Law of Settlement and Removal. This law gave authority to the overseers of the poor to return people to their former place of residence within the first 40 days of their arrival if the person needed assistance, or even if it was thought that the individual might need assistance at some time in the future. This law had two purposes:

1. To keep wages low by restraining people's movement from place to place to find employment with better wages
2. To limit the number of people who might require assistance so that local taxes would be kept as low as possible

Points to Ponder

De Schweinitz (1943) considered this law to be "The most extreme and cruel form of localism that England had known previously or has known since . . . it still stands in history as the ultimate on the negative side of the Elizabethan system of assistance by neighbors to neighbors" (p. 39).

The Law of Settlement and Removal set the stage for residency requirements for public assistance in the American colonies. This remains a political issue in the United States even today.

The American Colonies and the Need for a Program of Public Social Welfare

While some of the settlers came to the American colonies because of intolerance of their religious beliefs, many had been poor in England and migrated with the hope of finding opportunities for a better life. Others who were convicts vagrants, beggars, or political prisoners were transported to the colonies by the English government and were sold to work as indentured servants (Quigley, 1996; Trattner, 1999).

The Need for Economic Assistance in the Colonies

Despite many opportunities for farming or other employment in the American colonies during the 1600s, there always were people in need of economic assistance. These included the elderly, the disabled, the sick, orphans, children of the poor, widows, and the physically and mentally ill whose families were not taking care of them.

In the frontier communities, where people were closely knit, the response to those needing help was through informal, mutual-aid systems (Mencher, 1967). However, by the mid-1600s, despite the fact that there were relatively few people who required help, it was clear that the informal systems of mutual aid were overburdened and that other approaches to the alleviation of poverty had to be found. The need for a different approach to helping the poor was particularly evident in the colonial towns, as both the numbers of people requiring assistance and the extent of their needs made it clear that the system of mutual aid had become inadequate.

The Growth of Cities and Their Social Problems

Although only about five percent of the colonists were living in cities during the 1700s, the cities grew in population and played a dominant role in the social, economic, and political direction of the colonies (Nash, 1982).

Population Changes: 1690–1720

	1690	1720
Boston	7,000	12,000
Philadelphia	4,000	10,000
New York	3,900	7,000

(Bridenbaugh, 1938)

According to Nash (1982), many of the colonists arrived with the ideal of a society that would reflect economic and social equality. However, economic development and population growth led instead to "brash, assertive, individualistic modes of thought and behavior—what would become known as 'the democratic personality' " (p. 215), and business interests were put before idealism. As the cities began to attract a great deal of wealth, the broadening inequalities between the wealthy and the poor became more and more apparent.

Points to Ponder

"Society in the colonies was more and more stratified, wealth became less evenly distributed, and impressively rich and truly impoverished classes emerged. . . . The aggrandizement of wealth became clearly apparent in all sections of the country. . . . In Boston, Newport, New York, Philadelphia, and Charleston stately town houses rose as testimony to the fortunes being acquired in trade, shipbuilding, and land speculation" (Nash, 1982, p. 215).

The cities, and particularly the seaport towns, also drew poor immigrants and transients looking for work. In addition, there was a steady influx of people who were dislocated from the frontiers as a result of the ongoing wars with Native American populations. Even by the middle of the 17th century, before the increase in the population of the cities, social problems had been described in town records. For example, official records in Boston in 1662 indicate that crime was prevalent: "Cases of assault, arson, breaking and entering, embezzlement, fighting and brawling, manslaughter, theft, and the reception of stolen goods appear in mounting numbers . . ." (Bridenbaugh, 1938, pp. 69–70).

With the growth of the population in the cities, the labor force increased, leading to additional unemployment. By the middle and late 1700s, there was even more widespread unemployment resulting from economic conditions, such as slumps in business and inflation. Consequently, poverty in the cities was rapidly increasing (Quigley, 1996).

There were only a few charitable or religious organizations to assist the needy. The first private welfare organization in America was the Scots' Charitable Society, which was established in Boston in 1657. It was not until the second half of the 18th century that other ethnic groups established charitable organizations. There also were no separate institutions for needy children until 1727, when the Ursuline Convent in New Orleans was established (Trattner, 1999). Thus the need for a more organized approach to helping the poor became evident. For this approach, the colonists turned to their familiar tradition of public assistance based on the English Poor Law.

Features of the Colonial Poor Laws

The Poor Laws in the colonies were established during the 17th century and bore a close resemblance to the English Poor Law of 1601. Colonial poor laws encouraged work for all but those who were clearly unemployable. Although each colony had its own poor laws, determined by its specific economic and social circumstances, there were common principles that were based on the Elizabethan Poor Laws. These included:

■ The principle of separation of the needy into categories of *worthy*, *unworthy*, and *needy children* was the basis for the poor laws in the American colonies, as it had been in England. Help was given to the worthy poor, either in the form of "indoor" or "outdoor" relief. Outdoor relief was help to people while they continued to live in their own homes, and indoor relief was help for those unable to live on their own. Indoor relief could be provided in institutions, such as almshouses or workhouses. These institutions often were used interchangeably, housing together those who were unemployable with the employable poor. Another approach to providing care in the northern colonies was what might be seen as an early form of foster care, called "auctioning off." People needing care were placed in the homes of families in the community who were willing to provide the care for the least amount of money. This was done at public expense.

The unworthy poor were treated in a manner similar to their treatment in England: They were offered public employment, such as work in public inns and on ferries, and if that was refused, they were considered to be sinful and were punished by being put in jail, or being whipped and sent out of town. Some were bound out as indentured servants.

Neglected children and young orphans were apprenticed to tradesmen. This arrangement served to keep children living within a family structure while also preparing them for employment. It also helped meet the need for labor, and did not present a financial burden to the town. Although there was no uniform policy regarding the length of apprenticeships, they generally lasted seven years. Both girls and boys could be apprenticed until they reached the age of 21, although in Virginia, girls remained in apprenticeships only until age 18. Boys were apprenticed to tradespeople such as merchants, goldsmiths, wagon makers, printers, or weavers, while girls usually learned cooking and sewing to prepare them for their future roles as homemakers (Bridenbaugh, 1938).

■ Responsibility to help relatives in financial need spanned three generations, including the responsibility of financially able adults for their children and grandchildren, and financially able children for their parents and grandparents.

■ Responsibility for the poor was left to the smallest unit of government so each community, whether a town or a city, was responsible for the support of its needy.

■ In the northern colonies, overseers of the poor were appointed to provide help to the needy, as well as assess and collect taxes for the care of the poor; while in the southern colonies, the Anglican church assumed these responsibilities in individual parishes.

■ Residency requirements were established in each town or city, stipulating that only people who had established residency in that locale would be eligible to receive aid. This served to limit the number of people requiring assistance by discouraging people who had no means of support from moving with the intention of receiving help.

Implementation of the Colonial Poor Laws

During the 18th century, the growing city of Boston, which had become the center of business in New England, came to be known as "a haven for the provincial poor" (Lee, 1982, p. 581). While very few people in all the colonies had been receiving assistance during the 17th century, by 1757, one thousand people were receiving poor relief in

Boston alone (Quigley, 1996). Some who were both poor and ill were cared for in the Boston jail. However, whenever possible, people were maintained in their own homes through outdoor relief.

Although it had been the policy to have people who could not live independently cared for by individuals or families who were paid to take the poor into their homes, this practice became less popular as the population grew. While people had been willing to board neighbors and people they had known, they were not willing to help those who were not part of their community.

As the population increased in the larger cities such as Boston, Plymouth, and New York, institutions such as almshouses or workhouses were established to house and care for the needy (Lee, 1982; Mencher, 1967). During the 1700s, these institutions were used not only for the poor, but also to house criminals and the mentally ill (Bridenbaugh, 1938).

Points to Ponder

In 1630, there were between 400 and 500 people living in Plymouth Colony, and by 1643 the population had increased to 700. Between 1630 and 1645, there were 57 relief cases on record (over 8 percent of the population), some of which were carried year after year, and others whose names appeared just once (Lee, 1982).

Issues of Social Justice and Oppression in Colonial America

Despite the help provided by the colonial poor laws, social injustice and oppression continued to affect many groups during the colonial period.

Issues of Social Justice

Social and economic policies in the colonies did not address issues of social justice, but rather served to sustain the economic and political power positions of wealthy, landowning white men. For example:

- Slavery, as well as the practice of indenture, were accepted throughout the colonies
- Educational opportunities for children of all but the rich were severely limited
- The right to vote was severely restricted, and the same group of wealthy, white, male landowners retained political power

Slavery throughout the Colonies

Although most slaves were located in southern colonies, slavery existed throughout the colonies and also played a significant role in urban areas (Quigley, 1996). In Boston, the number of slaves rose from 400 in 1708 to 2,000 by 1720, when they comprised 17 percent of the population (Bridenbaugh, 1996). By 1746, slaves made up more than 21 percent of New York's population (Abramovitz, 1988). In New York, as in other northern cities, many slaves did the same work as free white laborers. In 1711, Wall Street was designated as the area where slaves could be taken by their owners to be hired out by the day or week (Bridenbaugh, 1938).

A growing awareness of the contradiction between slavery and the ideals of the American Revolution were articulated in the abolitionist movement during the Pre-revolutionary period. Slavery was identified as a degradation for whites as well as for blacks. According to Nash (1982), "The imprisonment of blacks was external and physical, while for the whites it was internal and spiritual" (p. 269). Although abolished in some of the northern colonies during this period, slavery and an economic dependence on slaves were increasing in the South.

Lack of Educational Opportunities for Poor Children

Although efforts were made to provide opportunities for public education for the poor, these opportunities were limited and were almost nonexistent for children of slaves and Native Americans. Some cities, such as Boston, Newport, and Philadelphia, became important centers for education. Boston had the most highly developed system of public education in the western world, and in 1738 it had almost 600 students in its schools. However, although these were called free schools they were only partially publicly funded, and students' families were expected to pay toward the support of the teachers. There was an effort to develop what were known as charity schools for the poor in Boston, but sufficient funding was not made available. In Charleston, money was contributed for tuition for some poor students (Bridenbaugh, 1938).

The need to educate apprentices, particularly in reading and writing, was addressed in some of the colonies. For example, in Massachusetts, a law was passed in 1648 specifying "compulsory book learning and religious instruction in all indentures of apprenticeship" (Bridenbaugh, 1938, p. 127), and twenty years later another law was passed to ensure its enforcement. New York took the lead in the development of evening schools, which were effective in providing educational opportunities for some apprentices (Bridenbaugh, 1938).

Limitations on the Right to Vote

Voting rights in the colonies were severely limited. In twelve of the thirteen colonies, the only people who could vote were white men who owned property. The exception was South Carolina, which extended voting privileges to white men who did not own property but were taxpayers. As indicated earlier, these policies served to keep all political power centered among the wealthy, white, male landowners.

Oppressed Population Groups

In addition to slaves and indentured servants, other groups were victimized by oppressive policies that restricted opportunities for economic and social advancement, keeping them disenfranchised and in a perpetual state of hardship. These included:

- Women, including slaves, indentured servants, and the poor
- Free blacks
- Native Americans
- Free workers

Women—Slaves, Indentured Servants, and the Poor

Women, both black and white, were oppressed during the colonial period. Motivated by economic gain, racism, and fear, slave owners often separated slave families. Black female slaves could not marry, and had no protection against sexual abuse. After 1808, when the slave trade became illegal, female slaves became even more valued for their childbearing. Some were promised freedom after giving birth to many children, and were given small amounts of money, extra food, and clothing (Quigley, 1996).

White women who were indentured servants also were denied legal rights. They were not permitted to marry and frequently were exploited sexually. An indentured servant who became pregnant was fined, and whipped if she did not pay the fine. Her term of indenture could be extended for up to two years to make up for her lost time at work (Abramovitz, 1988).

Poor, free white women were also vulnerable. Many who had no means of support moved to the cities, especially those who were widowed, who were abandoned by their husbands, or who were unmarried mothers. In some colonial cities, one-third to one-half of the poor were women (Quigley, 1996).

Free Blacks

There were many free blacks in the cities. Among them were the indentured servants whose term of service was completed, slaves who had been freed, runaway slaves who found shelter in northern communities, slaves who had purchased their freedom, and refugees who came from the West Indies.

Abramovitz (1988) described the life of free blacks during the early years in the colonies: "For a short while, colonial leaders tolerated the growth of a free black population. . . . Free blacks voted, intermarried with whites, held minor elective office, owned property, and a few amassed huge fortunes and became slave-holders" (p. 83). However, as the economy of the colonies became more dependent on slave labor, free blacks with civil rights were seen as a threat to the institution of slavery. Laws, known as "slave codes," were introduced in the colonies to restrict the activities of both slaves and free blacks. As a result, both of these groups were oppressed and kept outside the mainstream of society. In Virginia, by the middle of the 18th century, slave codes included such requirements as registration of free blacks with the town official. In other areas, free blacks were prohibited from entertaining slaves without permission from their masters. Servitude for free blacks was introduced as the punishment for failure to pay fines, and slave owners were required to post a bond before freeing their slaves (Abramovitz, 1988; Quigley, 1996).

Free blacks generally were denied any public assistance under the colonial poor laws, and they turned to mutual aid groups instead. When this was not available, some free blacks who were destitute resorted to voluntary enslavement as their only way of survival. Such enslavement might last up to twenty years (Quigley, 1996).

Although social and economic mobility for free blacks was severely limited in the colonies, some opportunities for education did exist in the cities. For example, a charity school, established by philanthropists in Philadelphia in 1741, admitted black students. In Boston, a school for "The Instructions of Negros [sic], in Reading, Catechizing, and Writing" (Bridenbaugh, 1938, p. 443) was started by James Pigett in 1728, where for a small fee, masters could send their black servants, and in Charleston, a Mr. Boulson established a school for blacks in 1740. He was accused in court of violation of the slave code because he was teaching blacks to read; however, he was allowed to continue (Bridenbaugh, 1938, p. 443).

Native Americans

Native Americans also were denied relief during the Colonial period. According to Quigley (1996), "Colonial laws that addressed concerns about the Indians were usually regulations of, rather than regulations for, them" (pp. 80–81). Laws that were passed limited their rights to enter towns, or, as in the case of Salem, Massachusetts, they were permitted to enter the town only in daylight hours (Quigley, 1996, p. 81).

Free Workers

Free laborers of all races were subject to laws intended to protect the interests of the employers rather than the workers. Such laws were established to guarantee sufficient labor while holding wages at a subsistence level. In some of the northern colonies, maximum wages were set, and in the middle and southern colonies, local authorities could set the maximum wage (Quigley, 1996).

Free male workers could also be subject to forced labor by local governments and could be required to accept work on public works projects even though they might be employed elsewhere. A worker was also required to complete a task before quitting a job or would face a fine (Quigley, 1996).

Conclusion

This chapter has begun the brief historical review of several processes, including: (1) the development of urban communities and the emergence of urban social problems; (2) the beginnings of public social welfare as a response to these problems; (3) changes in the understanding of the causes of poverty and the role of the community in alleviating poverty; and (4) the development of policies to deal with oppression. These processes have been viewed historically, beginning in 17th century England and concluding with the colonial period.

The following chapter will continue this brief review, looking at the growth of cities in the United States during the 19th and 20th centuries, and at the social problems that emerged during that period. Government efforts to respond to these problems will be reviewed, and the development of the social work profession in the United States will be traced within the context of its response to urban social problems. The ongoing issues related to social justice and oppression will be addressed.

REFERENCES

Abramovitz, M. (1988). *Regulating the lives of women.* Boston: South End Press.

Bridenbaugh, C. (1938/1955). *Cities in the wilderness: The first century of urban life in America, 1625–1742.* New York: Knopf.

de Schweinitz, K. (1943/1961). *England's road to social security.* New York: Perpetua/A. S. Barnes.

Lee, C. R. (1982). Public poor relief and the Massachusetts community, 1620–1715. *The New England Quarterly, 55*(4), 564–585.

Mencher, S. (1967). *Poor law to poverty program.* Pittsburgh, PA: University of Pittsburgh Press.

Mollat, M. (1986). *The poor in the Middle Ages: An essay in social history* (A. Goldhammer, Trans.). New Haven, CT: Yale University Press.

Nash, G. (1982). *Red, white, and black: The peoples of early America* (2d ed.). Englewood Cliffs, NJ: Prentice-Hall.

Quigley, W. P. (1996, Fall). Work or starve: Regulation of the poor in Colonial America. *University of San Francisco Law Review, 31,* 35–83.

Rice, E. F. & Grafton, A. (1994). *The foundations of early modern Europe, 1460–1559* (2d ed.). New York: W. W. Norton.

Tawney, R. H. (1926). *Religion and the road to capitalism.* New York: Harcourt, Brace.

Tierney, B. (1959). *Medieval poor law.* Berkeley: University of California Press.

Trattner, W. (1999). *From poor law to welfare state* (6th ed.). New York: Free Press.

5 The Urban Roots of Social Welfare and Social Work in the United States

Newly arrived immigrant children in New York City learn English, 1922. The mother of one of the authors was in this class. Courtesy of Norma Phillips

Although the colonial Poor Laws involved local governments in providing help for people, as the extent of need swelled during the 1800s, local and even state governments no longer had the resources to provide for everyone. During the 19th century, the United States experienced dramatic growth, particularly in the cities. While immigrants and migrants settling in urban areas made critically important contributions to the social, cultural, and economic development of the cities, this rapid growth also meant that there were more people living in poverty, and that the social problems of the cities had become vast. In addition, the profound social upheavals brought about by the Civil War demanded new approaches to meeting human needs.

Failed efforts to involve the federal government with the social welfare of people in need left the tasks of helping to the voluntary sector of social services. This chapter provides a brief overview of the development of the voluntary sector of social work in the cities during the 1800s and explores the early development of the social work profession. It traces:

- The impact of immigration, migration, industrialization, and urbanization during the 1800s

- Changes in attitudes toward the poor and their care prior to the Civil War
- Social reform efforts during the Civil War and during the Reconstruction period
- The development of voluntary agencies, including sectarian and nonsectarian agencies
- The development of social work as a profession

Immigration, Migration, Industrialization, and Urbanization: Driving Forces of the 1800s

During the 1800s several important processes that shaped the development of social welfare in the cities were occurring simultaneously. These processes included immigration, migration, industrialization, and urbanization.

The Growing Nation

By the time the Civil War began, the population of the United States was six times larger than it was at the time of the Revolutionary War. This phenomenal growth took place in less than 100 years. While some of the increase in population was due to births; to immigration from China and Japan; and to the inclusion of 80,000 Mexicans who became part of the United States following the annexation of Texas, the Mexican-American War and the Gadsden Purchase (Marden, Meyer, & Engel, 1992); by far the greatest impact was made by the six million immigrants from Europe who arrived in the Unites States between 1800 and 1860 (Trattner, 1999).

Most European immigrants arrived through northeastern ports and settled in the cities, where industry was developing and jobs would most likely be available. Consequently, the population of the cities increased from 202,000 in 1790 to 6.2 million

Points to Ponder

The first census in the U.S. was taken in 1790. As can be seen from this chart, the population of the U.S. steadily increased between 1790 and 1860. These numbers underestimate the population because Native Americans were excluded from the count:

1790	3,929,000
1800	5,297,000
1830	12,901,000
1840	17,120,000
1850	23,261,000
1860	31,513,000

(Axinn & Levin, 1997, p. 36)

people in 1860. New cities were formed in New England and the Middle Atlantic states, as well as in the South and West (Axinn & Levin, 1997).

Changes in Attitudes and Care of the Poor during the Pre-Civil War Period

Most of the 6 million immigrants were Catholics from Ireland and Germany. Their religion, cultural patterns, lifestyles, and language differed from the Protestant majority then living in the United States, and resulted in an atmosphere of mistrust and resentment. In addition, many of the immigrants arrived destitute, without resources, skills, or social supports. Trattner (1999) states, "That many of the immigrants were victims of malnutrition, exploitation, the Irish potato famine, the cruel voyage across the sea, thieves and swindlers waiting to fleece them as soon as they stepped off the boat, vile slums and substandard wages, and other wretched living and working conditions, was ignored by the dominant majority" (p. 55).

Discrimination against the new immigrants, and particularly against those who were poor, increased. The myth that opportunities for employment were available to all who wanted to work, and the denial of the existence of economic causes of poverty, such as low wages, economic depressions, and seasonal employment in some industries, led to a blaming of the poor for their poverty. The belief that poverty was caused by laziness or immorality was held by many, and was supported by the Protestant ethic, which emphasized the value of hard work, morality, and independence (Trattner, 1999).

The Movement from Local to Centralized Responsibility for the Poor

As a result of resentment and mistrust toward immigrants, people were less willing to assume responsibility for them and treatment of the poor became more punitive. Consequently, local governments objected to supporting the poor and the principle of local responsibility was replaced by a centralized approach to providing help. This shift began by moving the responsibility for caring for the poor first from the towns to the counties, and then some of the responsibility was assumed by the states. As a result, the experience of both giving and getting help became more and more depersonalized.

Points to Ponder

"The changes in the nation's socioeconomic life—the influx of immigrants, the expansion of an industrial–capitalist economy, the growth of cities and a vast network of canals, railroads, and highways, the increase in travel and mobility, the westward movement . . . all of which helped to change the poor from 'neighbors' to members of the 'lower classes'—made it impossible to maintain a completely local and insular poor relief system" (Trattner, 1999, p. 59).

The Shift from Outdoor Relief to Indoor Relief

The punitive attitude toward the poor led to severe criticisms of the existing outdoor relief programs—those programs that were aimed at making it possible for people to be given help while remaining in their own homes. According to Bremner (1956), "The aim of public relief in the nineteenth century was to prevent starvation and death from exposure as economically as possible" (p. 47).

As was the custom during the colonial period, some of the destitute lived with families through the system of auctioning off the needy to those who asked the least payment for their care. However, the homes and the type of care given were unsupervised and the poor were often deprived of food, clothing, and other essential needs.

This system, which was used for both adults and orphaned or abandoned children, continued to be used until 1875 (Bremner, 1956), by which time there was a growing movement from outdoor to indoor relief. In cities such as New York, Philadelphia, Providence, and Baltimore, studies were carried out that justified assistance in institutions such as almshouses and workhouses, rather than providing for people's needs within a family context, as had been favored during the colonial period (Trattner, 1999). Consequently, fewer people were supported in their own homes, and outdoor relief was used only in cases of emergencies. In its place, more and more institutions were built. By 1900, public outdoor relief had completely ended in cities such as Atlanta, Baltimore, Cincinnati, Charleston, Denver, Indianapolis, Kansas City, Louisville, Memphis, New Orleans, New York, Pittsburgh, St. Louis, San Francisco, and Washington, DC (Trattner, 1999).

Points to Ponder

In Massachusetts, the number of almshouses increased rapidly:

Year	Number of Almshouses
1824	83
1839	180
1860	219

(Trattner, 1999, p. 59)

Social Reform during the Pre-Civil War Period: The Example of Dorothea Lynde Dix and Her Work for the Mentally Ill

The young and old, the sane and mentally ill, the healthy and sick, and criminals and alcoholics were all placed together in the same institutions. The terrible conditions in these institutions became the focal point for social reformers, who identified and raised public awareness about the needs of particular groups who were institutionalized. Consequently, specialized state institutions, such as orphanages, penitentiaries, and mental hospitals were eventually established (Trattner, 1999).

Points to Ponder

". . . the public complacently considered that the community's responsibility to its dependents was met if . . . an institution was available, with almost no regard for the quality of care actually given. The result was that most almshouses held a conglomerate mixture of very young, feeble-minded, insane, handicapped, ill, and aged persons in all stages of deterioration. Where even such an almshouse was lacking or an inmate proved troublesome, often the local jail was the only custodial resource" (Pumphrey & Pumphrey, 1961, p. 124).

Dorothea Lynde Dix was a social reformer who had a major impact on the care of the poor mentally ill during the mid-1800s, and who ultimately had a profound and lasting effect on the delivery of social services in the United States. Dorothea Dix identified:

- The importance of separating the needy into categories based on their individual needs, so that appropriate services could be provided
- The need to involve the federal government in the funding of costly social welfare programs

Identifying the Mentally Ill as a Group with Special Needs

While teaching Sunday school to incarcerated women in the city of Cambridge, Massachusetts, Dorothea Dix witnessed the cruel treatment of the indigent mentally ill, who, for lack of other facilities, were kept in prisons or in almshouses. Determined to find a way to improve their treatment, Dix traveled through twelve states, observing the care of the mentally ill in various institutions, and studying and recording the conditions under which the mentally ill were confined. Dorothea Dix "described vividly how many of the unfortunate crazed were impounded in cabins, cages, closets, stalls, and other pens of one kind or another, often chained and then abandoned to filth and neglect, or else brutally beaten . . ." (Trattner, 1999, p. 65). Guiding her approach to achieving social change was the belief that "Reform comes from patient, factual research" (Trattner, 1999, p. 65)—a model for social change that is equally important today.

Based on her research of the type of care the mentally ill were receiving in almshouses, workhouses, and prisons, Dorothea Dix made the case for caring for the mentally ill in separate institutions, where specialized care could be provided. Although some states already had both public and private institutions specifically for the care of the mentally ill, these were not sufficient to meet the needs.

Early Efforts to Involve the Federal Government in Helping the Mentally Ill

Dix saw the lack of specialized institutions as a national problem. She recognized that the costs of developing hospitals for the indigent mentally ill were beyond the resources of the counties or even of the states, so she turned to the federal government to request additional funding. Unlike today, when social workers might apply for federal grants for particular projects, such grants were not yet in existence and the federal government had no formal commitment to helping people in need. In spite of that, though, there had been some history of federal assistance, such as provision of land grants to educational institutions, help given to victims of fires and floods during the early part of the 1800s, and the establishment of a pension program for war veterans in 1818 (Trattner, 1999).

So it was not without precedent that Dix turned to the United States Congress in 1848 to propose that the federal government set aside land as a national endowment for the care of the mentally ill. Although her bill was finally passed by Congress in 1854 and ten million acres of public land were to be appropriated to establish hospitals for the mentally ill, the bill was vetoed that same year by President Franklin Pierce in what has come to be known as the "Pierce Veto." In his veto, President Pierce maintained that the states were responsible for the care of the needy, and that this was not a function of the federal government. The veto also raised the concern that if the federal government were to provide for the care of one group of the needy, it would then be expected to provide for all groups.

Points to Ponder

In his veto, President Franklin Pierce stated, "If Congress have power to make provision for the indigent insane . . . it has the same power to provide for the indigent who are not insane, and thus to transfer to the Federal Government the charge of all the poor in all the States. It has the same power to provide hospitals and other local establishments for the care and cure of every species of human infirmity, and thus to assume all that duty of either public philanthropy, or public necessity to the dependent, the orphan, the sick, or the needy, which is now discharged by the States themselves, or by corporate institutions, or private endowments existing under the legislation of the States" (quoted from the Pierce veto, 1854, in Pumphrey & Pumphrey, 1961, p. 132).

Although Dorothea Dix was not successful in establishing the precedent for federal funding for programs for the needy, she did bring this problem to the awareness of the public, and she obtained funding from other sources for building thirty-two institutions for the care of the mentally ill (Axinn & Levin, 1997).

Social Reform during the Civil War Period and Reconstruction

Attempts to provide public social services were also made in response to the social disorganization brought about by the Civil War. Efforts were made by local, state, and federal governments to provide help to specific groups of people, both during and after the war. Groups requiring help included soldiers and their families, veterans, freed slaves, and others dislocated by the war.

Government efforts included bounties paid to the families of soldiers to encourage enlistment (Bremner, 1956); assistance given by state and county governments to the dependents of soldiers; a federal pension system for disabled soldiers and families of servicemen who were killed in the war, followed by a pension based on need rather than disability; a national military and naval asylum for totally disabled soldiers and sailors of the Union Army; and a system of homes for veterans. During the war, the United States Sanitary Commission was established to address the health and welfare needs of people in the military, and to sensitize the nation to the needs of veterans (Axinn & Levin, 1997).

In the South, many families of Confederate soldiers became impoverished, and special legislation to provide emergency assistance was enacted by southern localities. As the Civil War progressed, responsibility for meeting the needs of soldiers and their families shifted from voluntary agencies to local governments, then to state governments, and finally to the Confederate Congress. Eventually, social welfare in the South was taken over by the federal government through the Freedmen's Bureau.

The Freedmen's Bureau

Known officially as the Bureau of Refugees, Freedmen, and Abandoned Lands, the Freedmen's Bureau was established by Congress in 1865, just two months before the Civil War ended. This bureau has great historical significance for two reasons:

- It was the first government program in the United States to provide services to blacks.
- It was the first *federal* relief agency.

Because government money was not appropriated specifically for the activities of the Freedmen's Bureau, it was operated out of the War Department and was dependent on the military for funding its programs and staff.

The Freedmen's Bureau helped former slaves make the transition to freedom and also provided help to whites who suffered from the upheaval of the Civil War. "Food and clothing were distributed; hospitals, schools, orphan asylums, and homes for the aged and infirm were established; plantation lands were leased to freedmen, jobs were found for them, and labor contracts were supervised; housing and transportation were arranged for job-seekers; courts were set up, and legal counsel about their rights was offered to Negroes" (Olds, 1963, p. 247). In addition, the Freedmen's Bureau supported schools for black children, and provided support for black colleges. The Freedmen's Bureau was directed by a General named Oliver Howard, a very effective and successful administrator. Howard University, a distinguished black university in Washington, DC, is named for him.

In spite of its important work, the Freedmen's Bureau was controversial. It raised questions about the role of the federal government in providing for the social welfare of specific groups, much the same as Dorothea Dix's proposal that the federal government act in the interest of the mentally ill. And, as Dix's proposed legislation was upheld in Congress and vetoed by President Franklin Pierce, the Freedmen's Bureau also was upheld in Congress, but its continuation was vetoed by the president at the time, Andrew Johnson.

In his veto message, President Johnson stated, "A system for the support of indigent persons in the United States was never contemplated by the authors of the Constitution, nor can any good reason be advanced why, as a permanent establishment, it should be founded for one class or color of our people more than another. Pending the war, many refugees and freedmen received support from the Government, but it was never intended that they should henceforth be fed, clothed, educated, and sheltered by the United States. The idea on which the slaves were assisted to freedom was that, on becoming free, they would be a self-sustaining population" (quoted in Axinn & Levin, 1997, p. 90).

With yet another obstacle to federal involvement in social welfare presented by the Johnson veto, the burden to help the needy remained confined to state and local governments and to voluntary agencies. Because the poorest communities had the least money available to help the needy, much of the responsibility for welfare programs fell to the voluntary sector.

The Urban Roots of Voluntary Social Agencies: Responding to the Social Problems of the Cities

Bremner describes the burgeoning cities of the 1800s: "It was in the slums of the larger cities that Americans discovered the new poverty that was invading the nation in the wake of industrialization, urban growth, and immigration. Here were new worlds of wretchedness characterized by ways of life foreign to American experience and menacing to conventional standards of decency" (1956, p. 4).

Points to Ponder

Jacob Riis, who was a journalist, photographer, and social reformer living and working in New York City during this period, said of the city, "Its poverty, its slums, and its suffering are the result of unprecedented growth with the consequent disorder and crowding, and the common penalty of metropolitan greatness" (1890/1971, p. 148).

It was in response to the critical social problems that arose in cities around the country that the voluntary sector of social work developed. As discussed in Chapter 3, agencies in the voluntary sector may be sectarian, which are religiously affiliated and supported, or nonsectarian, which are secular and are not connected to or supported by any religious group.

Among the voluntary agencies that began in the United States around the middle of the 1800s, and which illustrate the various approaches taken to help people in urban areas were:

- The Association for Improving the Conditions of the Poor
- Charity Organization Societies
- The Children's Aid Society
- Settlement Houses
- Various sectarian agencies

The Association for Improving
the Conditions of the Poor

Organized nonsectarian agencies began in the United States toward the middle of the 1800s. The Association for Improving the Conditions of the Poor, known as the AICP, was started in New York City in 1843 under the leadership of Robert Hartley, and similar organizations were developed in other cities around the country. Despite the fact that the organization was formed in the years following the economic depression of 1837, which resulted in widespread unemployment and poverty, the AICP was based on the assumption that poverty was an individual matter and that the poor were responsible for their own economic state. According to Hartley (1882), "Almost all pauperism comes from indolence, intemperance and other vices. To remove the evil we must remove the causes, and these being chiefly moral, they admit only moral remedies. . . . Apart from death, and accident, and unavoidable disease, the wretchedness of humanity is resolvable to moral causes" (p. 307).

The AICP used male volunteers to visit the poor in their homes, with the goal of reeducating and achieving personal reform of the poor. The giving of financial assistance was seen as a less important objective. Most of the volunteers were white, middle-class Protestants, while their clients were white, European-Catholic immigrants who had settled in the cities. According to Trattner (1999), the AICP "evolved into a leading spokesman for an urban middle class bewildered by the rapid spread of poverty and anxious over its possible effects" (p. 68).

However, as the volunteers visited the poor in their homes, their assumptions about the causes of poverty were challenged. They became aware of the lack of jobs, and they saw the consequences of low wages for those who were working. The AICP abandoned its early approach of personal reform, and instead began providing financial support for those who needed it. It also addressed the need for government enforcement of safety standards in housing construction and sanitation in slum areas. In addition, the agency fought against the practice of the adulteration of milk, which involved the watering down of milk and selling it as whole milk. As a result of this practice, children were not getting proper nutrition, and illnesses such as rickets were common among urban poor children.

While the AICP started out to re-educate the poor and influence their morality, the agency administrators and volunteers were instead educated by the poor in how they understood the causes and consequences of poverty. Personal responsibility for poverty was replaced by an appreciation for the economic and social causes of poverty. Contrary to its beginnings, the AICP ultimately served as "a leading advocate of social reform" (Trattner, 1999, p. 71).

Charity Organization Societies

The charity organization movement originated in London in 1869. In the United States, the first Charity Organization Society, referred to as the COS, was started in Buffalo, New York in 1877, and others followed in all the major cities around the country. Just as the AICP was started during an economic depression, so did the Charity Organization Societies come at a time when three million people were left unemployed because of the depression during the 1870s.

The Charity Organization Societies, also known as Associated Charities, did not originally provide financial assistance to clients. Rather, the agency was based on a "scientific approach" to poverty, looking into requests for help and trying to prevent duplication of services by various philanthropic organizations, preventing fraud in applications for assistance, and exerting a moral influence on the poor to help them overcome their poverty. The theme of the "worthy" and "unworthy" poor that was introduced by the Elizabethan Poor Laws was perpetuated, as applicants for relief had to be certified as "worthy" by COS agents before being referred to a participating relief-giving agency.

Similar to the AICP, the COS used volunteers, called friendly visitors, for its work. However, unlike the AICP before it, the COS recruited women as well as men to serve as volunteers. By 1892, of the 4,000 COS volunteers in cities around the country, women were in the majority (Bremner, 1956). The friendly visitors were expected to work toward changing the behavior of the poor. Toward the end of the 1800s, the volunteers were replaced by paid workers, with the mainly wealthy volunteers taking on an advisory and fund-raising function.

Points to Ponder

According to Bremner (1956), "Friendly visitors were expected to be combination detectives and moral influences. They were to ascertain the reason for the applicants' need and to help them overcome it. Their function was not to help the poor obtain charitable assistance, but by advice and example to stimulate them to become self-supporting" (p. 52).

The outcome of the work of the friendly visitors should not be surprising. As they "investigated" the reasons for the poverty of individual cases, they discovered the same economic and social causes of poverty that the AICP volunteers had discovered earlier, including "involuntary unemployment, industrial accidents, and low wages, not in intemperance, improvidence, and the like. It became quite clear, then, that preconceived notions about the poor had to be discarded, or at least seriously reconsidered . . ." (Trattner, 1999, p. 100).

The COS workers also worked toward social change. According to Trattner, (1999), "Organized charities . . . were taking part in . . . activities which, if not aimed at altering the social order, at least sought to mitigate some of its worst effects—housing reform, antituberculosis work, publication of reform-oriented journals, and the like, including juvenile court, probation work, and other measures for child welfare" (p. 103).

Another important outcome of the work of the Charity Organization Societies was the development of *casework* as a method of helping, and the recognition of the need for professional workers who were educated and experienced in the casework method. Consequently, the organized charities developed special training schools for charity workers—the first step in the development of social work as a profession.

The Children's Aid Society

Illness, poverty, and desperate living conditions of newly arrived immigrants who settled in the cities, combined with the lack of social services to assist them, resulted in neglect and abandonment of hundreds of thousands of children of all ages. Jacob Riis (1890/1971) photographed and vividly described the plight of the poor living in tenement buildings on New York City's Lower East Side. Riis wrote about infants abandoned by their destitute parents, left in gutters to be picked up by the police, or in hallways of buildings during the winter months. Three or four infants could be found every night, 90 percent of whom died.

It was during this time that children were being removed from almshouses and that the practices of apprenticeship and indenture came to an end. Institutions for children, known as orphan asylums, were established mostly by religious and ethnic groups. These institutions became overcrowded; food was scarce; and child care staff was minimal (Trattner, 1999).

It was in this social milieu that Charles Loring Brace, a minister who worked in New York City's poorest district, came to know the conditions in which the very poor and their children lived. Brace was horrified by the conditions he saw on the streets. Children were homeless and starving, and many joined gangs. Ten thousand homeless children were living on the streets of New York, and 5,000 of these children were on the streets at all times. The police arrested vagrant children as young as five years old, and put them in prison with adults. Social reformers urged that these children be sent to orphan asylums instead of prison, but Brace thought the idea of sending the children to asylums was unacceptable because children were not taught useful skills there.

Instead, Brace devised a plan that would serve two functions. On the one hand, he wanted to remove these children, whom he described as being part of the "dangerous classes" of society (Brace, 1872/1973), because he considered them disruptive to life in the city. On the other hand, he wanted to rescue the children by sending them to live with families in rural areas in the Midwest, with the intention that they would remain permanently with their new families. In 1853, he established the Children's Aid Society in order to implement this plan. This was the first voluntary agency to place children in the care of families rather than in institutions.

Traveling west on what came to be known as the *Orphan Trains*, 100,000 boys and girls were sent away from their homes in the cities. The program began in 1853 and was terminated in 1929. These children were removed forever from their families and their familiar environment and sent to live with strangers thousands of miles away.

Points to Ponder

"Foster care practice in the 19th century was a terminal service: its purpose was achieved once the child was removed from his or her home of origin—and from the pernicious influences of the city—and placed with the substitute family in a nonurban environment" (Holody, 1997, p. 137).

This approach of placing needy children in homes rather than institutions was replicated by other agencies and in other cities, such as the Boston Children's Aid Association, and the Children's Aid Society of Pennsylvania (Trattner, 1999).

A documentary film produced in 1995 by the public television station, WGBH in Boston, titled *The Orphan Trains* tells us a great deal about the impact of this program on its participants. Research for this film, including poignant interviews with now-elderly individuals who were among the children sent away from their urban homes, teaches us how children in need can best be helped. For example, some of the features of the program that had detrimental effects on the participants were:

■ Communication with parents was cut off, leaving the children with no information or contact with their families. Letters that parents gave to children when they left were taken from them by agency staff, and letters sent to the agency by the children for their parents were never delivered. The children experienced feelings of abandonment, confusion, and anger. It is apparent today that this approach to foster care is detrimental to all involved.

■ Siblings were separated, and the children were given no information about their brothers and sisters. Many never found each other again and felt sorrow about this loss throughout their lives.

■ Placements were haphazard, with families choosing children on the spot. There was no attempt to "match" personal qualities or needs and there was no ongoing support for the children or the foster parents from the agency. The outcomes were uneven, with some of the placements working well, while others led to disappointment for the children and families.

■ There was no supervision of the foster parents. Some of the children were well received and treated well, while others were exploited and abused.

The reflections of the participants on their experiences are invaluable to understanding the long-term impact of separation of children from their families, whether through foster care or adoption. This film holds critical and timeless lessons. As the social work profession continues to struggle with difficult issues surrounding child welfare today, such as permanency planning for children in foster care, the reflections of the participants in this program need to be revisited by students and professionals alike.

The Settlement House Movement

While the voluntary social service agencies responded to individuals requiring assistance in the cities, a different approach to urban social problems was taking place through the Settlement House Movement. Started in London in 1884, Toynbee Hall served as a model for the *settlement house movement* in the United States. This movement, which took hold toward the end of the 1800s, introduced a new direction for helping people. It expanded the approach of direct service to individuals and communities by working on the broad societal level to achieve social reform. Some of the goals of the movement were to improve the social, economic, and health conditions for the poor in the cities, particularly poor immigrants, to expand opportunities for education and employment, and to protect vulnerable populations, such as children and youth.

The most famous settlement house leader in the United States was Jane Addams, who established Hull House in a crowded, poor working-class neighborhood in Chicago in 1889. Addams chronicled her work in her books, *Twenty Years at Hull House*, and *The Second Twenty Years at Hull House*, which offer a vivid picture of the work of settlement houses, and describe how well-educated young men and women, generally from wealthy families, moved into the settlement houses so they could live and work closely with the poor, many of whom were migrants and immigrants.

Points to Ponder

"Among her other achievements, Addams introduced the notion that a well-organized community life and culture can exist even among poor people and that one means by which to make society better is to attend to and nurture that community life and culture" (Specht & Courtney, 1994, p. 21).

Much of the work at the settlement houses took place in "clubs," which were gatherings for people with special interests. Settlement house workers also started kindergartens and nurseries for the children of working parents, and offered a variety of classes. The Henry Street Settlement on the Lower East Side of New York City, under the direction of the social reformer, Lillian Wald, began a program of visiting nurses, and Hull House in Chicago opened a boardinghouse for working women, as well as a branch of the public library (Bremner, 1956).

According to Bremner (1956), settlement houses were seen more as homes than institutions; they served as "a comfortable sociable annex to each drab tenement flat" (p. 62). The movement grew rapidly. By 1900 there were 100 settlement houses in existence in United States cities, and by 1910 there were as many as 400 (Trattner, 1999).

Settlement house workers and clients tended to be white, and diversity in the settlement houses was based on socioeconomic status rather than on race (Bremner, 1956). Although some of the settlement house leaders advocated against racial discrimination and were participants in the formation of the National Association for the Advancement of Colored People in 1909, and the National Urban League in 1911, this was the exception rather than the rule. As in the communities surrounding them, racism persisted in most of the settlement houses. Following the migration of blacks to urban areas after World War I, separate settlement houses for blacks were started in several cities, including New York, Tuskegee, Atlanta, and Hampton, Virginia (Trattner, 1999). While not generally involved in the struggle for racial equality, the Settlement House Movement directed its attentions to other forms of social change.

Starting with neighborhood reform, such as supporting the development of public parks, public health facilities, improved school curriculum, and improved sanitation, the settlement workers then addressed broader reforms. They worked on the citywide level in the interest of developing a juvenile justice system, and during the first two decades of the 1900s, known as the "Progressive Era," they joined with other social reformers in activities to address broad social problems, both on the state and national level.

It is hard to imagine a time when there were no government protections that we take for granted today, such as minimum wages, safety standards in buildings and the workplace, and laws preventing child labor. However, at the start of the 20th century, these issues had not been addressed successfully in the United States.

It was during the Progressive Era that social reformers worked to achieve both *protective legislation* that would protect people from exploitation, and *preventive legislation* that would help prevent problems from developing. In addition to the work of social reformers, interest in social problems was stimulated by popular culture. Writers, known as muckrakers, brought to the attention of the public the life circumstances of people who were exploited for profits in industry. One such book, *The Bitter Cry of the Children*, written by John Spargo and published in 1906, addressed the issue of child labor. It described how young children were exploited in factories, and pointed to the need for child labor laws to prohibit this practice. Another book, *The Jungle*, written by Upton Sinclair, and published in 1905, portrayed the difficult circumstances faced by immigrants working in the meat packing industry in Chicago, and identified the need for government regulations in the workplace.

Working with labor unions, leaders in the Settlement House movement joined in efforts to gain protective legislation, such as minimum wages, laws prohibiting child labor, and legislation limiting work to six days a week and eight hours a day (Straussner & Phillips, 1988). In addition, they worked to gain preventive legislation, such as establishment of safety standards in the workplace, building safety codes, and regulation of health and sanitary conditions in housing. Settlement House leaders also played an important role in the creation of the U. S. Children's Bureau in 1912, which greatly influenced education and child-rearing practices around the country (Cremin, 1988).

In spite of this important work, the settlement movement weakened after the outbreak of World War I. Several developments contributed to decreased interest in it among professional social workers and its loss of public support (Trattner, 1999):

- Leaders of the settlement movement took what was an unpopular position against World War I, and were outspoken in their opposition to the involvement of the United States in the war.
- With the economic prosperity of the 1920s, less attention was paid to social reform movements.
- New agencies, such as the YMCA, neighborhood youth centers, and agency-sponsored summer camps, took on some of the direct service functions of the settlement houses.
- Expanded opportunities for work and for service opened up for women during and after the war. Trattner (1999) states, "Living in the slums of New York City was no longer as attractive as previously when compared to teaching school in Africa, working with the Red Cross in war-ravaged Europe, or even just living in Greenwich Village" (p. 186).

Rather than focusing on social reform, social workers were educated in casework, and the profession increasingly identified itself with helping individuals with emotional problems. It was not until the 1930s, during the Great Depression, that the social work profession once again concerned itself with problems in the social environment. It was then that the federal government redefined its position with regard to human suffering and human need, and, consequently, the social work profession became involved with the greatly expanded public sector of social welfare.

The Growth of Sectarian Agencies

Religiously-affiliated social agencies expanded in response to the needs of the large numbers of people migrating to cities in the United States from Europe at the end of the 19th century. Some of the agencies that will be recognized today are:

- The Salvation Army
- Young Men's Christian Association
- Local agencies and organizations sponsored by religious groups, including numerous agencies under Catholic and Jewish auspices

Missionary work in urban slums was started toward the end of the 1800s. Among the largest missionary groups was the Salvation Army, an independent Protestant group that established missions throughout the country, starting first in Boston. By 1880 there were 30 missions in various cities, engaging in both religious activities and relief for the poor, including housing, education for children, equipping libraries, and providing summer vacations for children living in the slums. The Salvation Army provided nursing and medical care in the cities, summer programs for poor children living in the cities, and homes for prostitutes and their children (Leiby, 1978).

The Young Men's Christian Association (YMCA) was started in 1851 to provide help to young men moving into the cities. Some YMCA's also provided financial assistance in their communities, such as those in Washington, DC and Chicago. Today the "Ys," which now also include the Young Women's Christian Association (YWCA), the Young Men's Hebrew Association (YMHA), and the Young Women's Hebrew Association (YWHA), provide a wide variety of other services, including recreational and educational programs, and special programs for children, teens, and the elderly.

Many other sectarian organizations provided social and educational services within a religious context. For example, in 1884 in Philadelphia, the Baptist Temple began a night school, which eventually grew and became Temple University (Bremner, 1956). In addition, numerous services for the sick and the aged, and services for families and children, were also sponsored by sectarian organizations. Those providing services to children grew rapidly, and by 1890 there were 600 institutions for children around the country, started by both religious and ethnic groups.

Today, sectarian agencies continue to provide numerous services to different population groups in the cities, such as immigrants, the elderly, children, families, adolescents, substance abusers, and people with HIV/AIDS. In addition, many sponsor programs for the poor, such as shelters, food pantries, and soup kitchens. They employ a large number of social workers, both as providers of direct services and as agency administrators.

Development of Social Work as a Profession

Two women, Mary Richmond and Jane Addams, were instrumental in identifying approaches to helping people and communities, and laid the foundation for the development of the profession of social work. They represented different approaches to helping; differences that continue to exist today.

The Social Casework Approach—Helping Individuals and Families

Mary Richmond began working with the Charity Organization Society in Baltimore in 1888. Her book, *Social Diagnosis*, which was published in 1917, was used as a guide for friendly visitors of the Charity Organization Societies in their "investigation" of people's applications for assistance. Richmond adapted the medical model—including fact gathering, diagnosis, and treatment—to helping people with problems in personal and social functioning. According to Specht and Courtney (1994), *Social Diagnosis* was remarkable for two reasons:

1. It stressed the importance of understanding people in the context of their social situations.
2. It highlighted the importance of talking with people in order to learn about their specific circumstances, rather than making assumptions about them.

The approach to individualizing each applicant applying for assistance became the foundation for what came to be known as *social casework*, and shaped the direction of the emerging profession of social work.

Points to Ponder

"It was a major contribution to modern casework when Mary Richmond contested the prevalent view of her time that poverty and other difficulties facing clients (family unhappiness, alcoholism and unemployment, among others) were the result of innate character defects, weak wills, or indolence. She stressed the *influences of surroundings and social relationships*, past and present, on individuals and their problems; she emphasized the need to study thoroughly environmental factors in order to understand a case . . . she urged that whenever possible the individual should be seen in the context of the family and home environment. She was also convinced of a 'fundamental truth' that 'mass betterment and individual betterment are interdependent' with 'social reform and social case work of necessity progressing together' " (Woods & Hollis, 2000, p. 8).

The Social Reform Approach—Development of Social Group Work and Community Organization

During the same time period, the Settlement House movement advocated a very different approach to helping. It was just a year after Mary Richmond began her career with the Charity Organization Society in Baltimore that Jane Addams established Hull House in Chicago. Although both women were working at the same time and had the same goals of improving the lives of people, their approaches to that goal differed. While Richmond advocated for individual change, taking the environment into account, Addams focused on changing the social conditions that had adverse effects on people. Out of this approach evolved two important methods of social work intervention:

1. **Social group work**—used the power of groups of people to effect personal and societal change.
2. **Community organization**—used the strengths and power of communities to influence city and community life and the social policies affecting them.

The popularity of the social reform movement during the Progressive Era was so widespread that the leaders of the Charity Organization Societies joined with leaders of the Settlement House movement in their efforts to achieve social reform.

Points to Ponder

"By 1912 the nineteenth-century concern about paupers, criminals, and institutions for their relief or correction was somewhat eclipsed by a bold new notion of 'social welfare' that addressed itself to impersonal causes of poverty and injustice and looked towards a more equal and just society. So philanthropy and social policy were brought closer together" (Leiby, 1978, p. 144).

Beginnings of Professional Education for Social Workers

The turn of the century also saw the beginnings of professional education for social work. With the changing approach to providing financial help for the poor that included individual casework services, the volunteer friendly visitors were replaced by paid professionals. In order to prepare people for this work, training programs for charity workers were established by the end of the 1800s. During the 1890s, Mary Richmond and others had advocated for the establishment of "schools of applied philanthropy." By 1910, schools of social work were established in New York, Chicago, Boston, and other large cities in the United States (Trattner, 1999).

Points to Ponder

Bertha Reynolds, a well-known social work educator during the first half of the 1900s, wrote in 1963 about the changes she witnessed in social work: "I grew up with a profession that first found its identity when it reached into the masses of people displaced by the industrial revolution and found individuals. It found them first in families, as economic units, and its mission was to restore them to self-maintenance. Then it discovered what the personal touch could do. When I first met the still-new thing called social casework, it was a cultivated personal touch between privileged people who gave of their time and interest and underprivileged folk who received guidance as well as financial help. Even then, fifty years ago, the 'retail' method of helping was challenged by reform movements that actually did wipe out important sources of human misery by legislative action" (1963, p. 317).

Conclusion

This chapter has traced some of the events and themes in the development of social welfare and the social work profession in the United States up to the Great Depression. Although some local public-sector programs were developed before the 1930s, the major thrust in terms of social work and social welfare prior to the Great Depression was in the voluntary sector. The voluntary sector has continued to grow and plays a critical role in social welfare today.

During and after the Depression of 1929, a major shift took place in social welfare, as the public sector of social welfare as we know it today got its start. The next chapter focuses on the development of public social welfare, with a concentration on the involvement of the federal government with social problems and social welfare policies.

REFERENCES

Addams, J. (1910). *Twenty years at Hull-House*. New York: Macmillan.

Addams, J. (1930). *The second twenty years at Hull House*. New York: Macmillan.

Axinn, J. & Levin, H. (1997). *Social welfare: A history of the American response to need*, (4th ed.). NY: Longman.

Brace, C. L. (1872). *The dangerous classes of New York*. NY: Wynkoop and Hallenbeck. Reprinted by National Association of Social Workers, 1973, Silver Springs, MD.

Bremner, R. H. (1956). *From the depths: The discovery of poverty in the United States*. New York: New York University Press.

Cremin, L. A. (1988). *American education: The metropolitan experience*, 1876–1980. New York: Harper and Row.

Hartley, I. S. (1882). *Memorial of Robert Milham Hartley*. Utica, NY: Author.

Holody, R. (1997). Children in out-of-home placements. In N. K. Phillips, and S. L. A. Straussner (Eds.). *Children in the urban environment* (pp. 135–153). Springfield, IL: Thomas.

Leiby, J. (1978). *A history of social welfare and social work in the United States*. New York: Columbia University Press.

Marden, C. F., Meyer, G., & Engel, M. H. (1992). *Minorities in American society* (6th ed.). New York: HarperCollins.

Olds, V. (1963, May). The Freedmen's Bureau: A nineteenth-century federal welfare agency. *Social Casework, 44*, 247–253.

Orphan Trains. (1995). Documentary produced by WGBH TV.

Pumphrey R. E. & Pumphrey, M. W. (Eds.). (1961). *The heritage of American social work.* New York: Columbia University Press.

Reynolds, B. (1963). *An uncharted journey.* New York: Citadel.

Richmond, M. (1917). *Social diagnosis.* New York: Russell Sage Foundation.

Riis. J. A. (1890/1971). *How the other half lives.* New York: Dover.

Sinclair, U. (1990). *The jungle.* Philadelphia, PA: Dutton.

Spargo, J. (1906/1972). *The bitter cry of the children.* New York: Crown.

Specht, H. & Courtney M. (1994). *Unfaithful angels.* New York: Free Press.

Straussner, L. A. & Phillips, N. K. (1988). The relationship between social work and labor unions: A history of strife and cooperation. *Journal of Sociology and Social Welfare, 15,* 105–118.

Trattner, W. (1999). *From Poor Law to welfare state: A history of social welfare in America* (6th ed.). NY: Free Press.

Woods, M. E. & Hollis, F. (2000). *Casework: A psychosocial therapy* (5th ed.). New York: McGraw-Hill.

CHAPTER

6

The Development of the Public Sector

A Bronx street during the Great Depression, 1936. Library of Congress/photo by Dorothea Lange

Key events between the 1930s and the 1980s—the Great Depression, the turmoil of the 1960s, the growth of inner city areas, and the dismantling of public assistance—have produced both social upheaval and social change. Along with these changes came a heightened awareness of the impact of the lack of social justice on individuals and groups of people.

This chapter discusses the following topics:

- The Great Depression and its impact on the development of new policies, such as the New Deal and the Social Security Act of 1935; responses of the social work profession
- The slow movement toward equality

- Economic and racial segregation in the cities during the post-World War II era
- Expansion of federal involvement with social welfare through the 1960s and the responses of social work
- Legislative reform during the 1970s
- The resurgence of poverty during the Reagan and George Bush administrations and its impact on the cities

Social Welfare and the Great Depression

In 1933, four years into the Great Depression, Franklin Roosevelt took office as President of the United States. During his first term in office, pivotal social welfare legislation was passed, and the federal government stepped into the role of providing for the financial needs of particular groups of people. Numerous government agencies were formed to implement the new mandated services, thereby establishing the public sector of social welfare on the federal level. While the extent to which the federal government should be involved with social welfare has been debated over the years, the precedent for this involvement was established (Phillips, 1985).

The Great Depression: Federal Involvement and the Public Sector of Social Welfare

Following years of prosperity during the 1920s, the collapse of the stock market in 1929 plunged the United States into a lengthy and severe economic depression, known as the "Great Depression." Unemployment soared, people lost their savings and investments, and poverty reached groups of people who had never been poor before. Jacob Fisher, a social worker who wrote about social work during the Great Depression, described those affected by the depression: "The family earner whose lack of a job drove him to apply for public aid was a bricklayer, a store clerk, a truck driver, a telephone operator, a machinist, a typist, a cloak cutter, a copper miner, a coal miner, a loom fixer, a tool-and-die maker, an assembly-line operator in an auto plant, a printer —occupational groups hitherto almost never touched by want" (1980, p. 10). State and local governments did not have adequate funds to provide for the millions of people needing help. In addition to unemployment, the problems of the cities were compounded by the resumption of the large migration of people from farms into urban areas after 1933 (Axinn & Levin, 1997).

Herbert Hoover, who was president of the country when the depression began, took the traditional view toward help, looking to the voluntary sector rather than to government intervention, as a way to relieve the widespread need. During the early years of the depression, it was expected that the economic conditions would be resolved quickly, as they had during earlier depressions. However, poverty was more widespread this time, and personal and social conditions grew worse. The voluntary sector did not have sufficient resources to meet the needs of all of the poor and by 1932 a third of the private agencies in the country had closed down because of lack of funds (Trattner, 1999).

As the depression not only lingered but also deepened, poverty came to be broadly recognized as a consequence of the nation's economy, rather than the result of personal failure. This shift in attitude toward the poor made it possible for the government to step in and introduce new ways of helping those in need.

Franklin Delano Roosevelt, usually referred to by his initials, FDR, was elected president in 1932 and took office in March 1933. At that time, 13 million people (about one quarter of the labor force) were unemployed. A quarter of a million families had lost their homes. In some states, as many as 40 percent of the people were receiving local relief; in some counties it reached 90 percent. By the time FDR was elected, every bank in the country had closed down, and many people wondered whether the capitalist and democratic systems could survive (Schlesinger, 1958).

Roosevelt's approach to the national problem was different than Hoover's. Rather than relying on voluntary contributions to help the needy, Roosevelt immediately introduced what he called the "New Deal." Making reference to a game of cards, he set out to encourage people with the idea that they would be dealt a new hand of cards—that there would be a "new deal" that would offer new opportunities. He introduced many new programs, including financial assistance to the needy, and work for the unemployed. He also began programs to promote economic stability and help for people who were losing their homes to foreclosure.

Federal Work and Relief Programs of the New Deal

Numerous federal work and relief programs designed to address the problems of unemployment and poverty were developed between 1933 and 1935. Among the programs were the:

- Federal Emergency Relief Administration (FERA), which gave almost $190 million to states and local relief agencies
- Civil Works Administration (CWA), which gave over half a billion dollars for wages to three-and-a-half million of the neediest unemployed, reflecting Roosevelt's belief that in order to feel good about themselves, people needed to work and be productive, rather than be given money
- Civilian Conservation Corps (CCC), which took 300,000 young men whose families were receiving public assistance and put them to work developing national parks and forests
- Works Progress Administration (WPA), which provided work to 8 million people in various industries, teaching positions, and the arts

These programs brought new hope to individuals and families, and over time, they restored confidence in the government.

All of these programs, however, were designed to be temporary. Although the scope of these work relief programs was much larger, in spirit they were not unlike the Freedmen's Bureau that was developed during the Civil War. Both gave the federal government a temporary role in relieving individual need during a period of crisis.

The Social Security Act of 1935

While improving the social and economic conditions of millions of people, the New Deal programs succeeded in helping only about one third of those who were unemployed. Consequently, millions of people were still living in desperate conditions. These circumstances led to the recognition of the need for a new national policy—one that would bring relief to the people and also prevent such severe economic and social devastation in the future. Roosevelt was clear about his belief that some residual programs would always be needed. However, he also believed that many services ought to be provided through an institutional system of social insurances.

Points to Ponder

Roosevelt's intention was to provide social insurance for all people throughout their lifetime. He said, "There is no reason why everybody in the United States should not be covered. I see no reason why every child, from the day he is born, shouldn't be a member of the social security system . . . from the cradle to the grave they ought to be in a social insurance system" (Schlesinger, 1958, p. 308).

The form that this insurance ultimately took was the Social Security Act, which was passed and signed into law in 1935. The Social Security Act was a compromise, as is the case with most critical pieces of legislation. Since there was a great deal of opposition to the Social Security Act, the highly controversial medical insurance program had to be dropped in order to secure its passage. Consequently, the Social Security Act did not offer the scope of protection against life's insecurities that Roosevelt wanted (Wyatt & Wandel, 1937).

In spite of its drawbacks, as the first permanent federal social welfare program in the United States, this Act instituted the *public sector of social welfare* at the federal level, and established the precedent of federal involvement with the welfare of the people. The Social Security Act of 1935 included programs for the elderly, the unemployed, and mothers with dependent children. A Social Security Board was established to implement the programs of the Social Security Act.

Subsequently, the Social Security Act has been amended to include many of the programs and benefits we take for granted today, such as Medicare, Medicaid, and Supplemental Security Income (SSI), to name but a few. It is important to remember that these programs and benefits grew out of the commitment that the federal government made in 1935 to become involved with the social welfare needs of the American people.

Points to Ponder

"With the Social Security Act, the constitutional dedication of federal power to the general welfare began a new phase of national history" (Schlesinger, 1958, p. 315).

Social Work during the Great Depression

Both Hoover and Roosevelt turned to social workers to assist with providing financial help for the unemployed during the depression. This caused an uneasiness among many in the social work profession, as caseworkers were reluctant to give up their counseling function in family agencies, and instead work with the newly formed public welfare agencies. Many of the caseworkers were more concerned about personal change than with addressing the existing poverty. In addition, some social workers also objected to the federal government's involvement with relief, preferring that these responsibilities remain with local public agencies and the voluntary sector. However, as economic conditions worsened, the profession unified in its support of federal government assistance to the poor. In fact, some of the key figures who made major contributions to the design and implementation of the social welfare programs of the New Deal were social workers. For example, Harry Hopkins headed the Federal Emergency Relief Administration, and Frances Perkins, who had worked with Jane Addams at Hull House, served as the Secretary of Labor throughout the Roosevelt administration (Phillips, 1985).

The Slow Movement toward Equality during the 1930s and 1940s

The programs of the New Deal did not address the existing racial discrimination. For example, some states excluded African Americans from federal work projects and relief programs. In addition, the Civilian Conservation Corps limited the enrollment of black men to ten percent, and it was not uncommon for camps to be racially segregated (Trattner, 1999).

Points to Ponder

". . . just as wealth was inequitably distributed, so too was poverty; blacks and other minority group members, who usually were the first to lose their jobs and the last to be rehired, and who in the interim received the least assistance, felt the crush of the depression even more than did their white counterparts" (Trattner, 1999, p. 282).

It was not until 1941, as the country was "about to enter a war for the defense of democracy and human equality" (Trattner, 1999, p. 306), that President Roosevelt established, by Executive Order, the Fair Employment Practices Committee, which prohibited "discrimination in the employment of workers in defense industries or Government because of race, creed, color, or national origin" (quoted in Trattner, 1999, p. 306). While the recommendations of this committee were not broadly accepted, and the government did not have authority to impose any penalties for failure to accept the recommendations, the Executive Order signified "gains unprecedented in American history" for groups that had been oppressed (Trattner, 1999, p. 306).

In addition, the need for labor in factories during the war and the decline in the labor force due to the draft opened opportunities for women, blacks, Mexicans, Mexican Americans, and Puerto Ricans (Axinn & Levin, 1997). For example, by 1943 there were a million black workers in factory jobs, 500,000 black workers were union members, and by 1944, 200,000 blacks had government jobs. In addition, about one million black men and women served in the military during World War II (Axinn & Levin, 1997).

Points to Ponder

"The most dramatic changes of the thirty-year period from 1940–1970 occurred during World War II. The upheaval of war brought full employment and rising incomes. For oppressed groups, particularly blacks and women, the period offered increased opportunity for economic, educational, and social equality and laid the groundwork for the civil rights and feminist movements of the 1950s and 1960s" (Axinn & Levin, 1997, p. 227).

Native Americans, who were denied state social service benefits, also found new opportunities for employment during World War II. Almost 500,000 Native Americans moved off their reservations to work in war-related industries, and many settled in the cities. Another 25,000 Native Americans served in the military during the war, returning with veteran's benefits in employment, housing, and education (Axinn & Levin, 1997).

People of Japanese descent who lived in the U.S. suffered from brutal discrimination, both before and during the war. For example, the San Francisco school board passed a resolution in 1906 barring Japanese children from white schools; however, this resolution was repealed as a result of pressure from the governor of California and the federal government. At the time of the attack by the Japanese on Pearl Harbor, there were 122,000 Japanese living in the United States—83 percent were living in Los Angeles, with small communities of Japanese immigrants in other cities, such as New York and Chicago.

In February 1942, two months after the attack on Pearl Harbor, the U.S. Army established "military zones" and the Army was authorized to evacuate and exclude whoever might be considered a threat to security, whether or not that person was a citizen of the United States. As a result, all those of Japanese descent who were living on the West Coast were told to move. With no state willing to accept them, 110,000 people, including over 77,000 Japanese Americans born in the United States, were taken to internment camps. Some were resettled in 1943, but others remained in the camps until 1945, when the war was over (Marden, Meyer & Engel, 1992). The experience of internment was devastating to many families, who suffered humiliation and resentment as their social structure and cultural patterns were destroyed. According to one former internee, "It was many years after the camp experience before the togetherness, filial strength, and dignity of her family were restored" (Marden, Meyer & Engel, 1992, p. 404).

The Crises of the Cities Following World War II

As the cities became more and more commercialized and industrialized, migration of people from farms to the cities increased. Approximately 6 million people came to the cities between 1920 and 1930, and during the first 30 years of the 20th century, urban centers with populations over 100,000 increased from 38 to 83 (Axinn & Levin, 1997).

Points to Ponder

According to Axinn and Levin (1997), the growth of the cities prior to the Great Depression "was haphazard, causing crowded, unsanitary, tenement living . . . the pressing need for housing, sanitation, fire protection, policing, traffic regulation, and educational facilities went unheeded" (p. 125).

Among the migrants were a large number of blacks who were drawn to the cities by the availability of jobs. The population of blacks in Chicago increased more than five times during the 20 years preceding the Great Depression, and that city came to be known as the "Black Metropolis" (Lemann, 1991). Harlem, in New York City, also attracted many blacks, and during the 1920s, when it welcomed black professionals, artists, and intellectuals, it enjoyed a period known as the "Harlem Renaissance" (Takaki, 1993; Wilson, 1974).

Nonetheless, racial discrimination was widespread. Housing outside existing black communities was denied to many, and the segregated ghetto communities became overcrowded. Ongoing job discrimination and the resulting unemployment contributed to the deterioration of living conditions (Axinn & Levin, 1997).

An even larger migration into the cities occurred after World War II. Between 1940 and 1970 more than 20 million people were forced off farmlands due to mechanization of farm production; about 80 percent were whites. Those migrants who were African American, Puerto Rican, Mexican American, and Native American, and who settled in the cities, suffered from discrimination in housing, employment, and the justice system (Marden, Meyer, & Engel, 1992; Trattner, 1999).

At the same time that this migration into the cities was taking place, there was a shift out of the cities to suburban areas. Little housing had been built in the cities during the war years, and the influx of migrants, followed by the returning veterans, led to a severe housing shortage. During the period of "economic boom and intense optimism" (Palen, 1995, p. 57) that followed World War II, home ownership increased dramatically.

Following the war, home ownership in the suburbs was encouraged by liberalized home mortgage lending policies of the federal government. Programs were administered through the Veterans Administration and also through the Federal Housing Authority for nonveterans. Down payments were less for suburban homes than for houses in the cities, and mortgages were easier to secure for homes outside the cities. Moreover, loans to veterans could not be used for apartments. Consequently, millions of low-cost homes were built in suburban subdivisions, supported by public transportation and new highway systems linking the suburbs with the cities. During the

1950s and 1960s, the number of people living in the suburbs increased from 35 million to 84 million people (Palen, 1995).

Most suburbs were ethnically and religiously integrated, but not racially integrated. According to Palen (1995), "The newcomers were Catholics and Jews as well as mainline Protestants; they were Irish, Italian, and Polish as well as English or northwest European; they were white-collar and factory workers as well as professionals and managers . . . suburbs were coming to mirror mainstream America" (p. 57). However, people who were not white were excluded. Acts of white mob violence occurred in some areas when people of color moved into suburban areas (Abrahamson, 1996).

Urban ghettos were enlarged as the government built public housing projects in these areas, contributing to even greater social, racial, and economic segregation. Isolated in the ghettos, little attention was paid to the poor during the postwar period of "social complacency" (Axinn & Levin, 1997, p. 233). However, according to Jansson, (2001), the movement of African Americans to the cities in the south during the 1950s, "allowed them to organize more easily against rampant discrimination" (p. 236), which enabled the start of the Civil Rights Movement.

In spite of the neglect of the poor and punitive welfare policies during the 1950s (Trattner, 1999), several critical pieces of legislation were passed that impacted the quality of life of the poor. For example, the Social Security Act was amended in 1950, changing the public assistance category of "Aid to Dependent Children" to "Aid to Families with Dependent Children," thereby recognizing the role of parents as caregivers. Other public assistance programs created during the 1950s were Aid to the Permanently and Totally Disabled, and Disability Insurance. The Social Security Board, which had been formed to implement the programs of the Social Security Act, led to the eventual development of the federal Department of Health, Education, and Welfare in 1953. This department, currently called the U.S. Department of Health and Human Services, continues to play a crucial role in the development and implementation of social welfare policies and programs (Trattner, 1999).

The segregation that took place during the 1940s and 1950s due to demographic changes led to the challenge and overturning of the "separate-but-equal" approach to race relations during the Truman administration. This was followed by the *Brown v. Board of Education* decision by the U.S. Supreme Court in 1954, which prohibited racial segregation in public schools. These critical events paved the way for the watershed social welfare legislation of the 1960s.

Expansion of Federal Involvement with Social Welfare through the 1960s

Paralleling the economic crisis that led to the passage of the Social Security Act and other social legislation during the 1930s, the social changes of the 1960s grew out of another crisis—this one due to turmoil in the cities and the efforts by people of all racial groups to achieve racial equality.

By 1960, when John F. Kennedy was elected president, there was a growing acknowledgement of unemployment, poverty, and discrimination as social problems.

Kenneth Clark, in his eye-opening book, *Dark Ghetto*, which was first published in 1965, described the plight of African Americans living in the ghetto in the early 1960s. "Sixty-four percent of the men in Harlem compared to only 38 percent of New York City's male population, and 74 percent of the women, compared to 37 percent for New York City, hold unskilled and service jobs" (1989, p. 35).

The focus on the poor, both black and white, was reinforced by the 1962 publication of Michael Harrington's book, *The Other America*. This book helped bring to light the conditions of the 40 to 50 million poor in the United States, as well as the discrimination suffered by the almost four million Mexican Americans who struggled to earn a living despite their poor education and limited job skills. There also were 450,000 Native Americans who Trattner (1999) described as "perhaps the nation's most desperate and deprived minority group—the poorest of the poor" (p. 318). Stressing the economic and societal causes of poverty and the ways in which it is perpetuated, books such as William Ryan's *Blaming the Victim*, and Piven and Cloward's *Regulating the Poor*, helped put the focus back on poverty. The impact of these books was felt by the society in general and the social work profession in particular.

During the 1960s and 1970s the cities continued to lose their middle class to the suburbs. Palen (1995) presents the credible argument that the movement to the suburbs after Word War II did not represent a flight from the cities, but rather was a response to the baby boom and the availability of government subsidies for suburban housing. Only after the desegregation of public schools during the 1960s did the movement to the suburbs reflect what has been called "white flight" from the cities (Palen, 1995, p. 63). By 1970, 37 percent of the people in the United States were living in the suburbs, and by 1990, the number increased to 48 percent (Palen, 1995), leaving a disproportionate number of the poor living in urban areas.

Efforts of African Americans to gain civil rights started with the attempt to break the policy of African Americans sitting in the back of public buses. Starting with a bus boycott in Montgomery, Alabama, in 1955, other attempts were made to protest racist policies, and these protests grew into a national Civil Rights Movement (Jansson, 2001). Riots protesting racist policies in the cities across the United States during the 1960s, which included the slum areas in Detroit, New York, Newark, NJ, and Los Angeles, resulted in increased public awareness of the desperate circumstances of the poor. President Kennedy's New Frontier, and President Lyndon Johnson's War on Poverty programs made social welfare policy a priority on the nation's political agenda:

■ The Civil Rights Act of 1964 made racial, sexual, or ethnic discrimination illegal in employment. The Equal Employment Opportunity Commission was established to enforce the Civil Rights Act.

■ The Economic Opportunity Act (EOA), an antipoverty bill, also passed in 1964, was implemented by the Office of Economic Opportunity (OEO). Numerous programs were introduced, such as Job Corps for training high school dropouts; Head Start for preschool children of low-income families; establishment of the domestic Peace Corps, called Volunteers in Service to America; Neighborhood Youth Corps, to help unemployed teenagers; and the Community Action Program, which was supposed to give power to community members as they attempted to build their own communities.

■ The Food Stamps Act, also passed in 1964, introduced the Food Stamp Program, which continues to play a central role in the lives of low-income people today.

■ The Social Security Act was amended to add two health care programs—Medicare for people when they reach the age of 65, regardless of their income, and Medicaid for those who met financial eligibility, including recipients of public assistance.

■ Also passed in 1965 was the Older Americans Act (OAA), which led to the development of Area Agencies on Aging (AAA) around the country. OAA subsidized services such as nutritional programs for older adults, and services for homebound older adults.

Social Work during the 1960s

During the 1960s, the social work profession again became aligned with social reform activities. Social workers helped mobilize the poor and the National Welfare Rights Organization was formed to advocate for the removal of punitive welfare measures (Piven & Cloward, 1971.) Changes were made in social work education to include material on public administration, community organization, and social welfare policy, thereby recognizing and valuing agency and policy practice. Social work schools, supported by federal funding, began actively recruiting students from a variety of ethnic and socioeconomic backgrounds. New organizations emerged, such as the Association of Black Social Workers, and within a decade, well-established agencies, such as New York City's Community Service Society, which was the oldest family service agency in the country, reshaped their programs to turn their attention to social reform rather than to providing direct counseling to individuals and families (Trattner, 1999).

Important Social Legislation of the 1970s

Richard Nixon's "New Federalism" programs advocated shrinking federal participation in social welfare and returned decision making about welfare matters to the states. However, despite his efforts, the forward thrust of the Kennedy and Johnson years pervaded his administration, and critical legislation was passed. In fact, spending for welfare programs during the Nixon era was almost twice that of the Kennedy and Johnson administrations (Trattner, 1999).

Some of the social welfare legislation passed was protective, such as the *Rehabilitation Act of 1973*, which gave federal protection from discrimination to physically disabled people, while other laws were preventive, such as the *Occupational Safety and Health Act* (OSHA), passed in 1970, which gave the federal government responsibility for monitoring safety standards in the workplace—an important step in preventing industrial accidents and protecting the health of all workers. The Department of Labor was responsible for its implementation.

Efforts were made to find more efficient ways to provide help to the poor. In 1969, President Nixon proposed the Family Assistance Plan. While this was an attempt to cut through some of the welfare bureaucracy, in fact it was a plan for a guaranteed minimum income for poor families. It was a highly controversial piece of legislation because it did not provide sufficient income for the working poor, and it also required mothers with children to work. The Family Assistance Plan was not passed, and Nixon did not pursue it.

However, another part of that proposed legislation was passed, leading to the creation of the *Supplemental Security Income (SSI)* program, established in 1972. Implemented at the start of 1974, this legislation consolidated the public assistance programs for adults, including Aid to the Blind, Aid to the Permanently and Totally Disabled, and Old-Age Assistance. Whereas previously funding for these programs had been shared by the federal government and the states, now they were moved from state authority into full funding and authority of the federal Social Security Administration. Although eligibility for SSI continues to be means-tested, both eligibility and benefits became uniform throughout the country, and both the program and the recipients of its benefits are less stigmatized.

Points to Ponder

"SSI ... which ... federalized all public assistance for the adult poor who clearly were considered unemployable, was a landmark in American social welfare history in that it created the nation's first guaranteed annual income program: The needy elderly, blind, and disabled were 'entitled' to such assistance; it no longer was a gratuity to be doled out at the discretion of some administrator" (Trattner, 1999, p. 348).

Other legislation was passed that addressed the quality of life of oppressed groups. These included:

- Title XX amendment to the Social Security Act in 1974, providing money to the states for social services, including services to welfare recipients
- The Earned Income Tax Credit, which was the first legislation providing fiscal welfare for the poor; it was passed in 1975

Although a judicial rather than a legislative decision, it is important to note that in 1973, during the Nixon administration, the U.S. Supreme Court issued the *Roe v. Wade* decision, legalizing abortion.

Another significant piece of legislation passed in 1980 while Jimmy Carter was president was the *Adoption Assistance and Child Welfare Act*. This act, which provided money to states to help pay the cost of foster care for children, also provided federal subsidies to eligible families adopting children, and required that states have a permanency plan for children remaining in foster care.

Cutting Back: Retreat from Federal Involvement with Social Welfare during the Reagan and Bush Administrations

President Reagan's conservative policies, which led to an even greater inequality of income and opportunities for different income groups, had a severe impact on the cities. For example, he introduced the largest tax cuts since World War II, giving the largest tax benefits to corporations and the wealthy. In addition, although Social Security and Medicare were not touched, there were major cuts in social programs for the poor.

Points to Ponder

Jansson (2001) described the resurgence of poverty resulting from the policy changes of the Reagan administration: "... Reagan managed during his administration to cut AFDC (Aid to Families with Dependent Children) by 17.4 percent; 400,000 persons were removed from the rolls. One million persons lost eligibility for Food Stamps; the program was cut by 14.3 percent ... funding for low- and moderate-income housing was reduced ... 57 percent. Reagan ... eliminated work-incentive payments in the AFDC program so that many working women could no longer receive welfare benefits, even if they were beneath official poverty lines" (pp. 319–320).

Between 1981 and 1983 the country fell into a deep recession and the national debt broke all records. Twelve million people were unemployed, with those hardest hit being women, people of color, and teenagers. Once again, poverty was most apparent in the cities.

Points to Ponder

Trattner (1999) describes "... the appearance in America's cities of vast sections populated by a so-called underclass of racial minorities—school dropouts, teen-age mothers, dope addicts, hustlers, criminals, and the like—who existed at the margins of society and frequently preyed on others" (p. 369).

In 1988, during his second term, Reagan signed the Family Support Act, which was his administration's response to the growing poverty in the country. Scheduled to begin in 1990, it introduced more stringent procedures for collecting child support from parents who were not in the home, extended Medicaid coverage for families for one year after the family became self-supporting, and provided money to families for transportation and child care for one year after beginning employment (Trattner, 1999). In order to help families become self-supporting, the Family Support Act created the Job Opportunities and Basic Skills (JOBS) program, requiring single parents with children over the age of 3 years to work or be in a training program in order to receive public support; states had the option to require single parents to work or be in a training program if their children were over one year old. However, research findings showed that in the 10 states that were studied, none had taken steps to implement the JOBS program, and in addition, the services that were to support families in their attempt to work, such as expanded child care funds, were not implemented by the states.

Also passed in 1987, during the Reagan administration, was the Stewart B. McKinney Homeless Assistance Act, supporting the establishment of programs and housing for the homeless. Specifically targeting the education of children in homeless families, this act required that each state facilitate equal access to education for homeless children. However, in 1990 the National Law Center on Homelessness and Poverty conducted a survey of 20 states and found that in spite of these regulations, this act was largely ineffective. A 1990 amendment to the McKinney Act expanded its provisions but in some states the act was ignored altogether (Danzig, 1997).

Points to Ponder

According to the findings of the 1990 survey of the National Law Center on Homelessness and Poverty, even after the passage of the McKinney Act, children in homeless families still had not gained access to education. ". . . 60 percent of the states denied access based on district residency, 40 percent denied access due to guardianship issues, and 70 percent delayed access without current immunization records or birth certificates. Furthermore, 55 percent of the states did not provide non-schooled homeless children with services that were comparable to those accorded to schooled children" (Danzig, 1997, p. 197).

Reagan's successor, George H. Bush, was elected in 1988. Trattner (1999) describes Bush's campaign:

> The more conservative Bush . . . campaigned on the Reagan administration's record and said very little else, other than that he favored school prayers, the death penalty, a lower capital gains tax, and a strong national defense—and he opposed abortion and a tax increase (p. 378).

Nonetheless, the Bush administration produced important protective legislation for two groups:

- The *Americans with Disabilities Act* (ADA), a pivotal piece of legislation passed in 1990, gave people with disabilities expanded civil rights protections. This act opened opportunities for people who had long experienced discrimination.
- The *Civil Rights Act of 1991* clarified one aspect of the Civil Rights Act of 1964, making it possible to sue for monetary damages if a hiring or promotion decision of a government or private employer was based on intentional discrimination of groups, such as women or people of color.

However, during the Bush administration, many urban social problems were not addressed. Between 1989 and 1991, poverty rose from 12.8 percent of the population to 14.2 percent. With more people turning to welfare, many states reduced their AFDC benefits. Social problems, many related to poverty, increased.

Points to Ponder

Trattner (1999) offers the following description of the impact of the lack of legislation to alleviate social problems during the years of the Bush presidency: "All sorts of related social problems continued to worsen, including homelessness—which reached an all-time high since the Great Depression—unemployment, child abuse, crime, racial tensions, and the like. Proposals to deal with these and other problems, especially the needs of drug addicts, alcoholics, and AIDS victims, went nowhere or were rebuffed by the President . . . Other major challenges, such as rapidly increasing medical costs and the lack of health insurance for millions of Americans, simply were ignored" (1999, p. 382).

Conclusion

This chapter has discussed the growth of the public sector, including some of the major federal policy responses to urban social problems from the Great Depression up to the Clinton administration. Some of the social problems and policy changes during the Clinton years will be discussed in the next chapter.

We have seen the development of agency and policy practice during the 1930s, and their expansion during the 1960s. During each of these two decades, there were growing concerns with broad social problems within the social work profession, as there was in society as a whole. During each of these two periods, the 1930s and the 1960s, the concerns of the social work profession shifted from "case to cause."

However, despite the overall dramatic advances in social welfare since the 1930s, persistent and demoralizing conditions have continued, including discrimination of population groups, the stigmatization of many services, and fragmented and inadequate social welfare programs. These problems continue to challenge our society, and as they persist, they impact severely on the lives of clients and, in fact, on the life of every person.

The next chapter explores some of the social problems that continue to affect millions of people in the United States today. Current policy approaches, and implications of these policies for clients and for social work practice, will be discussed.

REFERENCES

Abrahamson, M. (1996). *Urban enclaves: Identity and place in America*. New York: St. Martin's Press.

Axinn, J. & Levin, H. (1997). *Social welfare: A history of the American response to need* (4th ed.). New York: Longman.

Clark, K. B. (1965/1989). *Dark ghetto: Dilemmas of social power* (2d ed.). Hanover, NH: Wesleyan University Press.

Danzig, R. A. (1997). Children in homeless families. In N. K. Phillips & S. L. A. Straussner (Eds.), *Children in the urban environment* (pp. 191–208). Springfield, IL: Thomas.

Fisher, J. (1980). *The response of social work to the Depression*. Cambridge, MA: Schenkman.

Harrington, M. (1962/1997). *The other America: Poverty in the U.S.* New York: Simon and Schuster.

Jansson, B. (2001). *The reluctant welfare state*. Belmont, CA: Brooks/Cole.

Lemann, N. (1991). *The promised land*. New York: Knopf.

Marden, C. F., Meyer, G. & Engel, M. H. (1992). *Minorities in American society* (6th ed.). New York: HarperCollins.

Palen. J. J. (1995). *The suburbs*. New York: McGraw-Hill.

Phillips, N. K. (1985, June). Ideology and opportunity in social work during the New Deal years. *Journal of Sociology and Social Welfare, 12*, 2, 251–273.

Piven, F. F. & Cloward, R. (1971). *Regulating the poor*. New York: Vintage.

Ryan, W. (1976). *Blaming the victim*. New York: Vintage.

Schlesinger, A. M., Jr. (1958). *The age of Roosevelt: The coming of the New Deal*. Boston: Houghton Mifflin.

Takaki, R. (1993). *A different mirror: A history of multicultural America*. New York: Little, Brown.

Trattner, W. (1999). *From Poor Law to welfare state: A history of social welfare in America* (6th ed.). New York: Free Press.

Wilson, W. J. (1974). *Coming of age: Urban America, 1915–1945*. New York: Wiley.

Wyatt, B. & Wandel, W. (1937). *The Social Security Act in operation*. Washington, DC: Graphic Arts Press.

7

The Policy-Practice Connection

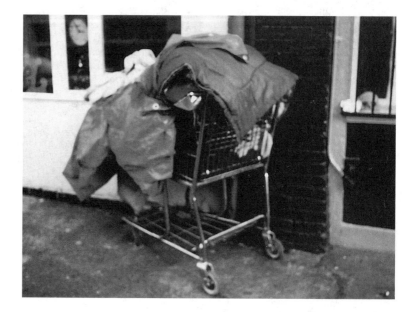

Homelessness in the new Millennium: Portland, Oregon, New Years 2001. Photo by Adrian Gaut

This chapter focuses on three current urban social problems and some of the social welfare policies relevant to them. The impact of these policies on clients, and the interrelationship of problems and policies with client, agency, and policy practice will be discussed. The problems and policies addressed are:

- Poverty and the impact of welfare reform
- Substance abuse and the complex and contradictory policies related to it
- Health care and the impact of the lack of a universal health care policy

Errata for
Phillips and Straussner
Urban Social Work
An Introduction to Policy and Practice in the Cities
0-205-29019-1

Page 107

The following chart shows the cities with high concentrations of families receiving welfare in 1994 and 1998, and reflects that a growing proportion of states' welfare recipients are living in the cities:

City	Percent of Families Receiving Welfare in the State Who Were Living in the City in 1994	Percent of Families Receiving Welfare in the State Who Were Living in the City in 1998
Chicago	66%	74%
New York	68%	70%
Baltimore	48%	56%
Detroit	42%	48%
Philadelphia	39%	47%
Los Angeles	34%	37%
Cleveland	19%	24%

(Pear, June 6, 1999, Sec. 1, p. 26.)

Urban Poverty and the Impact of Welfare Reform

The economic and social changes brought about by the development of a global, technology-based economy have led to a new level of prosperity for many, and also to new social problems. In spite of this prosperity, poverty continues to grow as an urban problem. As in the past, poverty often is accompanied by a range of other social problems such as inadequate housing or homelessness, unemployment or underemployment, hunger, substance abuse, and violence.

The country's largest cities are home to a disproportionate number of the poor. Even though the number of people in the cities who received welfare declined between 1994 and 1998, the concentration of the poor in the big cities—those with populations over 470,000—continued to increase ("Out of Sight, Out of Mind," 2000, p. 28).

When we look at cities with the highest percentage of their population receiving welfare, we find that in 1998, all of them had an increase in the percentage of families receiving welfare, as compared to the previous four years:

City	Percent of Families Receiving Welfare in 1994	Percent of Families Receiving Welfare in 1998
Chicago	66%	74%
New York	68%	70%
Baltimore	48%	56%
Detroit	42%	48%
Philadelphia	39%	47%
Los Angeles	34%	37%
Cleveland	19%	24%

(Pear, June 6, 1999, Sec. 1, p. 26.)

According to the federal Department of Health and Human Services, 75 percent of people who received welfare lived in the inner cities. It is also these poverty-stricken areas that typically have the greatest rates of unemployment.

Unemployment among the Poor in the Cities

The problem of unemployment is an obvious place to start when trying to understand poverty in the cities. Despite the availability of jobs, people in inner city communities still have a high rate of unemployment due to lack of transportation and personal problems that interfere with obtaining or maintaining a job.

Lack of transportation becomes a critical issue as more and more jobs are created outside the cities. For example, in 1999, close to three-quarters of newly-created jobs were located outside urban areas. Lack of public transportation and the high cost of owning a car, including the particularly high rates of automobile insurance for people living in the inner cities, lead to difficulties in commuting to available jobs (Pear, 1999).

In addition to looking at the availability and accessibility of jobs, it is also important to consider the personal problems that can contribute to unemployment. For example, the outcome of Milwaukee's "Project New Hope," which was an effort to help the poor gain economic self-sufficiency through employment, helps us to understand the complexity of circumstances that can lead to unemployment and poverty. In this project, individuals receiving public assistance were given jobs with the guarantee that their families would be lifted out of poverty if they worked 30 hours a week. However, 73 percent of the 677 participants failed to achieve a significant change in their lives after two years in spite of the availability of a job. This study demonstrated that there are important personal factors in addition to the availability of jobs that need to be considered when thinking about policies to reduce poverty. For example, many of the participants had mental health problems, such as depression, which were not affected by the opportunity to work. Other personal and social problems were also found to play important roles in the ability of people to become economically self-sufficient: "The problems that kept people from maintaining steady employment comprise a catalog of inner-city ills: drug and alcohol abuse; jealous or violent boyfriends and husbands; conflicts with employers; unreliable baby-sitters and cars, and generally flagging spirits" (DeParle, 1999, p. 1).

Points to Ponder

Project New Hope made it clear that causes of poverty can be complex and that a comprehensive approach is needed when planning social welfare programs to help the unemployed.

The Current Policy Approach to Poverty: Temporary Assistance to Needy Families (TANF)

In 1996, during the Clinton administration, federal welfare reform legislation was passed in the United States. This law, entitled the *Personal Responsibility and Work Opportunity Reconciliation Act*, altered a basic assumption that had existed in the United States since the passage of the Social Security Act in 1935—the assumption that people have a *right* to public assistance. Title 1 of the 1996 legislation, called *Temporary Assistance to Needy Families*, referred to as TANF, replaced three entitlement programs that had been in effect—Aid to Families with Dependent Children, Emergency Assistance, and the Job Opportunity and Basic Skills Training Program (JOBS).

The new law introduced, for the first time, a maximum period that a person could receive public assistance throughout his or her lifetime. A lifetime maximum of 60 months of eligibility for public assistance was set. However, each state can decide if it wants to accept the five year limit, or reduce it further. In addition, the law stated that assistance ends after two years if the person is not working or involved in a work-connected activity. In order to qualify for assistance under TANF, recipients are required either to work, participate in community service, provide child-care for people who are participating in community service, or receive on-the-job or vocational training.

Some of the other provisions included in this 1996 legislation are:

- More stringent eligibility requirements for benefits through the Supplemental Security Income (SSI) program, which operates through the Social Security Administration
- More aggressive laws regarding child support by absent parents, and the repeal of the previously required monthly pass-through, which gave families the first $50 collected by the state for child support from the absent parent
- Denial of eligibility of legal immigrants entering the United States after 1996 for means-tested federal programs, such as Medicaid, Food Stamps, and Supplemental Security Income, during their first five years in the United States; however, states could determine less stringent eligibility requirements for their residents

Points to Ponder

According to the Children's Defense Fund (1999), eight states have opted to lower the five year time limit of eligibility for assistance.

The New Role for States in Administering TANF

TANF redefined the role of the federal government in public welfare. Through the mechanism of block grants to each state, TANF turned much of its decision making and standard setting over to state governments. Consequently, 43 states and the District of Columbia provide benefits at a rate of less than half the poverty line for a family of three (Children's Defense Fund, 1999).

Points to Ponder

"States now have both the authority and the responsibility to establish all eligibility requirements, and they are under no obligation to serve any particular type of family—or any particular family. No longer are there specific federal requirements states must follow in determining eligibility for welfare, and states have wide latitude to impose additional behavioral conditions on the receipt of welfare" (Hagen, 1999, p. 80).

Outcomes of TANF

Although reports of TANF outcomes indicate that welfare rolls have dropped dramatically, it would be a mistake to assume that those who are not receiving assistance are working and living even reasonably well. In spite of the economic boom in the second half of the 1990s, in the year 2000, one in eight people in the United States was living in poverty, including almost one in five children. The poverty rate is even higher than it was in the 1970s, and "single urban mothers living in poverty still make up a big proportion of the poor" ("America's unfinished agenda," 2000, p. 24).

Points to Ponder

According to Frederick Seidl, chair of NASW's Peace and Justice Committee, although welfare reform was labeled a success because fewer people were receiving welfare, this assessment of the legislation fails to consider "the consequences of this reduction or the degree to which the problem of poverty in America had been addressed" (Slavin, 1999, p. 5).

A survey of 25 midsize and large cities, including Denver, Detroit, Los Angeles, Miami, Nashville, Philadelphia, Phoenix, Providence (Rhode Island), San Diego, and Trenton, carried out by the United States Conference of Mayors at the close of 2000, showed that:

> Requests for emergency food rose about 17 percent from last year, while requests for emergency shelter were up 15 percent . . . Demand for emergency food by families with children increased 16 percent. Not all the requests were filled. On average, 13 percent of the requests for emergency food were not met last year, as well as 23 percent of requests by homeless people for emergency shelter ("Need for Emergency Aid Rises . . .," 2000).

Policy Practice: Advocacy for Policy Change

Since TANF removed the responsibility of making many of the decisions about assisting the poor from the federal government and instead gave these decisions to the individual states, social action on the part of social workers must be directed at both national and state levels. For example, TANF restored state residency requirements for public assistance, despite the fact that they had been declared unconstitutional by the Supreme Court in 1969. TANF gave states the right to adjust welfare benefits to people residing in that state for less than one year to the level of benefits provided in their home states. However, on May 18, 1999, in the *Saenz v. Roe* case, the U.S. Supreme Court ruled in a 7 to 2 vote that this residency requirement was unconstitutional (Greenhouse, 1999, p. 1).

Points to Ponder

Quoting from the 14th Amendment to the Constitution, Supreme Court Justice John Paul Stevens said, "Citizens of the United States, whether rich or poor, have the right to choose to be citizens 'of the State wherein they reside' . . . The states, however, do not have any right to select their citizens" (Greenhouse, 1999, p. 1).

In addition, the constitutionality of certain aspects of TANF legislation has been raised by advocacy groups, and consequently, in some states the courts have challenged parts of the legislation. For example, New York State's 1997 Welfare Reform Act excluded documented immigrants from coverage under Medicaid, as stipulated in TANF. However, according to a May, 1999 decision in the Supreme Court of New York County, "state and welfare laws that condition benefits on citizenship and duration of residency violate the Fourteenth Amendment's Equal Protection clause. This court also concluded that the law ran afoul of Article 17 of the State Constitution, which requires the state to provide aid, care and support for the needy" (cited in *New York Law Journal*, May 27, 1999, p. 25). One can see from this policy change that advocacy can have an impact on social policy, not only legislation but also in the courts throughout the judicial system.

Agency Practice and the Provision of Services to the Poor

A critical agency practice issue concerns the provision of emergency services to uninsured clients, including both medical and social services. How an agency can maintain a humanitarian service, particularly during times when funding is cut back, is an ongoing dilemma that all agencies must deal with.

As part of agency practice, social workers seek out resources in the community that are appropriate for their clients. Social workers need to assess the needs of their clients and locate agencies that can meet these needs. For example, it is important to locate agencies whose staff is familiar with the language and culture of the clients in order to provide quality service and reduce stress on family members who may be put in the position of serving as translators.

Client Practice with People Facing Poverty: The Case of Luba and Vadim

TANF has serious implications related to clients' eligibility for services and for the range of services that an agency can provide. It also raises critical questions about the role of government in helping the poor and the need for social work advocacy. The potential impact of TANF and other social welfare policies is illustrated in the case of Luba:

> Luba, 41 years old, emigrated to the United States from Russia four years ago with her husband and her son, Vadim, who is now 14 years old. They settled in Kansas City, Missouri, where their cousins were living. Her husband worked "off the books" as a driver for a small taxi company. Five months ago her husband suffered a massive heart attack while on his way to work and died instantly. Luba used their limited savings to pay for her husband's burial, and to pay rent and daily expenses for the next three months.
>
> Yesterday, Luba started having abdominal pain and when she could not stand it anymore, she went to the emergency room at a nearby hospital. She was told that she had appendicitis, and needed surgery immediately. Luba, who spoke very little English, asked Vadim, who visited her after the surgery, to tell the nurse that she was worried about paying for the surgery. The nurse made a referral to the hospital's social worker.
>
> The social worker did not speak Russian, and Vadim translated for them. It was awkward for him because his mother was crying. He seemed embarrassed and upset as he translated and tried to rush it along. During the course of the conversation about paying the hospital bill, Luba confided that her money was all gone and that she sold all the jewelry she had. Moreover, she had received a dispossess notice from her landlord at the beginning of the month, and she did not know where to turn for help.
>
> In answer to the social worker's questions, Luba stated that she never felt "at home" in the United States and that she had few friends and spent most of her days in bed. Even when her husband was alive, she was unhappy and cried frequently, and now she felt even worse and she worried about how this was affecting Vadim. She never learned much English even though she took a class for a couple of months when she first got here, and she never worked in the United States, although she did try to get a job.

In an effort to help Luba and her son, the social worker needs to address two areas of concern: the immediate financial situation, and the emotional issues that Luba talked about—her isolation and depression, and their impact on Vadim.

First, the social worker needs to determine whether Luba and Vadim are eligible for any benefits and services, including the services of social workers. Therefore it is important to ask the following questions:

- Are Luba and Vadim in the United States legally? Did they arrive on refugee status? This information is crucial in order to determine what, if any, assistance they will be eligible to receive, such as public assistance under TANF, Medicaid, and Food Stamps. Although TANF stipulates that documented immigrants must reside in the United States for five years before being eligible for assistance, some states have lowered that requirement. What are the current policies regarding eligibility for assistance for documented immigrants in Missouri? For undocumented immigrants? For refugees?
- Did the family have any medical insurance while Luba's husband was working? How has the family managed to pay for medical care in the past? If they do not have medical insurance, do they meet the eligibility requirements for Medi-

caid? If not, is Vadim eligible for Missouri's Child Health Insurance Program (CHIP)?

■ Is Luba familiar with any of the local voluntary agencies in her area that are providing service to the large number of immigrants from Russia?

Although Luba has not requested help with other concerns, the social worker needs to listen carefully as Luba talks to see if she might be open to other kinds of help. For example:

■ What is her support network? Are any of her friends or relatives available to help get them through this critical time? Are they involved with any religious or ethnocultural organizations?

■ How has Luba been coping with the sudden death of her husband? What has the impact been on Vadim? Does she think counseling would be useful for either or both of them?

■ It sounds like Luba might have been depressed even before this loss. Has she tried to obtain help before?

■ Did she work outside the home before coming to the United States? What did she do? Does she want to look for a job or obtain vocational training once she is feeling better?

■ What arrangements were made for Vadim's care while Luba is in the hospital? If he is alone and no other arrangements for his supervision can be made, does the social worker have a legal responsibility to notify child protective services?

Substance Abuse: Contradictory and Confusing Policies

Many people think substance abuse refers only to illegal drugs, such as heroin or cocaine. However, it is important to remember that abuse of substances also refers to "legal" drugs. These include tobacco, prescription drugs that might be abused, and alcohol. In fact, it is alcohol, which was legalized in 1933 with the repeal of Prohibition, which is the most destructive to individuals, families, and communities and is the most closely associated with criminal behavior (Straussner, 1994).

Points to Ponder

The National Center on Addiction and Substance Abuse (CASA) at Columbia University found that "of 1.7 million prisoners in 1996, 1.4 million had violated drug or alcohol laws, had been high when they committed their crimes, had stolen to support their habit or had a history of drug and alcohol abuse that led them to commit crimes. Twenty one percent of state prisoners convicted of violent crimes committed them under the influence of alcohol alone . . . three percent were high on crack or powder cocaine and only 1 percent on heroin" (Wren, 1998, p. A-14).

Substance Abuse in the Cities

While substance abuse exists in all communities, it is a particularly devastating problem in many cities. For example:

- Police in New York City made close to 900,000 drug arrests between 1989 and 1999, more than in any other city worldwide (Egan, 1999, p. 1)
- "No region in the country is having a deadlier struggle with heroin than the Pacific Northwest. . . . Deaths from heroin overdoses have more than doubled in Kings County, which includes Seattle, over the last decade. They have risen so much in the nearest metropolitan area, Portland, Oregon, during the same time that the drug is now ranked among the leading causes of death among white men there age 25 to 54" (Sanchez, 2000)
- 1 out of 6 adults in Baltimore, or about 60,000 people, are addicted (Metropolitan Washington Council . . . , 1999)

Points to Ponder

"Substance abuse and addiction have changed the nature of everyday life in urban America. This epidemic affects how city residents play, learn, worship, receive medical care, go to and from work and school, shop, litigate, wear jewelry, carry their pocketbooks, drive and park their cars, secure their apartments and homes, and raise their children. Mothers are reluctant to let their children play unsupervised in the parks; children walk to school on police-protected safe corridors and often pass through metal detectors as they enter the building; some teachers are locked in classrooms for their own safety. Joggers avoid parks after dark. Churches that once never closed are open only during services. Patients wait for hours in crowded emergency rooms. Cars are put in attended and locked garages and in outdoor lots fenced by barbed wire; storekeepers unlock their doors only in response to a ringing bell; and lawyers manipulate clogged court calendars to their clients' advantage" (CASA, 1996, pp. 11–12).

Impact of Substance Abuse on Families

In addition to the profound impact of substance abuse on urban communities as seen above, the abuse of alcohol and other drugs has a devastating impact on families.

Points to Ponder

Parents who are preoccupied with obtaining and using drugs are likely to have difficulty providing their children with an environment conducive to optimal psychological and social development" (Nadel & Straussner, 1997, p. 159).

Substance abuse is a primary factor in domestic violence and in child neglect and abuse.

The negative impact of substance abuse on the welfare of a child can occur even before the baby is born. For example:

- Smoking during pregnancy increases the incidence of infant death from Sudden Infant Death Syndrome (SIDS).
- Use of heroin during pregnancy leads to children born addicted to heroin and subsequently suffering withdrawal symptoms.
- Use of cocaine during pregnancy may result in newborns who are premature and who may suffer from various medical and cognitive complications.
- Alcohol consumption during pregnancy may lead to fetal alcohol syndrome, a devastating condition that is characterized by stunted growth, mental retardation, behavioral problems, and physical deformities.

Points to Ponder

Fetal alcohol syndrome is "the leading preventable cause of mental retardation" (CASA, 1996, p. 18).

Substance abuse by parents increases the need for child welfare services, and particularly foster care. For example, between 1985 and 1991, the number of children in foster care rose in proportion to the increase in the use of crack cocaine by women (CASA, 1996; Straussner, 1994). The need for foster care is particularly acute in urban communities.

Points to Ponder

"In New York State . . . two-thirds of the children in care are from New York City, though the city is home to less than half of the state's residents" (Holody, 1997, p. 135).

Many state policies attempt to prevent substance abuse during a woman's pregnancy through particularly harsh policies. For example, in May 1999, legislation was passed in Sioux Falls, South Dakota, making South Dakota the first state to consider drinking during pregnancy a form of child abuse, and making it possible for friends, relatives, and judges to commit pregnant women who are alcoholic to treatment centers during the pregnancy (Pregnant Drinkers . . . , 1999). In other states, numerous women have been arrested for drug use during pregnancy.

Points to Ponder

"Recognition of the special needs of pregnant addicted women has resulted in more programs targeting this population. However, social policy directed at this problem has been inconsistent and conflicting. In some states, these women face prosecution under child abuse laws, thereby discouraging women from seeking addiction treatment and prenatal care" (Smyth & Miller, 1997, p. 133).

Policy Practice and Substance Abuse

The policy responses of the society to substance abuse are complex and often contradictory, creating difficulties for social workers and other helping professionals attempting to assist clients. Like all policies, federal and state laws and regulations regarding substance abuse change over time. It is important that social workers be aware of policies related to the use and abuse of substances, both on the national level and in the state and city in which they work.

Drug Prevention Policies

Current federal substance abuse policies are aimed at controlling either the supply of, or the demand for drugs. *Supply approaches* try to prevent drugs from reaching people and are part of various federal "war on drugs" legislations. They include funding to foreign governments to eliminate the growing of drugs in their countries and the arrests of drug distributors and dealers in the United States. *Demand approaches* seek to decrease the use of drugs by individuals and include the development of various educational and prevention activities, treatment programs, and research on treatment effectiveness and program evaluation (Nadel & Straussner, 1997).

Points to Ponder

According to former President Clinton, the disparities in sentencing of people using crack compared to powdered cocaine "are unconscionable. . . . I tried to change that. The Republican Congress was willing to narrow but not eliminate them, the theory being that people who used crack were more violent than people who used cocaine. What they really meant was: People that used crack were more likely to be poor—and coincidentally, black or brown. And therefore not to have money. Those people that used cocaine were more likely to be rich, pay for it and therefore be peaceful" (quoted in Kiefer, 2000, p. A26).

Institutional Oppression and Drug Policies

Current federal policies regarding drug use reflect institutional oppression. This can be seen in the lower mandatory federal sentencing laws for those who use powdered cocaine compared to those who use crack cocaine. Cocaine powder is a more costly substance that is used more widely by those who have more money, while the inexpensive crack cocaine is readily available in inner city communities and more commonly used by people with lower incomes.

Harm Reduction Approaches

Federal and state regulation also impact the availability of what has been termed *harm reduction* approaches to substance abuse treatment. Unlike the *abstinence* model, where the ultimate goal of treatment is complete abstinence from all substances, the harm reduction model is based on the assumption that abstinence is not a realistic plan for everyone, and it aims at controlling some of the negative consequences of substance abuse. For example, harm reduction may include the availability of needle exchange programs aimed at minimizing the spread of AIDS. Moreover, unlike most treatment approaches for substance abuse, which tend to be determined by agency policies, the provision of *methadone maintenance* services are determined by government policies. Federal laws regulate the criteria for admission to a methadone maintenance program, as well as the dosage given (Friedman, 1993).

"Criminalization" of Mentally Ill Substance Abusers

Many substance abusers also have other mental disorders and some use drugs to medicate themselves. When found in possession of an illegal drug, mentally ill individuals may be prosecuted as criminals. This results in what has come to be called the "criminalization" of the mentally ill. Once caught up in the criminal justice system, the option for rehabilitation becomes limited.

Some states are introducing drug courts and other legislation that give nonviolent convicted criminals who were under the influence of drugs at the time they committed the crime a choice of prison or drug rehabilitation. However, opportunities for rehabilitation for substance abusers in the criminal justice system are inadequate. They are even more limited for those who are dually diagnosed with mental illness, with the vast majority receiving neither psychiatric treatment nor drug rehabilitation.

Points to Ponder

In 1996, 840,000 federal and state prisoners needed treatment for drugs, but less than 150,000, not even 18 percent, received treatment prior to their release. The remaining 82 percent were released with no intervention (Wren, 1998).

Agency Practice: Lack of Availability of Treatment and Fragmentation of the Service Delivery System

Despite the enormity of substance abuse problems in many communities, there is a general lack of funding to provide adequate rehabilitation services. For example, "Baltimore currently has about 6,400 treatment slots, up by 2,300 over the last 2 years, but 12,000 to 15,000 slots are needed" (Metropolitan Washington Council, 1999, pp. 9–10). Lack of opportunities for rehabilitation contributes to high rates of crime committed by abusers, including buying and selling drugs.

Lack of Services for Dually Diagnosed Clients

With the recognition of the co-occurrence of mental illness and substance abuse, often referred to as "dual diagnosis," special services for *mentally ill, chemical abusing* (MICA) clients have been developed, but are limited in many communities. In many cities, funding and services for dually diagnosed clients are fragmented, with different agencies providing mental health services and substance abuse services to the same client without any coordination.

The Impact of Managed Care

The current policy of managed health care further complicates services for substance abusing clients. As with treatment for physical and mental illnesses today, most treatment for substance abuse also falls within the parameters of managed health care by medical insurance companies. This approach to health care defines the limits of help for which an agency can receive reimbursement for their services and may interfere with the continuation of treatment services to clients. It also impacts the helping relationship between clients and social workers or other helping professionals because the time allowed for treatment is determined by managed care staff and not by the client or the agency providing the services.

Points to Ponder

"In 1998 . . . 57 percent of America's addicts who needed treatment did not get it" (Donnelly, 2001, p. A1).

Client Practice with Substance Abusing Clients: The Case of John

The story of John illustrates the complexity of client need, agency regulations, and social welfare policies relating to substance abusing clients, particularly those who are dually diagnosed.

John, a 55-year-old divorced Vietnam veteran, had returned from the military in 1972 with both a substance abuse problem and a psychiatric problem. While he drank heavily and smoked marijuana before going into the army, at the time he went into the military he had a regular job as a store clerk and was married and the father of a two-year-old daughter. Once in Vietnam, John started using heroin, which initially helped him cope with his fears. However, after a few months of fighting, he became so anxious that he could no longer function and was given a medical discharge.

After returning home, John was in a Veteran's Administration Hospital for two months for psychiatric treatment and was discharged with medication and an appointment for outpatient treatment. However, he did not follow up with either treatment or his medication.

Things went steadily downhill for John at that point. He returned to using heroin and later started using cocaine. He had trouble holding a job, and after five years of supporting John and hoping he would get his life straightened out, his wife pursued a divorce. At that point he became abusive, and she moved with their child to another state.

John gave up their apartment and moved in with a friend, sleeping on the couch in the friend's single-room apartment. Although he had jobs from time to time, his drug use continued and he was an unreliable employee. Finally, he went to see a doctor at the Veterans Administration Hospital, and was diagnosed with post-traumatic stress disorder. Based on this diagnosis, he was referred to and approved for Supplemental Security Income.

John felt encouraged by this and thought he would be able to start functioning again—at least to get his own place to live. He was able to get a small apartment in a public housing project, felt better about himself, and cut back on his drug use. However, after a while he resumed his drug use, was unable to manage his money, and was evicted from his apartment.

Shortly afterward, John was arrested for possession of narcotics after being questioned by police who found him living in an abandoned building. After a brief stay in jail, John was put on probation and released to a community residence for nonviolent drug offenders. He was also assigned to a social worker at a mental health facility for dually-diagnosed clients.

In trying to help John, the social worker had to address the following issues:

- Does his arrest have any impact on his receiving SSI benefits, including Medicaid?
- Is John eligible for another city housing apartment given his previous eviction and later arrest?
- Because the onset of his psychiatric disability might have been service connected, does the Veteran's Administration offer any benefits or services that can be helpful to John?
- Assuming his readiness, what are the opportunities for education or vocational rehabilitation for John? Is he protected from job discrimination by the Americans with Disabilities Act?
- Does John meet the federal eligibility requirements for a methadone maintenance treatment program?

- Assuming that he wants to, and is eligible to receive methadone maintenance treatment, can John still receive treatment for his mental illness? How will the treatments be coordinated?
- Can the social worker keep any information confidential or does she have to tell the probation officer everything that John reveals to her?
- If John expressed interest in reestablishing a connection with his daughter, is there any agency that could help him with his search?

Health Care: The Lack of a Comprehensive National Policy

The lack of a comprehensive medical care program in the United States affects every person. The number of people without any medical insurance rose from 38 million in 1992 to 44 million in 1998, affecting 18.4 percent of the population (Rosenbaum, 2000). It is important to note that, with the exception of South Africa and the United States, a program of universal health care exists in all the developed countries. In the United States today, the elderly are underinsured through Medicare, the poor are in danger of losing Medicaid if they work, health-care programs designed especially for uninsured children are underutilized, and policies related to women's health differ from state to state.

As noted in the previous chapter, the United States has struggled with health-care legislation since the 1930s, when unsuccessful efforts were made to include health insurance in the Social Security Act. Subsequent efforts also failed, as did President Clinton's proposal for a universal health-care plan, which met with overwhelming opposition from insurance companies and other health care-related businesses, and lacked general support from the public.

Points to Ponder

"Two-thirds of Americans tell pollsters they would like a government program to make sure people have insurance, but fewer than 40 percent favor a sweeping measure that would require higher taxes" (Rosenbaum, 2000, Sec. 4, p. 1).

The lack of a comprehensive program of health insurance in the United States has had the most devastating effects on the working poor and people in the middle class who do not have adequate health-care coverage. Unlike most other benefits in our society, health care is available for the poor through the Medicaid program, but it is not available for many others who need it. For most low-wage earners, health insurance is not provided through their jobs. Many people earn just enough to keep them ineligible for Medicaid, while at the same time they find that paying for private medical insurance for a family is not only unaffordable, but may require most of the person's earnings.

The first piece of legislation signed into law by President Clinton was the Family and Medical Leave Act, which gave job protection for 12 weeks a year to people needing time away from work to care for a newborn or an adopted child, because of the employee's own health, or to care for a family member with a serious medical condition. The fact that the person would be without pay for the period of the leave meant that people with marginal incomes could not take advantage of this law, nor did it apply to people working in small businesses with fewer than 50 employees. However, for many people it has offered the opportunity to take care of health-related family responsibilities while at least preserving their jobs.

Policy Practice and Health Care

The health-care programs that do exist in the public sector form a complex and confusing patchwork of services. Social workers not only need to be able to help their clients make some sense of the services and find access to them, but they also need to take an active role in advocating for needed health care services. With no mandate in the United States to proceed with a comprehensive health-care program, it is left to different groups, each with its own special interest, to attempt to shape health-care policy in the United States. Many of these groups, such as insurance companies, drug companies, hospitals, and health-care providers, have vested financial interests in particular programs. It is easy for the needs of patients to be overpowered by these big-business interests. Under these circumstances, it becomes even more urgent that social workers take a leadership role in advocating for health-care services needed by their clients.

Social workers have a wealth of information about the impact of current health care programs on clients, and are in the position to provide feedback to legislators about their clients' needs. They also can take an active role in mobilizing professional and client groups to speak out for clients' needs and interests.

Following is a brief overview of some of the current health-care policies and programs, including their strengths and weaknesses. These are organized according to groups of people who may benefit from the programs:

- People who are financially eligible for *Medicaid*
- Older adults and *Medicare*
- Children and the federal *Vaccines for Children's Program* and the *Children's Health Insurance Program*
- Groups with special health needs, including persons with HIV/AIDS and persons with disabilities
- Health care for women, including policy issues related to reproductive rights and adolescent health

Medicaid for Those Who Are Financially Eligible

Medicaid was passed in 1965 as an amendment to the Social Security Act. It is the most comprehensive of the health-care insurances in the public sector in terms of the services it covers, and includes medical, hospital, and long-term care expenses. However, it is a means-tested program restricted to those who meet stringent financial eligibility requirements. Currently it covers about 36 million people, including:

- Children
- Older adults
- The blind
- The disabled
- People who are eligible for federally assisted income maintenance programs

Medicaid is funded jointly by the federal government and state governments and is administered by the states. In addition to income requirements, there are also residency requirements—as a consequence of TANF legislation, legal immigrants are not eligible for Medicaid until they have been in the United States for five years. Undocumented immigrants are not and cannot become eligible for Medicaid.

Both the income levels to establish eligibility for Medicaid and the scope of benefits provided differ from state to state. In some states, Medicaid recipients are monitored by managed care organizations called health maintenance organizations (HMOs), which control the type and extent of services provided.

Medicare for Older Adults

Medicare is not as comprehensive as Medicaid, and in fact covers only a portion of medical costs of older adults. Medicare—Part A is an institutional program available to all people when they reach age 65. As such, it is not means-tested and is not stigmatizing to people who use it. Part B of Medicare supplements the benefits of Part A and can be purchased separately; it works like private health insurance.

The major drawback of Medicare is that it leaves older adults underinsured. It does not provide the full cost of medical care and offers limited hospital coverage. Further, it does not cover the very high costs of long-term care. Consequently, when a person is in need of these very costly services, they must "spend down" their assets by paying for medical services until they reach the poverty level and become eligible for Medicaid.

Points to Ponder

In 1966, when Medicare was implemented, 19 million people enrolled in it. In 1972, Medicare was extended to include the disabled and also people with permanent kidney failure, regardless of their age, to cover the particularly high costs of dialysis. This brought 2 million more people into the program. By the year 2000, 39 million older adults and persons with disabilities received Medicare. It is anticipated that by the year 2030, 77 million people will be using the program (<www.medicare.gov>, accessed December 5, 2000).

Points to Ponder

Jansson (2001) has identified another critical failure of Medicare: "Because, in line with the disease model of medicine, it was confined to financing existing curative services, Medicare did not promote innovative alternatives to nursing home care, failed to foster preventive services for elderly persons, and did not provide outreach services to the frail elderly. In short, Medicare funded conventional services for a population that needed innovative programs, and it covered only a small fraction of their medical needs" (p. 250).

Programs for Children

Two important health programs for children were started during the Clinton administration. The federal *Vaccines for Children Program*, established by legislation passed in 1994, provides for vaccinations against childhood diseases for uninsured infants and young children, and for all Native American children, with no cost to the recipients.

Another, the *Children's Health Insurance Program (CHIP)*, was started in 1997 as part of Title XXI of the Social Security Act. CHIP is funded by states with matching funds from the federal government. Each state has its own version of the program. In some, it is attached to Medicaid, and in others it is a separate program. Some states charge monthly premiums for each child who is covered. However, in 1999, it was reported that less than 20 percent of federal money that was made available by Congress for CHIP was being used by the states, despite the fact that there were still at least 10.7 million uninsured children in the United States (Pear, 1999).

One of the problems facing agencies is the need to find strategies to let clients know about available services. This problem has affected many programs. It was seen in the Women's, Infant's and Children's Program, which was underutilized, and is currently seen in the Child Health Insurance Program, which is severely underutilized in some states. For example, in Texas, 1.5 million children, or 37 percent of youngsters in low-income homes, remain uninsured in spite of the fact that this program is underutilized.

Points to Ponder

As pointed out by Marian Wright Edelman (1999), President of the Children's Defense Fund, "The problem is not that there is too much money for the Children's Health Insurance Program and too few children to enroll. The problem is letting parents know that the program exists. . . . Now is the time to step up efforts to inform working families about health insurance for their children. Only then will they get the healthy start in life they deserve" (Sec. 4, p. 16).

Programs for Persons with HIV/AIDS and Persons with Disabilities

While there are many groups with special medical care needs, we will limit this discussion to particular programs for persons with HIV/AIDS and persons with disabilities.

Persons with HIV/AIDS: Access to Treatment

The number of people in the United States who were diagnosed with AIDS dropped for the first time in 1996; the decrease in AIDS has been attributed to both improved treatment and extensive public education campaigns. However, side effects of drugs used for treatment discouraged their use, and many people discontinued using them. In 2000, it was estimated that between 800,000 and 900,000 people in the United States were infected with the HIV virus. Of these, one-third did not even know they were infected (www.hhhs.gov/news/press/2000pres/00fsaids.html, accessed December 16, 2000). According to Jansson (2001), "As the panic about the (AIDS) epidemic abated, many persons stopped using safe sex so that rates of infection, having dropped for several years, began to rise again. The epidemic began to spread . . . the Board of Supervisors in Los Angeles County declared a state of medical emergency in late 1999, calling for an all-out campaign of education and outreach to arrest its spread, particularly in low-income areas" (p. 403).

About half the people with HIV/AIDS are Medicaid recipients. However, many people who are HIV-positive are not Medicaid eligible. Through state and federal funding, some states are sponsoring demonstration programs to extend Medicaid coverage to HIV-positive people early in the course of the disease, before they are considered disabled, so that drug therapies and treatment can be available to them. Other sources of funding are also available. For example, the *Ryan White Care Act*, enacted by Congress in 1990, has been instrumental in providing funding for agency services to help thousands of individuals in metropolitan areas that were hard hit by AIDS.

Health Care for Persons with Disabilities: The Work Incentives Improvement Act

Signed into law in 1999 during the Clinton administration, the Work Incentive Improvement Act makes it possible for people with disabilities to work without losing health care coverage. Previously, many people with disabilities lost their Medicaid and Medicare eligibility when their incomes increased due to their employment. This created serious problems because even those who had private insurance through their employment could not afford to pay the out-of-pocket expenses for the costly medical equipment and health care that they needed. Consequently, many disabled people could not work because working meant they would lose eligibility for Medicaid. The *Work Incentive Improvement Act* provides federal government grants to states so that the disabled who are working can buy into Medicaid. Each state determines the cost of premiums that the workers pay for their coverage (Lacey, 1999, Section 1, A 14).

Health Care for Women—Reproductive Rights

Perhaps the primary issue related to women's health has to do with policies and services regarding reproductive rights. Because policies in this area are so volatile and subject to change, we will present some of the issues rather than specific policies, and look at the impact that some of these policies can have on clients and on social work practice.

Starting with the *Roe v. Wade* Supreme Court decision in 1973, abortion has been legal in the United States. However, many groups, particularly fundamentalist religious groups, continue to battle this decision. Related issues hotly debated include:

- How long into the pregnancy can an abortion take place? How is a "late-term" abortion defined?
- What role should the government assume in protecting women who are seeking abortions, and in protecting doctors from attack?
- Should parental notification be required in the case of an abortion for a minor? Currently, this decision is made at the state level; at least 29 states require some form of parental notification or counseling before a minor has an abortion (Gray, 1999).
- Efforts have been made to make it a federal crime for an adult to take a minor to another state for an abortion, thereby bypassing the parental-notification law in the girl's home state (Rosenbaum, 1999).

Agency Practice and Health Care Services

Many of the issues raised in the discussion of health care pertain to agency practice. For example:

- Funding for services, as seen in the discussion of HIV/AIDS is variable, depending on the political scene.
- Reimbursement to agencies by Medicaid and Medicare is lower than private insurance and can be slow in arriving.
- The growth of managed care has interfered with the autonomy of agencies.
- Even when funding is available, as for the CHIP program, agencies may have difficulty getting the word out to potential clients about the programs.
- The lack of a holistic approach to health care leads to fragmented services, highlighting the need for case management in social agencies.
- Policies, whether on the federal, state, or city level, or by the agency itself, can interfere with the provision of services that are needed by clients, as can be seen in the case of Melissa in the following section.

Client Practice and the Impact of Policies: The Case of Melissa

How can social workers be effective helpers when policies seem to work against their clients' goals for themselves? Following is the story of Melissa, whose life during the last nine months has been driven by state policies related to reproductive rights. And the rest of her life will also be driven by these policies.

Melissa is 17 years old and has just been arrested. A police investigation found her to be the mother of a newborn baby boy who was found abandoned on a park bench. The baby was taken to the hospital suffering from dehydration and cold. What were the circumstances that led to this abandonment?

Melissa became pregnant after going to a rave party with a friend. The last thing she remembered was drinking a soda given to her by a good-looking guy she met there. As it turned out, she was given a "date rape" drug and although she didn't remember what had happened, her friend told her that she had left with the guy she was talking to. She found herself in the living room of her home early the next morning, confused and disheveled, and two months later she realized that she was pregnant.

Her high school graduation was a few months away and Melissa was planning to go to a community college in her city, hoping to become an elementary school teacher. Melissa did not feel ready to be a mother. She had no idea who fathered the child, and she was eager to get on with her life. She could not talk to her parents about the pregnancy because they were very religious, and she knew they were vehement in their opposition to abortion.

She asked her girlfriend to come with her to a hospital to find out about having an abortion. The social worker at the hospital told Melissa they no longer perform abortions because this hospital merged with the nearby Catholic hospital and the new policies no longer allowed abortions, even in cases of rape.

Melissa and her friend decided to go to a family-planning agency nearby. There, Melissa was told that yes, they could help her with an abortion, but because she was under 18, she would need her parent's permission for the abortion. Melissa became very angry, and said this was her pregnancy, not her parents', that her parents were "crazy religious" and they would never, ever, sign for this. The social worker told her she was really sorry, but that was the state's policy, not her own or even the clinic's, and the only way she could get an abortion was to have parental approval.

A few weeks later, Melissa heard about the legalization of the "morning after" pill and asked a doctor if she could give it to her. The doctor told Melissa that she could lose her license to practice medicine in the state if she gave it to her without parental consent.

Feeling desperate, Melissa asked her friend's 22-year-old brother to drive her to a neighboring state, where, she heard, parental approval was not needed. He told her that he would really like to help her out but that one of his friends had gotten into trouble because it is illegal in their state to take a minor to another state for an abortion. So he was afraid to do it.

Melissa graduated from high school, and carefully hid her pregnancy from her family. During the summer she gave birth by herself to a little boy in the bathroom of her family's apartment while her parents were at work. She did not look at the baby, but wrapped him in a large towel, and when she felt strong enough she carried him to the park near her home and left him on a bench in a secluded area.

Melissa's choices were severely limited. While she would not have run into these obstacles in a different state where parental consent for abortion for a minor was not required, she was not able to get the help she wanted and needed where she lived. Although she knew the baby could be adopted, she did not want to let anyone know of the birth—especially her parents. She did not want to have a child. She also was not given the option to go out of state to get help. Melissa felt trapped by her situation.

This case raises many difficult and important questions that social work students need to think about.

- What went wrong? What was the combination of circumstances and policies that so adversely affected Melissa?
- What other steps could both of the social workers involved have taken in order to try to be helpful to Melissa?
- What are the pros and cons of parental notification laws?
- What are the pros and cons of laws prohibiting adults from taking minors to another state for the purpose of having an abortion?
- What kinds of programs could agencies develop in order to educate young men and women about date rape?
- What changes in policies do you think are needed in order to prevent this from happening again?
- How do you think the criminal justice system should react in this case? What should Melissa's penalty be? What should the penalty be for the young man who raped her, assuming he could be found?
- Melissa's baby recovered and developed nicely. What planning do you think should be made for him?

Conclusion

The notion that social workers need to become familiar with all social welfare policies affecting their clients and their practice can be daunting. The fact is there are more policies than any one social worker can, or even needs to, keep track of, particularly as policies change. Also, many policies differ from state to state. It is, however, necessary for social workers to be aware of how social problems, social welfare policies, and social work practice are connected and how one can influence the other. They also need to know where to go to locate information about specific policies that affect their clients, and what information is needed from clients in order to help determine eligibility for services.

The cases presented in this chapter raised questions about the values and ethics, the knowledge, and the skills needed for social work practice. The next section moves on to discuss each of these aspects in depth. Throughout those discussions, the impact of social problems and of social welfare policies will be evident.

REFERENCES

DeParle, J. (1999, May 15). Project to rescue needy stumbles against the persistence of poverty. *New York Times*, p. A1.

Edelman M. W. (1999, May 16). Letter to the Editor. *New York Times*, Section 4, p. 16.

Egan, T. (1999, October 19). A drug ran its course, then hid with its users. *New York Times*, p. B27.

Friedman, E. G. (1993). Methadone maintenance in the treatment of addiction. In S. L. A. Straussner (Ed.), *Clinical work with substance abusing clients* (pp. 135–152). New York: Guilford.

Gray, J. (1999, May 18). New pressure for Whitman on abortions. *New York Times*, p. B1.

Greenhouse, L. (1999, May 18). Newcomers to states have right to equal welfare, justices rule. *New York Times*, p. A20.

Hagen, J. L. (1999). Public welfare and human services: New directions under TANF, Part 2. *Families in Society, 80*, 78–96.

Holody, R. (1997). Children in out-of-home placements. In N. K. Phillips & S. L. A. Straussner (Eds.), *Children in the urban environment* (pp. 135–153). Springfield, IL: Thomas.

Join Together Online. (2000, May 5). Researchers provide heads-up on emerging drug trends, <www.jointogether.org>, pp. 3–4. Accessed December 22, 2000.

Kiefer, J. (2000, December 7). Clinton says he felt forced into setting gay policy. *New York Times*, p. A26.

Lacey, M. (1999, December 18). Clinton signs law to help workers with disabilities. *New York Times*, p. A14.

Meredith, R. (1999, May 30). Testing welfare applicants for drugs. *New York Times*, p. A14.

Meredith, R. (1999, November 11). Judge halts drug tests of welfare applicants. *New York Times*, p. B3.

Metropolitan Washington Council of Governments public hearing. (1999, October 18). *Changing the conversation: A national plan to improve substance abuse treatment*. Washington, DC: Center for Substance Abuse Treatment and Substance Abuse and Mental Health Services Administration.

Nadel, M. & Straussner, S. L. A. (1997). Children in substance abusing families. In N. K. Phillips & S. L. A. Straussner (Eds.), *Children in the urban envi-*

ronment: Linking social policy and clinical practice (pp. 154–174). Springfield, IL: Thomas.

Need for emergency aid rises, city study shows. (2000, December 15). *New York Times*, p. A30.

New York Law Journal, May 27, 1999, p. 25

Out of sight, out of mind. (2000, May 20). *The Economist*, 28.

Peabody, C. (2000, October). Is it possible to engage in social work without engaging in social work policy? NASW, New York State Chapter, *Update, 25*, (3), 5.

Pear, R. (1999, May 9). Many states slow to use children's insurance fund. *New York Times*, p. A1.

Pear, R. (1999, June 6). As welfare rolls shrink, cities shoulder bigger load. *New York Times*, p. A26.

Pregnant drinkers face a crackdown. (1999, May 24). *New York Times*, p. A16.

Ray, O. & Ksir, C. (1999). *Drugs, society, and human behavior* (8th ed.). Boston: WCB/McGraw-Hill.

Rosenbaum, D. E. (1999, July 1). House passes bill to restrict minors' abortions. *New York Times*, p. A17.

Rosenbaum, D. E. (2000, September 10). What if there is no cure for health care's ills? *New York Times*, Sec. 4, pp. 1, 3.

Sanchez, R. (2000, October 9). Northwest heroin use is epidemic. *Washington Post*, p. AO3.

Slavin, P. (1999, April). Welfare reform: Good news, bad news. *NASW News, 44*, 4, 5.

Smyth, N. J. & Miller, B. A. (1997). Parenting issues for substance abusing women. In S. L. A. Straussner & E. Zelvin (Eds.), *Gender and addictions: Men and women in treatment* (pp. 123–150). Northvale, NJ: Jason Aronson.

Straussner, S. L. A. (1994). The impact of alcohol and other drugs on the American family. *Drug and Alcohol Review 13*, 393–399.

U.S. Department of Health and Human Services (1999). *Mental health: A report of the Surgeon General*. Rockville, MD: U.S. Department of Health and Human Services, Substance Abuse and Mental Health Services Administration, Center for Mental Health Services, National Institutes of Mental Health <www.hhhs.gov/newspress2000/pres/00fsaids/html>.

SECTION THREE

Social Work Practice in the Cities

Introduction

In the previous sections we have seen that the social work profession developed as a response to urban social problems, and that it functions within the context of social welfare policies that impact on the lives of clients, on the services available to them, and on the ways in which social workers and social service agencies function.

While social work is influenced in many ways by policies, over the years it has, like all professions, refined its mission, and developed its own values, knowledge, and skills that define what the profession does and how it does it. The development of social work values, knowledge and skills is a dynamic process that is related to social and political change, changes in social welfare policies, and advances in scientific knowledge and technology. It is these aspects that unify the profession and guide social workers in their practice.

Understanding and applying the values, knowledge, and skills of the profession is not something that one accomplishes in a semester's work in college. It is an ongoing process of learning that requires the participation of every social worker throughout his or her career.

This section consist of four chapters that explore the various aspects of social work practice:

Chapter 8 discusses social work values and ethics. It discusses the Code of Ethics of the National Association of Social Workers, and applies principles of the Code to situations involving client, agency, and policy practice in urban settings.

Chapter 9 provides an overview of the broad scope of knowledge needed for client, agency, and policy practice. In addition, it provides an overview of knowledge of research needed for practice.

The second knowledge chapter, Chapter 10, is devoted specifically to the topic of diversity. This is a critical aspect of social work knowledge, particularly in urban communities.

The range of skills required for professional practice is discussed in Chapter 11. It identifies the various roles that social workers perform, the phases of social work intervention, and identifies specific skills needed for direct practice with clients, and for agency and policy practice.

CHAPTER

8

Values and Ethics in Social Work Practice

San Francisco's Mayor Willie Brown and leaders of the gay community raise the rainbow flag celebrating the gay community in City Hall in 1999—the first time this flag was raised in a city hall in a major city in the United States. AP/Wide World Photos

All professions are based on a set of values that guides professional behavior. The specific values of the social work profession are reflected in its Code of Ethics. It is this code that identifies the standards for ethical behavior for social work practice. Learning about these values and the Social Work Code of Ethics are crucial components of social work education.

As indicated in earlier chapters, social work practice in urban areas involves dealing with many different people who hold many different values. Social workers, however, deal not only with clients and their unique values, but also with agencies and policies, which reflect their own sets of values. Not infrequently, the values of these different systems conflict with each other. Therefore, in the course of their work, social workers may be faced with a variety of ethical dilemmas. Guidelines for ethical behavior presented in the Social Work Code of Ethics can be useful in dealing with such conflicts.

This chapter explores the following:

■ Definitions of values and ethics
■ The different value systems encountered by social workers
■ A summary and discussion of the ethical standards in the Social Work Code of Ethics
■ A discussion of client self-determination and confidentiality, including their importance and their limitations in social work practice
■ Value conflicts and ethical dilemmas encountered by social workers in urban areas

Understanding Values

Values are the underpinnings of the social work profession, and play an important role in how social workers respond to situations on a day-to-day basis. In urban areas, where there is a broad range of clients representing a variety of cultures with different value systems, social workers are more likely to confront value conflicts than in other areas. Therefore, it is important that social workers understand the meaning and significance of values, and be able to cope effectively with situations representing conflicts in values.

Values are assumptions of what is good or bad. These assumptions may derive from religious beliefs, cultural and family traditions, peer groups, or an individual's own beliefs of what is right and wrong and how to live one's life. They guide decisions about priorities, or what is most important at any given time. Values are purely subjective and may differ from person to person and culture to culture. Also, as Carol Gilligan's (1993) research has shown, values may differ by gender.

Values can be so deeply rooted that individuals may not be consciously aware of them. For some people, values remain unchanged throughout their lifetime, despite their changing environment and experiences. Others may be more open to new experiences that may influence them and cause a shift in their value system. Conflicts may occur when there are interactions between systems, whether individuals or institutions, which hold different values.

Values can also be influenced by knowledge and new research findings. For example in the past smoking had been widely accepted as a symbol of "masculinity" and "independence," so much so that photos of politicians and movie stars usually included a dangling cigarette. Today, with the scientifically-proven correlation between cigarette smoking and lung cancer, the social value of smoking has changed dramatically.

Values of Different Systems

Social workers need to deal with five different systems, each of which holds its own set of values. These include the values of:

■ Clients
■ Agencies or organizations

- The social work profession
- Society
- Personal values of the social worker

Knowing the values of each of these systems makes it possible for social workers to evaluate the extent to which the systems validate and support each other. Conversely, knowing where there are differences in values makes it possible to identify points of potential conflict so they can be acknowledged and addressed. In addition to conflicts for the social worker, there may also be conflicts among these systems, such as between the client and the society, the client and the agency, or the agency and the social work profession.

Values of Clients

All social work clients have their own sets of values. These values may or may not be in agreement with those of the worker. In order to be helpful, social workers need to be open to learning about their clients' values and the impact of these values on the lives of their clients. Moreover, different members in a family may have different values leading to stress and conflict within the family.

Values of the Agency

Social service agencies and institutions also reflect a set of values. These values determine the mission of an agency, and the services that it provides. They also reflect the auspices that support it. For example, as described in Chapter 3, the particular value systems of sectarian (religiously affiliated) agencies have a profound impact on their policies and programs.

Values of the Social Work Profession

Social work, as every other profession, is based on a set of values. The six core values of the social work profession are identified in the Preamble to the profession's Code of Ethics (NASW, 1996/1999). They are:

- Service
- Social justice
- Dignity and worth of the person
- Importance of human relationships
- Integrity
- Competence

Throughout its history, these values have been at the root of the profession, shaping its purpose and perspective. These core values represent the ideals of the profession. They include helping people who are in need; challenging social injustice; respecting the inherent dignity and worth of all clients; recognizing the importance of human relationships; dealing with clients, agencies, other professionals and the public in an honest, responsible, and trustworthy manner; and practicing competently while enhancing professional expertise.

Values of Society

Societal values are those values that are "recognized by major portions of the entire social system or, at least, by the leading members or spokespersons of that system" (Loewenberg, Dolgoff & Harrington, 2000, p. 56). Societal values impact on the policies adopted by government and other institutions and may influence laws and regulations, as discussed in the previous chapters. Values also influence the level of support given to implement existing policies. For example, while proposals for social programs may receive approval from government and voluntary agencies, these programs may not receive funding because they are not sufficiently valued by funding sources.

Societal values change over time. For example, tremendous changes in values relating to the role of women, to racial equality, to people's sexual orientation, and to sexual mores have occurred since the 1960s. These rapid changes may lead people to question their personal values, resulting in anxiety and confusion. On the agency level, these societal changes might result in different programs and services to meet the changing needs of the community.

Personal Values of the Social Worker

Social workers, too, have their own values, perhaps reflecting the family and culture in which they grew up, or the peer group with whom they currently associate. In spite of the fact that social workers may have strong convictions that influence their personal lives, it is important that their personal values do not interfere with their professional behavior.

Social workers need to become consciously aware of their own personal values before they can help their clients identify their values and pursue their goals. This occurs through the process of developing self-awareness. As they develop self-awareness, social workers become better able to separate their personal values from their clients', and are better able to respect the autonomy of clients in making their own decisions. Gaining self-awareness is an ongoing process that continues throughout one's lifetime. Ensuring that students engage in this process is one of the most important functions of social work education.

Understanding Ethics

Values can be seen as the building blocks of ethics. While values reflect judgments, *ethics determine behavior and represent a set of underlying values.* Levy (1976), has described ethics as "values in action" (p. 233). The word "ethics" comes from the Greek root "ethos," which means "custom, usage, or habit." Ethics are concerned with "the question of what actions are morally right and with how things ought to be" (Loewenberg et al., 2000, p. 6).

Points to Ponder

"We toss around the word 'unethical' whenever someone does something we don't like. . . . But painting every kind of bad behavior as a lapse in ethics cheapens a term that should be reserved for discussions of core moral values and their implications . . . Ethical does not always equal legal. It is possible to break the law—say, doing 40 in a 25 m.p.h. zone—and be perfectly ethical in the process, if speeding was necessary to get out of the way of an approaching ambulance. Conversely, unethical people have always found ways to do wrong even while hewing strictly to the law. Ethical doesn't always equal nice, either. People can treat you rudely, veil their motives from you, shock you, inconvenience you, or drive you nuts with their pigheaded intransigence without clocking up any automatic debits on the ethics register" (Seglin, 2000, p. BU4).

Although ethics do not provide answers for all situations, they do provide guidelines that assist in making difficult personal and professional decisions.

The Social Work Code of Ethics

The Code of Ethics for the social work profession is compiled by the National Association of Social Workers (NASW), and is revised every few years to reflect the changing professional knowledge and social environment. The most recent Social Work Code of Ethics was adopted in 1996, and revised slightly in 1999. (In addition to NASW's Code of Ethics, there are separate codes put out by the National Association of Black Social Workers, Clinical Social Work Federation, the Canadian Association of Social Workers, and the International Federation of Social Work.)

NASW's Code of Ethics provides a standard for professional behavior for social workers. Requiring professionals to adhere to a Code of Ethics protects the public from charlatans and incompetent practitioners, and also protects social workers from claims of unprofessional conduct. It is therefore important that all social workers become familiar with this Code.

Points to Ponder

"Professional ethics are at the core of social work. The profession has an obligation to articulate its basic values, ethical principles, and ethical standards. The NASW Code of Ethics sets forth these values, principles, and standards to guide social workers' conduct. The Code is relevant to all social workers and social work students, regardless of their professional functions, the settings in which they work, or the populations they serve" (NASW, 1996/1999, p. 2).

The social work Code of Ethics includes four sections: the *preamble*, which includes the mission of Social Work, quoted in Chapter 1, and the core values of the profession; the *purpose* of the Code of Ethics; *ethical principles* underlying social work practice; and the *ethical standards* for behavior of social workers. The entire Code is included in Appendix I.

Ethical Standards of the Social Work Profession

The NASW Code of Ethics identifies 155 specific ethical standards that describe in detail the ethical responsibilities of social workers (Reamer, 1999). These ethical responsibilities are clustered into six categories and identify specific responsibilities to clients, to colleagues, to practice settings, as social work professionals, to the profession, and to the broader society, as summarized below.

Ethical Responsibilities to Clients

Among the social workers' ethical responsibilities are those aimed at "promoting the well-being of clients." At the same time, it is recognized that "social workers' responsibilities to the larger society or specific legal obligations may on limited occasions supersede the loyalty owed to clients, and clients should be so advised (examples include when a social worker is required by law to report that a client has abused a child or has threatened to harm self or others)" (Standard 1.01).

Other important ethical responsibilities to clients include supporting clients' self-determination and respecting their rights to privacy and confidentiality (Standard 1.02; 1.07). These responsibilities will be discussed later in the chapter.

Social work ethics forbid social workers to engage in sexual activities or have sexual contact with current or recent clients, "whether such contact is consensual or forced" (Standard 1.09). Although many might think this is such a commonsense requirement, sexual activity with clients is one of the most common complaints of ethical violation for all mental health practitioners, including social workers (Kagle & Gielbelhausen, 1994; Perry & Kuruk, 1993). In their role as social workers, practitioners hold power over their clients. Unethical social workers can exploit their position in relation to clients, and clients may try to seduce social workers. Engaging in a sexual relationship with the client, moreover, redefines the relationship, and the client loses the opportunity to receive the help sought in the professional relationship.

Points to Ponder

A sexual relationship with a client is not only unethical, but is also considered to be a criminal activity that is subject to legal action in many states (Perry & Kuruk, 1993).

The Code of Ethics also addresses the issue of physical contact with a client, other than a sexual relationship. It specifies that social workers "should not engage in physical contact with clients when there is a possibility of psychological harm to the client as a result of the contact (such as cradling or caressing clients). Social workers who engage in appropriate physical contact with clients are responsible for setting clear, appropriate, and culturally-sensitive boundaries that govern such physical contact" (Standard 1.10).

There are many situations that arise during the course of working with clients when social workers have to make decisions about physical contact. Even such a common act as offering to shake a client's hand might be culturally inappropriate. For example, an Orthodox Jewish man cannot shake hands with a female social worker, or any woman other than his wife, because of religious law. The social worker needs to understand that this in no way reflects personal feelings toward her. Under other circumstances, though, some contact may be appropriate, and even advisable, such as holding the hand of an elderly person in a hospice. It is therefore important to always keep in mind the notion of "psychological harm" and "appropriate physical contact" when dealing with social work clients.

Among social workers' ethical responsibilities to clients is an awareness and avoidance of "conflicts of interest" (Standard 1.06), including what is referred to as "dual or multiple relationships." This occurs when social workers "relate to clients in more than one relationship, whether professional, social or business" (Standard 1.06c). Therefore, social workers in a professional relationship with a person, or group of people, must exclude personal interests from the relationship. While in small communities social workers may need to provide services to neighbors and other people with whom they may have professional, social, or business contacts, in large urban areas with numerous service providers, it is generally possible to avoid such potentially conflicting relationships.

Social workers also need to avoid conflict of loyalty when working with different members in a family. In such cases, social workers need to "clarify with all parties which individuals will be considered clients and the nature of the social worker's professional obligations to the various individuals who are receiving services" (Standard 1.06d).

Social workers are ethically bound to take "reasonable" steps to "safeguard the interests and rights" of clients who lack the ability to make their own decisions (Standard 1.14). Thus, social workers have special responsibilities to take appropriate steps to ensure the protection of the interests and rights of children, or those who are mentally handicapped, or other individuals who are in any other way unable to make their own decisions.

Finally, social work practitioners need to make sure that their clients receive appropriate services, should they be unable to continue working with them. Failure to do so is a violation of the Code of Ethics (Standards 1.15 and 1.16).

Ethical Responsibilities to Colleagues

As professionals, social workers also have ethical responsibilities to their colleagues. This includes treating colleagues with respect, and cooperating with social work colleagues and other professionals on behalf of their clients (Standards 2.01 and 2.03).

Social workers also have an ethical responsibility to take steps to help colleagues whose "personal problems, psychosocial distress, substance abuse, or mental health difficulties interfere with their practice effectiveness" (Standard 2.09). The same applies when a colleague is believed to be incompetent or whose conduct is unethical (Standards 2.10 and 2.11). On the other hand, social workers experiencing those problems also have an ethical responsibility to address them (Standard 4.05). For example:

> Andrea Greene, a social worker at a shelter for the homeless in Detroit, often smells of alcohol when she comes to work in the morning. Lately, her clients have remarked to other staff members about Andrea's slurred speech and unusual behavior. Her colleagues are wondering what they should do about this.

> According to the Code of Ethics, her colleagues should first consult with Andrea and assist her in taking action to get help for her problem. However, if Andrea does not take the steps necessary to do this, her colleagues need to take action, which may include talking to agency administrators, and if necessary, turning to NASW and/or state licensing and regulatory agencies.

Points to Ponder

A pamphlet entitled "Helping Social Workers with Alcohol and Other Drug Problems: Options for Interventions with Colleagues" (written by members of the NASW's New York City Chapter Addictions Committee) provides specific guidelines on how to help a colleague with a substance abuse problem. This publication is also available on the website of the Alcohol, Tobacco and Other Drugs Section of NASW: <www.naswdc.org/sections/ATOD/helpswers.htm>.

Ethical Responsibilities as Professionals

In addition to their direct responsibilities to their clients, the Code of Ethics points out that social workers have an ethical obligation to keep current with new knowledge related to social work, be competent in their job performance, and have cultural competence and knowledge regarding social diversity (Standards 1.05c and 4.01). Furthermore, social workers have an ethical responsibility to not participate in or condone "dishonesty, fraud or deception" (Standard 4.04), or take credit for the work of others (Standard 4.08). An example might be claiming someone else's writings as one's own, which is referred to as plagiarism.

Points to Ponder

"Social workers should obtain education about and seek to understand the nature of social diversity and oppression with respect to race, ethnicity, national origin, color, sex, sexual orientation, age, marital status, political belief, religion, and mental or physical disability" (Standard 1.05c).

Points to Ponder

"Social workers should engage in social and political action that seeks to ensure that all people have equal access to the resources, employment, services, and opportunities they require to meet their basic human needs and to develop fully. Social workers should be aware of the impact of the political arena on practice and should advocate for changes in policy and legislation to improve social conditions in order to meet basic human needs and promote social justice" (Standard 6.04a).

Ethical Responsibilities to Practice Settings and to the Social Work Profession

Because the majority of social workers are employed in agencies, the Code of Ethics addresses ethical responsibilities related to practice settings. It points out that social work administrators and supervisors have an ethical responsibility related to those roles, such as: having the necessary knowledge and skills to fulfill their jobs, being fair and respectful in evaluating their supervisees' work, and not exploiting their position with staff members (Standards 3.01, 3.03). It also identifies social workers' ethical responsibilities to their employers and to the maintenance of accurate client records (Standards 3.04, 3.09).

Social workers have an ethical responsibility to uphold the "integrity of the profession" and promote high standards of social work intervention (Standard 5.1). They need to be involved with evaluation and research at all levels of intervention, including monitoring and evaluating policies, implementation of programs, and practice interventions. All evaluation and research activities should be conducted at the highest level of "responsible research practices" (Standard 5.02).

Ethical Responsibilities to the Broader Society

An important component of social work's mission is to "promote the general welfare of society" (Standard 6.1). Social workers "should promote social, economic, political, and cultural values and institutions that are compatible with the realization of social justice" (Standard 6.01). Additionally, they need to advocate for "policies that safeguard the rights of and confirm equity and social justice for all people" (Standard 6.04c).

Points to Ponder

"A code of ethics cannot guarantee ethical behavior. Moreover, a code of ethics cannot resolve all ethical issues or disputes or capture the richness and complexity involved in striving to make responsible choices within a moral community. Rather, a code of ethics sets forth values, ethical principles, and ethical standards to which professionals aspire and by which their actions can be judged. Social workers' ethical behavior should result from their personal commitment to engage in ethical practice (NASW, 1996/1999, p. 4).

Personal Commitment to the Code of Ethics

Although the profession has articulated its mission, values, ethical principles, and ethical standards, a code of ethics is not something that can be imposed on anyone. It is voluntarily adopted by those who respect the profession of social work and believe in what it stands for.

Client Self-Determination and Confidentiality

Respecting the clients' right to self-determination and maintaining confidentiality of work with clients are ethical standards that can be particularly challenging when there are value conflicts, or when the social worker is concerned that a client's behavior may be harmful to other people.

Client Self-Determination

According to the Code of Ethics, "Social workers respect and promote the right of clients to self-determination and assist clients in their effort to identify and clarify their goals" (Standard 1.02). Respect for a *client's right to self-determination* requires that social workers refrain from imposing their personal values on clients, either directly or indirectly. Rather, they respect the rights of clients to hold their own values and make their own decisions about their lives. Maximizing opportunities for clients to make decisions for themselves is inherent in applying the principle of client self-determination and can be quite empowering for the client (Freedberg, 1989). This can occur in spite of the fact that the clients' values and goals may be different than the social workers' personal values and goals. The standard of client self-determination is one of the unique contributions of the social work profession.

At times, social workers may find that respecting client self-determination is extremely difficult for them because of the clash of the clients' values with their own convictions. While social workers do not need to abandon their own personal value system as it affects their personal life, they will need to establish a professional identity that is compatible with social work professional values, and with the ethical principles and ethical standards of the profession.

Adhering to the principle of self-determination may be particularly challenging when working with involuntary, or mandated clients. These clients do not come to a social worker looking for help, but rather they are required to be there, such as by a court order. There are many settings in urban areas where social workers work with clients who are mandated for services. For example, clients may be required to enter substance-abuse treatment programs in lieu of going to jail or suffering some other negative consequences, such as having their children removed from home. While mandating clients to get help from a social service program may be seen as negating the clients' right to self-determination, the clients ultimately have the option of accepting the consequences of refusing these services.

Limitations of Client Self-Determination

The Code of Ethics also recognizes that there are limits to self-determination, but offers only broad guidelines for identifying these situations. It states that limitations occur at times that "in the social workers' professional judgment, clients' actions or potential actions pose a serious, foreseeable, and imminent risk to themselves or others" (Standard 1.02). However, the definition and understanding of what constitutes "serious, foreseeable, and imminent risk to themselves or others" is left open to interpretation.

There are times when social workers are required to take action to limit what the client is doing or is planning to do. Some of these limitations are set by social service agencies and organizations, and some are set by society through its laws.

Limitations Set by Agencies

Social work agencies establish policies setting requirements for eligibility for services. Failure to meet these requirements may result in negative consequences for the clients. For example, drug-free substance abuse treatment agencies may require that clients abstain from the use of all substances. Clients who continue to use alcohol or other drugs are then excluded from these programs. Or, children who provoke fights with their peers might be excluded from a community center recreation program. In these instances, while the clients retain the right to self-determination, they also experience negative consequences for their action.

Limitations Set by the Legal System

In addition to following professional guidelines, social workers must also follow state and federal laws, which may, in the interest of protecting potential victims, limit the rights of clients to self-determination. For example, all states have laws requiring social workers to report suspected cases of child abuse and neglect to state authorities, and some states also have laws protecting the elderly from abuse. Some states also have laws relating to perpetrators of domestic violence.

Since many laws differ from state to state, it is important to act in accordance with the laws in the state where the social worker is practicing (Landers, 1998). When confronted with these difficult situations, it is important that social workers talk with their supervisors and, when necessary, use appropriate legal resources.

Privacy and Confidentiality

Social workers show respect for the privacy of clients by seeking only that information that is directly related to their work together. They do not ask for information to satisfy their own curiosity. Additionally, *all information a social worker receives from a client must be treated confidentially.*

But to what extent is a client's confidentiality protected, even within the agency? Social workers in social service agencies are hired and receive a salary to carry out the mandate of that agency. The agency has the ultimate legal responsibility for the professional actions of the social workers on its staff. Likewise, clients seek the services of a particular agency—not a particular social worker employed there. It stands to reason, then, that the agency not only has the right, but also the responsibility, to know what is going on between its social workers and its clients. Therefore, communication between the social worker and client must be shared with the agency, whether through documentation in a case record, discussion with a supervisor or a consultant to the agency, and/or presentation of cases to an interdisciplinary team of professionals at the agency or organization, as might happen in a nursing home or hospital. This sharing of information within an agency must be made clear to clients at the outset so that they are not working under the assumption of "secrecy" of their communications with the social worker.

What confidentiality *does* mean is that social workers do not:

- Talk about their clients to people outside of the agency, including their own family members and friends, even though the situations may be intriguing
- Discuss their clients with colleagues in public places, such as on elevators, on buses, or in crowded restaurants during lunch, even when the discussion seems urgent
- Discuss their clients with colleagues in offices when the conversation can be overheard by passersby or by other staff who are not involved with the case
- Leave case material unattended on desks

When social work students discuss their clients in classes, it is essential to disguise identifying information so that the client could not be recognized. This is done by disguising not only the name, but also other recognizable aspects of a client's life. However, any changes that are made should not distort the situation and the understanding of its dynamics.

Points to Ponder

With reference to confidentiality, the social work Code of Ethics states, "Social workers should protect the confidentiality of all information obtained in the course of professional service, except for compelling professional reasons. The general expectation that social workers will keep information confidential does not apply when disclosure is necessary to prevent serious, foreseeable, and imminent harm to a client or other identifiable person" (Standard 1.07c).

Use of Informed Consent

Social workers are frequently required to provide information about a client to professionals outside the agency or organization. They also may wish to get information about a client from other professionals or from individuals who are familiar with the situation. For example, a social worker in a nursing home might need to talk to a hospital social worker about the medical condition of a resident, or a social worker working with a court-referred client will need to provide feedback to a probation officer. In such situations, the social worker must first obtain *informed consent*, or written permission, to give out or seek information about the client. Social workers working with children need to obtain informed consent from a parent or a legal guardian.

Limitations to Confidentiality

There are many difficult and complex issues related to confidentiality. For example, many managed care organizations require extensive and ongoing detailed information about clients' physical or mental health status in order to pay for services. This situation has raised serious questions for both clients and social workers about confidentiality. The fact that clients have signed informed consent does not detract from these concerns.

Duty to Warn

In addition to the guidelines regarding confidentiality provided in the Code of Ethics, judicial decisions have affected social workers' ethical responsibility regarding confidentiality. For example, as a result of a well-known 1976 legal case in California (*Tarasoff v. Board of Regents of the University of California*), professionals who know that a client plans to harm a specific individual have a *duty to warn* that individual in order to protect the person. Although this ruling may not apply in every state, it has been widely accepted as a requirement for helping professionals, including social workers.

Giving Legal Testimony

Social workers are sometimes required to give testimony about their clients in court. In addition, social work records can be subpoenaed by courts. This may occur in situations such as determination of parental custody or in child welfare cases. For example, Jamila Stevens, a social worker working for a city child welfare agency, was ordered to testify regarding a complaint of child abuse against an immigrant Egyptian mother brought by the district attorney's office. Although Ms. Stevens thought that this situation would be best resolved by providing home services to help this family and that it was an issue of a culturally accepted pattern of discipline, she was still required to testify against the mother. As written in the Social Work Code of Ethics, social workers must disclose information to "prevent serious, foreseeable, and imminent harm to a client or other identifiable person," such as a child.

Points to Ponder

"Social workers . . . strive for a balance between responsibility to the community and responsibility to the self-determination of the individual client system" (Freedberg, 1989, p. 33).

Legal Protection of Client–Worker Confidentiality

In contrast to legal requirements to reveal information about their clients, there have been some situations when the courts have protected the rights of social workers to the confidentiality of their records. The most notable example is the case of *Jaffee v. Redmond* that went all the way to the U.S. Supreme Court. In this case, Mary Redmond, a police officer who killed a man while on duty, sought the help of a licensed clinical social worker to deal with her distress over the killing. Carrie Jaffee, who was the administrator of the estate of the man killed by Redmond, sought access to the social worker's case notes. The social worker refused to turn her notes over to the court, claiming that her conversations with her client, Mrs. Redmond, were privileged. In 1996, the Supreme Court ruled that conversations between a social worker and her client are protected from forced disclosure in court and affirmed the *right of confidentiality of a client-social worker relationship*. As pointed out by Lens (2000), "as a result of *Jaffee*, the confidentiality of a social worker's therapeutic relationship with a client stands on the same ground as the confidentiality between a lawyer and her client and a husband and wife" (p. 273).

Value Conflicts and Ethical Dilemmas in Client, Agency, and Policy Practice

Ethical dilemmas, or difficulties deciding how to act in a professional situation, may arise when social workers experience conflicts in values. These conflicts may occur in all areas of social work practice, including work with clients, work in agencies, or in policy practice. In these situations, priorities may be confusing and there may be no clear answers.

Points to Ponder

"The range and variety of ethical issues and dilemmas which face practitioners is enormous. . . . Neat and universal solutions are illusionary. . . . Practice demands require consideration of whether it is ever permissible to break implicit promises of confidentiality, whether violations of agency regulation is appropriate, and when client self-determination can/cannot/should not, be honored" (Mishne, 1992, p. 9).

Value Conflicts and Ethical Dilemmas in Client Practice

The most commonly-experienced conflicts occur when there are value differences between the social worker and the client, resulting in ethical dilemmas for many social workers. This might be in relation to such decisions as abortion, placement of an elderly parent or other relative in a nursing home, the decision of an adolescent to drop out of school, birth control, divorce, or end-of-life decisions, among many other decisions that clients may have to make. The case of Robert Carlsonn is one such example:

Robert Carlsonn left his friend's apartment in a run-down section of New Orleans around midnight and was shot twice in the chest while standing in the lobby of the building. He was taken to the university-affiliated hospital, where he was put on life support. The doctors diagnosed Robert to be brain dead and unlikely to ever regain consciousness. The next day, Robert's mother, Sandra Carlsonn, met with Jeannine Pontey, the social worker on the trauma unit. Mrs. Carlsonn told her that the doctors were saying that she should give them permission to take Robert off life support and that she should just let him die. She said that she was a God-fearing woman and that she did not want to hear such sinful talk. Then she broke down crying and talked about her son—he was only 17 and she could not stand to lose him. Ms. Pontey, who had seen this kind of situation many times, felt strongly that keeping someone for whom there was no hope on life support was a futile effort. It prolonged the misery for the family, was extremely expensive, and used up resources that would be better spent in situations where there was at least some chance of recovery. In addition, she knew that Robert may be a possible match for an organ donation that might save someone else's life.

This case raises a number of challenging questions:

- To what extent does a social worker try to influence a client in a case where continuing life support is seen as futile?
- To what extent does a social worker advocate for the mother with the hospital staff when continuing life support is seen as futile, but the mother needs more time to grieve?
- How should the worker handle the issue of organ donation?

Value Conflicts and Ethical Dilemmas in Agency Practice

Value conflicts and ethical dilemmas also arise for social workers in their agencies. Agencies have their own value systems that may conflict with those of their clients, or with the values of social workers on their staff. Agencies may also have value conflicts with communities. An example is the case of the expansion of the Ex-Offender Community Program:

The Ex-Offender Community Program was started two years ago in several apartments on the ground floor of a public housing project in Cleveland. When a large apartment adjacent to it was vacated, Ms. Olivia Tucker, the social worker who was the executive director of the agency, recommended to the board of directors that the agency rent the apartment so they could expand the agency's services to help additional clients. She was able to get a grant to fund the necessary renovations. However, the residents of the housing project were angry when they got the news of the expansion, and the head of the tenants association called the mayor's office to complain. Asher Katz, the social worker who worked as the community liaison for the mayor, met with the tenants to discuss this issue. Although there had not been any incidents in the neighborhood related to the program's participants, neighborhood residents said that they had enough trouble and did not need more from the people coming to this agency. Anyway, they said, what they really wanted was a day care center for the kids in the building. But nobody had asked them.

This is an example of what is referred to as NIMBY—"Not in My Backyard." Although many people are in favor of services, such as halfway houses for the physically or mentally disabled, programs for ex-offenders, or methadone maintenance programs for substance abusers, they do not want these facilities in their neighborhoods. They worry about safety issues and deterioration of their neighborhood. This example also illustrates what can happen when services are brought into a community without first discussing it with community residents, who may see such programs as disruptive. The questions raised in this situation include:

- What are the value conflicts and the ethical dilemmas raised for Olivia Tucker? For Asher Katz?
- How can these social workers best address the issues raised in this case?

Value Conflicts and Ethical Dilemmas in Policy Practice

The laws and traditions of all societies are value-based and may raise a variety of ethical dilemmas for social workers.

Among the many commonly-held societal values in the United States today are: self-sufficiency, social equality, social justice, the right to privacy, freedom of speech, primacy of family life, and protection of helpless individuals.

Despite the ostensible acceptance of these values, at times they may lead to conflict. For example:

- While society values free speech and the right of privacy, such freedoms may be limited by the "duty to warn" mandate.
- Free speech is limited when it is seen as leading to hate crimes that interfere with the value of social equality.
- The value of protection of helpless individuals may conflict with the value of primacy of family life, as may be seen in situations when children endangered by their families are removed from their home. This conflict also arises when there are laws or regulations mandating the arrest of a batterer in cases of domestic violence, even though the victim does not want to press charges.

There is no end to situations that pose ethical dilemmas for social workers in policy practice. It is important for students of social work to be able to identify these conflicts and to be aware of those situations that would be most challenging for them because of their own value systems.

Points to Ponder

"There are deep divisions in American society about such issues as euthanasia and the right to commit suicide, abortion, gay and lesbian marriage, the responsibilities of individuals, families and governments, and on another level clashing values among immigrants, racial, generational, religious, sexual-orientation, and ethnic and cultural groups, among others. Social workers are increasingly confronted by a diversity of values and moralities; they practice in a society where there is less and less consensus about what is *the* proper moral stance" (Loewenberg, et al. 2000, p. 23).

Conclusion

Social work practice takes place in an environment that is value laden. In order to be effective in their work, social workers must be prepared to understand and accept values that are different from their own. The Social Work Code of Ethics offers a set of values, principles, and standards to guide social workers in their professional conduct and in the decision-making process. However, it cannot provide a fixed set of rules that prescribe how social workers should act in *all* situations.

In order to be better able to handle the numerous unforeseen situations that take place when working with people, social workers need to develop self-awareness and they need to be able to use the supports available in their agencies. In addition, they need to learn about the knowledge base of social work practice, including knowledge of social work theories, of human development in the social environment, and an understanding of diversity that will be useful as they work with the multicultural populations in the cities. This is the subject matter for the following two chapters.

REFERENCES

Freedberg, S. (1989). Self determination: Historical perspectives and effects on current practice. *Social Work, 34*, (1), 33–38.

Gilligan, C. (1993). *In a different voice* (Revised Ed.). Cambridge, MA: Harvard University Press.

Kagle, J. D. & Gielbelhausen, P. N. (1994). Dual relationship and professional boundaries. *Social Work, 39*, 213–220.

Landers, S. (1998, May). Balancing confidences, law and ethics. *NASW News, 3*.

Lens, V. (2000). Protecting the confidentiality of the therapeutic relationship: *Jaffee v. Redmond. Social Work, 45* (3), 273–276.

Levy, C. (1976). The value base of social work. *Journal of Education in Social Work, 9*, 34–42.

Loewenberg, F. M., Dolgoff, R., & Harrington, D. (2000). *Ethical decisions for social work practice* (6th ed.). Itasca, IL: F. E. Peacock.

Mishne, J. (1992). Ethical assessment and moral reasoning in child therapy. *Child and Adolescent Social Work, 9*, (1), 3–18.

National Association of Social Workers. (1996/1999). *Code of Ethics*. Washington, DC: Author.

Perry, C. & Kuruk, J. W. (1993). Psychotherapists' sexual relationships with their patients. *Annals of Health Law, 2*, 35–54.

Reamer, F. G. (1999). *Social work values and ethics* (2d ed.). New York: Columbia University Press.

Seglin, J. L. (2000, April 16). Bad behavior can be perfectly ethical. *New York Times*, p. BU4.

9 Knowledge for Client, Agency, and Policy Practice

Social work students learn about policy at an NASW sponsored program in Washington, DC. Copyright, National Association of Social Workers, Inc.

All social workers today learn a body of knowledge that prepares them for *generalist social work practice*. Generalist practice includes the provision of direct services to clients, the development of needed resources and services in agencies and organizations, and advocacy for social welfare policies that are responsive to the needs of both individuals and society. Moreover, it is important that outcomes of social work practice are assessed through research and evaluation, and through constant self-assessment.

This chapter provides an overview of basic social work knowledge that is needed in all areas of social work practice. It discusses:

- The application of systems theory to social work
- Knowledge needed for *client practice*, which includes direct services to, or on behalf of, individuals, couples, families, groups, and communities
- Knowledge needed for *agency practice*, which includes working within a social service agency or organization, administering agencies, developing new programs, and supervising staff and students
- Knowledge needed for *policy practice*, which refers to impacting social welfare policies on all levels of government
- Knowledge of the range of *research methods* that can be used to evaluate client, agency, and policy practice

Application of the Systems Perspective to Social Work

According to systems theory, which originated in the natural sciences, a *system* is defined as a holistic unit composed of interrelated and interdependent parts, including smaller units, known as subsystems. The traditional view of systems theory in social work has been enhanced by the incorporation of an ecological perspective, developed within the environmental movement. The ecological perspective stresses the mutuality of various systems, with each system being impacted by, and impacting on the other (Germain & Gitterman, 1996). This has become known as the ecological systems model, also referred to as the ecosystemic model or perspective.

The *ecological systems model* views individuals as engaging in constant transactions with other systems in the environment, including other people and social institutions. All these systems reciprocally influence each other. Consequently, rather than merely react to the environmental forces around them, the reactions of individuals to their environment further shape the responses of other systems, or subsystems. Ecological systems theory, as applied to social work, focuses on the interrelatedness of people; the environment, which includes social agencies and other community resources; and society, including those social welfare policies that impact on clients and on social work practice.

Points to Ponder

"A major advantage of the ecological system model is that it is so broad in scope that typical human problems involving health care, family relations, inadequate income, mental health difficulties, conflicts with law enforcement agencies, unemployment, educational difficulties, and so on can all be subsumed under this model, enabling the practitioner to analyze the complex variable involved in such problems. Assessing the sources of problems and determining the focuses of interventions are the first steps in applying the ecological systems model" (Hepworth, Rooney, & Larsen, 1997, p. 18).

Open and Closed Systems

Each system, whether it is an individual, a family, a group, an agency, a community, or even a society, can be described as open or closed, based on the extent to which it accepts new information and is open to new views and behaviors. Closed systems have relatively rigid boundaries, preventing the introduction of new information, while open systems have relatively permeable, or flexible, boundaries that allow for freer exchange with the environment.

Points to Ponder

According to Compton and Galaway (1999), "to grow and develop, systems must be open to input from other systems" (p. 29).

___

For example, Edith Miller is a 91-year-old woman who has been living in the same apartment in Detroit for the past 40 years. She has been afraid to go outside since her husband died 13 years ago, and depends on her 60-year-old son to bring in food, pay bills, and help her clean the apartment. She has not removed anything that belonged to her husband, including his clothing and papers, and has left the apartment exactly as it was 13 years ago. She has also refused to go out to see the doctor, even though her son has urged her to do this and was ready to accompany her.

Clearly Mrs. Miller is an example of an individual with rigid boundaries, which is characteristic of a closed system. Only after her son suffered a stroke did Mrs. Miller allow a local agency providing services to the homebound elderly to come in and arrange for the provision of needed medical and psychiatric care, food, and other social services. As is typical for all kinds of systems, any change in a system, such as the illness of Mrs. Miller's son, tends to create a chain reaction—for better or for worse—further affecting other parts of the system.

Agencies can also be open or closed to new information. For example, an open agency will encourage its staff members to attend professional conferences to obtain the most recent professional information, and will adjust its services to reflect the latest knowledge and the changing needs of its community and clients. A closed agency, on the other hand, will resist change, trying to maintain its traditional way of functioning.

Knowledge for Client Practice: Human Behavior in the Social Environment

In order to provide direct services to individuals, couples, families, groups, and communities, social workers need to have a good understanding of the interrelationship between human behavior and the environment in which people live and work.

While no single theory guides the profession in understanding human behavior (H. Goldstein, 1990), there is general agreement that the social work profession is based on a *biopsychosocial* view of people. Today, there is a trend within the social work profession toward adding both spirituality and culture to the traditional biopsychosocial focus, viewing human nature in a more holistic framework.

Biopsychosocial Understanding of Human Behavior

Different professions tend to view the nature of human behavior from their own perspective:

- Biologists see behavior as reflecting the genetics and the inborn biological predisposition of humans.
- Psychoanalysts see people as reacting to unconscious conflicts and innate drives.
- Behavioral psychologists look at people's behavior as reflecting learned behavior and social conditioning.
- Cognitive psychologists focus on how people think about themselves and the world around them.
- Sociologists see people's behavior as a function of social structure, which includes groups, communities, and cultures.
- Family therapists see individuals as reflecting the family in which they grew up, which they refer to as the family of origin, and look at people in the context of their current family dynamics.
- Cultural anthropologists focus on the impact of diverse cultures on human behavior.
- Spiritual counselors emphasize the importance of spirituality and values for individuals and society.

Using the ecosystems framework, social workers recognize the value of each of these perspectives to our understanding of people and society. Therefore, social workers need to have some knowledge about the biological, psychological, sociological, cultural, and spiritual aspects of human development and functioning.

Knowledge of Biology for Client Practice

Biological knowledge includes a basic understanding of genetics, neurobiology, physiological development, physical and mental health, intellectual or cognitive development, and learning abilities. Biological knowledge emphasizes awareness of genetic endowment or predisposition, which is inherited, as well as the neurological functioning of our brain. These aspects of biology must be taken into account when working, for example, with a depressed woman whose mother and grandmother also had a history of depression, or with a hyperactive child who is unable to sit still in a classroom for more than a few minutes at a time.

Knowledge of biology also increases our awareness of the strengths and limitations of the physical body. For example, it is impossible for a social worker to make a satisfactory discharge plan for a hospitalized elderly man without paying attention to the man's gradual loss of vision and hearing, or to the fact that he is no longer physically able to walk to the supermarket around the corner to shop for his groceries.

However, biology does not exist in a vacuum. A person's genetic endowment can only be expressed, or developed, in interaction with a specific environment. For example, a young girl who has the potential to become a great tennis player will only do so if she lives in an environment that will allow and encourage her to play this game. Similarly, a boy who is born with Down syndrome will need an environment that can encourage the development of his full potential despite some biological limitations.

Knowledge of Psychology for Client Practice

Psychology teaches us that human behavior is not random, but is based on a cause and effect relationship (Brill, 1998). Consequently, human behavior can be understood, and if it is problematic, it can be treated and improved. For example, when dealing with a mother who has been accused of neglecting her six-month-old son, it is important to understand whether such behavior is due to her lack of knowledge of how to care for such a young child, to a postpartum depression that makes it difficult for her to get out of bed and care for him, to her addiction to alcohol or crack cocaine that interferes with her ability to parent, or to a variety of other possible causes. An understanding of the causes of a particular behavior, an important component of the *assessment process*, is essential, as different causes may require different interventions.

Three useful theoretical approaches for helping social workers understand human behavior are *ego psychology* (E. Goldstein, 1995), *life cycle stages*, particularly Erik Erikson's (1960) psychosocial stages of development, and *crisis theory* (Golan, 1978; James & Gilliland, 2001).

Ego Psychology and Its Application to Social Work

Ego psychology evolved out of classical psychoanalytic theory based on Sigmund Freud's structural theory of the mind (Freud, 1923/1961). Freud conceptualized the *ego* as one of the three structures of the mental apparatus of the personality, which also includes the *id* and the *superego*. The function of the ego is to regulate the internal psychic conflict between the id, which is the seat of the instincts, and the superego, which is the source of our conscience and idealized aspirations. The ego also mediates between the individual's internal needs and the demands of the outside world by developing our capacity to engage in rational behavior.

Building on Freud's views, theoreticians and clinicians, (including Freud's daughter, Anna Freud, Heinz Hartmann, and Erik Erikson, among others), have expanded our understanding of the importance of the ego in helping people navigate through life's challenges. Ego psychology focuses on the different aspects of the ego and how to assess their functioning in an individual (Bellak, Hurvich and Gediman, 1973). For example, in assessing ego functions, the social worker might look at:

- The quality of a person's judgment, or his or her decision-making ability
- The accuracy of an individual's reality testing, or the ability to distinguish between reality and fantasy
- The person's use of conscious coping and unconscious defense mechanisms in dealing with stressful and anxiety producing situations

- The quality of the person's thought processes, including age-appropriate thinking and logical reasoning
- The ability of the individual to control his or her impulses
- The quality of interpersonal relations (also referred to as "object relations")
- The individual's sense of mastery and competence
- The overall integration, or coherence, of the personality of an individual

Assessing each of these qualities makes it possible to evaluate the individual's ego strengths and weaknesses, and, based on this assessment, determine what interventions are most appropriate. For example, a social worker helping a teenage girl who gets into frequent fights in school because of her poor impulse control will want to focus the intervention on helping the client develop strategies that will help her stop and think before she reacts impulsively.

Points to Ponder

"The assessment of ego functioning permits an evaluation of the internal capacities that the individual brings to his or her life transactions. But such an assessment always must consider the nature of the individual's needs and capacities in relation to the conditions of the surrounding environment" (E. Goldstein, 1995, p. 71).

Knowledge of Stages of the Life Cycle

All systems have a life cycle that starts and ends at a certain point in time. While it is easy to understand and accept the life cycle of individuals, it is also important to keep in mind that families, groups, communities, and even social agencies and other organizations in which social workers are employed have a life cycle of their own. One can even think of social welfare policies as having a life cycle. The application of life cycle stages to agencies and policies will be discussed later in this chapter.

LIFE CYCLE STAGES OF INDIVIDUALS

In addition to understanding the various functions of the ego, social workers need to be familiar with human development during different life stages and within different environments. It is obvious that the needs of a seven-year-old girl are very different than those of a seventy-year-old woman. But what *are* the unique needs of each age group? To answer this question, it is important to know the typical dynamics and needs of people at different ages.

One way of conceptualizing those differences was offered by Erik Erikson in his well-known book, *Childhood and Society*, which was first published in 1950. Erikson, an elementary school teacher who became a renowned child psychoanalyst, described how, beginning from early life until old age, people go through eight different stages of development, which he called *psychosocial stages*. During each stage, the individual encounters specific tasks, or "crises." The individual's successful negotiation of each of these developmental stages results in new capabilities. These capabilities then become the building blocks for the next stage, while failure to negotiate any of the stages will interfere with the person's ability to master the tasks of the next stage.

Healthy human development, according to Erikson (1950), is based on the interplay between the needs of the individual and the family's and society's expectations and supports: "an individual life cycle cannot be adequately understood apart from the social context in which it comes to fruition. Individual and society are intricately woven, dynamically interrelated in continual exchange" (Erikson, 1997, p. 114). Although some modern feminists have found Erikson's (and Freud's) views to be based on a male model and quite sexist (Miller, 1976), many social workers still find that Erikson's conceptualization of human development can be useful in their work. This knowledge offers an understanding of the important role that the society plays in the psychological growth and development of individuals. It also helps to guide the kinds of social work services needed by individuals and families during the different stages of life.

According to Erikson (1959), during the first stage of human development, the infant needs an environment that will allow him or her to establish a sense of *basic trust*. During this stage, a consistent relationship with a parental figure helps children develop a sense of trustworthy dependence upon someone who can provide for their needs. This sense of trust serves as a solid foundation for all later personality development. Thus a very young child who is removed from a heroin addicted mother, and is then put into a series of foster homes, may be less likely to develop a sense of basic trust than is a child who grows up with a substance abusing mother who, in spite of her addiction, is able to provide a "good enough" and relatively consistent environment for the child.

The task of the second stage is the successful development of *autonomy*, while failure to master this task leads to a sense of shame and doubt. This stage takes place when children are around 2–3 years old. In their efforts to develop autonomy, children struggle to develop a sense of control over their bodies and their environment. It is during this stage, which includes the child's toilet training, that struggles between a child and a caregiver may take place. At this age, often referred to as the "terrible twos," children tend to assert their autonomy through temper tantrums and other oppositional behavior. In extreme cases, power struggles with a caregiver may lead to child abuse.

During the third stage, the task for the child focuses on developing *initiative*, while failure to accomplish it leads to guilt. During this stage, preschool-aged children actively explore the world around them and search for role models with whom to identify. A successful resolution of this stage leads to the development of a sense of purpose and courage, while a negative resolution leads to a sense of ruthlessness and guilt.

The fourth stage of development focuses on the development of *industry*, or a sense of accomplishment. During this stage, which occurs roughly between the ages of 6 and 11, children's interests shift from the family to school and peer group. Successful adaptation to school helps a child develop a sense of competence in his or her skills, and an ability to persevere and complete tasks. The consequences for a child whose sense of industry is not recognized is a sense of inferiority and diminished self-esteem. Thus, a boy who attends an overcrowded inner-city school, and whose achievements are not recognized at home or by teachers too busy trying to address the multiple demands on their time, may have a harder time in successfully resolving this stage of development.

The fifth stage, occurring during the adolescent years, focuses on developing *ego-identity*. At this stage, the peer group and other role models become crucial as adolescents begin to search for a sense of their own identity and to take their place in society. The danger at this stage is role, or identity, confusion: "adolescents who suffer from role confusion often may adopt dysfunctional or antisocial behavior as a way of achieving some type of identity, even a negative one, that is, an identity considered undesirable by one's family or by society" (E. Goldstein, 1995, p. 94).

The sixth stage, that of early adulthood, deals with developing intimacy, rather than its alternative, isolation. During this stage people begin to establish deeper relationships with others. However, the individual who in previous stages has not been able to achieve a sense of self may avoid close relationships with people, or may cling to others in a futile attempt to connect. The failure to achieve intimacy may lead to isolation or to constant longing for a relationship.

Erikson labeled the seventh stage of growth as the stage of generativity, with the alternative being stagnation. The major feature of this stage is the need to guide the next generation. Generativity also includes productivity in various areas of life, as well as creativity. "Thus the generation of new beings as well as of new products and new ideas, including a kind of self-generation concerned with further identity development" (Erikson, 1997, p. 67).

The outcome of this stage has an impact on the ability of the individual to address the psychosocial crisis contained within the eighth stage, which Erikson called *ego integrity*. This last stage of life focuses on the need to come to terms with one's past. Acceptance of self, or a sense of ego integrity, helps the individual feel that life has been worth living and that he or she accomplished important personal goals. In contrast, the individual who has been unable to successfully build on the previous stages of development may end life in despair, with regret for what he or she has not accomplished in life.

A more recent book by Erikson (1997), with additional chapters written by his 93-year-old wife, Joan, identifies a ninth stage of psychosocial development that addresses issues for the very elderly. This stage is particularly important as more people, known as the "old old," are now living well into their 90s. The ninth stage centers on the development of *wisdom*—a sense of knowledge of oneself, and a more spiritual state of *transcendence*—a "new feeling of cosmic communion with the spirit of the universe, a redefinition of time, space, life and death, and a redefinition of the self" (Tornstam, 1993, quoted in Erikson, 1997, p. 124). Joan Erikson also points out the importance of the elderly for the community:

> When, in this country and especially in our crowded cities, we began to consider how we could support and care for our elders, we made a giant step forward. . . . But how can we learn from our elders how to prepare for the end of life, which we all must face alone, if our role models do not live among us? One solution, though probably only a dream, would be for every city to have parks—fine, well-guarded parks—available to all. In the middle of each park could be a residence for elders. When able, they could take short walks or rides in wheelchairs within the park with their relatives and close friends, who could also visit, sit, and talk with them on terraces and decks. We all could speak to them and hear their stories, learning what they still have to offer of their wisdom (Erikson, 1997, pp. 116 and 118).

LIFE CYCLE STAGES OF FAMILIES

While the life cycle stages discussed above focus primarily on the development of an individual, families also have their own life cycles. Carter & McGoldrick (1999) have identified five stages that can apply to some, but not all, families:

- *Leaving Home: Single Young Adults*—during this stage the individual has to assume responsibility for him- or herself
- *The Joining of Families through Marriage: The New Couple*—the existing family relationships have to change as a couple commits to a new system of its own
- *Families with Young Children*—the family has to readjust to accept new members into a family
- *Families with Adolescents*—the parent/child relationship has to change as children mature and become more independent. At the same time, the grandparents may become less independent and more reliant on their adult children
- *Launching Children and Moving On*—at this stage the parents once again need to renegotiate their relationship with each other, as well as their role in relation to their adult children
- *Families in Later Life*—need to adapt to aging not just of an individual, but of all family members, and to address issues of loss and grief

With the changing structure of families over the years, the family life cycle has been reconsidered based on current family patterns, such as families from different cultures, single parent families, and other forms of modern families including remarried, blended, and gay/lesbian families. These diverse family patterns are discussed in the next chapter.

LIFE CYCLE STAGES OF COMMUNITIES

One can also think about communities in relation to their age and life cycle stages. Communities become established, change, and even disintegrate over time. While many urban communities, particularly inner-city areas, tend to be structurally old and relatively stable in their population, some are renewed, or become regentrified, either through formal processes, such as urban renewal projects, or by having new populations, such as new immigrants or artists, moving in and revitalizing both the physical structures and the community as a whole. While the process of regentrification may improve the physical aspects of a community, it may also displace many long-time residents who no longer can afford to pay the increased rents and the higher costs of living in the community. How these processes impact on individuals, families, and urban communities is an important aspect of social work assessment.

Knowledge of Crisis Theory

Crisis theory applies to all systems, including individuals, families, groups, communities, agencies, and even countries (Golan, 1978). Crisis is an outcome of overwhelming stress. All human beings, organizations, and societies experience stress. Most people have appropriate coping mechanisms to deal with daily stressors, even those resulting from living in large urban environments. However, there are certain situations that are so challenging that one's ability to cope becomes insufficient. In these cases, the person becomes overwhelmed with a high degree of anxiety and experiences a state of *crisis*. A crisis is a sudden disruption to a previously existing state of equilibrium, or balance, known as *homeostasis*.

Research studies have identified different types of crises, including:

- Anticipated, or developmental, crises, which are related to normal developmental processes, or predictable stressors, such as the birth of a child, graduating from high school, migration to a large city, and even the movement of a social agency to a new location
- Unanticipated, or accidental, crises, which might affect an individual, family, group, community, organization, or society, such as those resulting from sudden illness or death of a family member or of a member of a group, job loss, economic depression, a house fire, or a natural disaster such as a hurricane or an earthquake

A crisis is usually seen as being time limited, typically lasting between 4 and 8 weeks (Hepworth, Rooney & Larsen, 1997). While the external stressors may continue for more than this time, at a certain point people reestablish a degree of equilibrium that allows them to function, even if it is at a lower level than previously. In order to help people regain their previous state of functioning, or even to function at a higher level, social workers need to provide rapid intervention that is focused on the immediate goal of regaining equilibrium. Crisis intervention does not address underlying conflicts or pre-existing problems.

Knowledge of Mental Disorders

While the theories of individual development discussed earlier are focused on normal human development, social workers also need to have some knowledge related to mental health problems. Many agencies use the American Psychiatric Association's *Diagnostic and Statistical Manual* (known as the DSM) that categorizes and identifies specific symptoms for diagnosing mental, neurological, and behavioral disorders such as adjustment disorders, attention deficit/hyperactive disorders, post-traumatic stress disorder, depression, schizophrenia, substance dependence, Alzheimer's disease, and various other problems that can affect individuals throughout their life span.

Points to Ponder

The causes of mental disorders need to be viewed in a systemic perspective. "The precise causes (etiology) of most mental disorders are not known . . . but the broad forces that shape them *are* known: these are biological, psychological, and social/cultural factors. What is most important to reiterate is that the causes of health and disease are generally viewed as a product of the *interplay* or *interaction* between biological, psychological, and sociocultural factors. This is true for all health and illness, including mental health and mental illness" (U.S. Department of Health and Human Services, 1999, Sec 3, p. 1).

Social workers need to be aware that although many of these disorders may not be curable at present, all of them are treatable to some degree. Particularly in urban areas, help for mental disorders is generally readily available. It is important to note that, just as with physical illnesses, psychological disorders also have a profound impact on others and that help needs to be offered not only to the affected individuals, but also to their families.

Knowledge of Social and Cultural Dynamics

Social and cultural dynamics are important components of the biopsychosocial perspective of social work. Among the numerous social and cultural aspects that social workers need to be familiar with are:

- Social roles
- The role of family
- The role of peer groups
- The role of culture, including religion and spiritual beliefs of diverse groups
- The effects of stigma, prejudice, stereotyping, and discrimination

Social Roles

Roles are defined as the behaviors expected from people in the various positions that they hold. Individuals usually hold several roles simultaneously. For example, a person can have the roles of a student, employee, spouse, parent, sibling, friend, and so on—all at the same time.

When roles conflict with each other, the individual generally experiences stress, which may lead to a crisis. For example, going back to school to study social work may be a dream come true for a 42-year-old woman. However it may lead to high levels of anxiety about her ability to fulfill this new role, on top of her ongoing responsibilities as a mother of two teenagers, a caretaker of her own mother, and her part-time job as a bank teller. People also experience stress when they lose a role, or when major changes occur in a particular role. For example, losing the role of an employee after being laid off from a job can lead to severe depression, family problems, and even substance abuse (Straussner & Phillips, 1999).

Role of Family and Peers

Our earliest social learning takes place within the family. That is where our primary sense of who we are and what we are is established. Thus, it is difficult to have an understanding of individual clients without having some appreciation of the nature of their family. Another important source of social learning is the peer group. This is particularly important as children move into a school environment, and the roles of family and parents, or parent substitutes, become less powerful (Harris, 1999).

Role of Culture

Social workers must become knowledgeable about the important role of culture, including spirituality and religious beliefs, in human development and behavior. They need to understand the impact of negative sociocultural dynamics related to diversity of people, such as *stigma, prejudice, stereotyping, and discrimination* (Allport, 1954; Goffman, 1963/1986), and the devastating impact of social injustice on their clients and on society as a whole. Since addressing these issues is such an important component of social work, they will be discussed in detail in the next chapter. At this point, it is sufficient to note that social workers need to know that people may have different ways of viewing the world around them and various ways of resolving their problems, which may, in large part, be determined by their culture.

Knowledge for Client Practice: Assessment and Intervention

Social work assessment and intervention are the basic components of what social workers do. In making an *assessment*, the social worker determines the needs of the situation or problem and forms the basis for how one can go about addressing or remedying the situation. Social work efforts to remediate an existing condition are referred to as *interventions*. Assessment and intervention are ongoing, interactive processes.

Client assessment includes determining the severity and impact of a problem on a client, and evaluating the impact of environmental influences and of appropriate preventative efforts. These factors become integrated into a comprehensive assessment that involves the pulling together of knowledge about the client from all perspectives. Assessment of clients typically focuses on:

- Reasons for seeing the social worker, often referred to as *the presenting problem*
- Goals that the client would like to achieve
- Strengths and limitations of both the client and the environment that impact the achievement of the goals
- Resources available to the client to help accomplish the goals
- Resources available to the social worker to provide the needed services
- The kinds of interventions that would be most helpful
- The kind of regulations and policies that would impact the clients' situation and the ability of the social worker to provide needed services
- The social worker's impression of the problem and of the client's stage in the process of change (Prochaska, DiClemente & Norcross, 1992).

Points to Ponder

"Assessment is the appraisal of a situation and the people involved in it. This process of assessment has two purposes: it leads to a definition of the problem, and it begins to indicate resources for dealing with the problem. Workers move from operating on the basis of general knowledge to operating on the basis of specific knowledge of a specific set of circumstances and persons. They collect pertinent data, test and analyze these data, and arrive at conclusions" (Brill, 1998, p. 114).

The focus of client assessment and the nature of intervention depends on the needs of specific clients, the services that are available in a particular agency or community, and the preferences and skills of individual social workers. Social workers need to be able to determine which approaches or *modalities* may be best for a client. This may include working with one, or a combination of approaches, including:

- Individuals
- Families
- Groups
- Communities

For example, an adolescent father may benefit a great deal from participating in a group with other young fathers (Mazza, 2000) instead of being seen individually. He could also benefit from couples-counseling with the mother of their baby, or even with the whole family, or by being helped to become part of a community group aimed at mentoring young boys in the neighborhood.

In addition to basic knowledge regarding assessment and intervention with the various modalities, many social workers develop a specialization in working with a particular population, such as children, or in a particular field of practice, such as substance abuse. Regardless of the modality, the population, or the field of practice, social workers need knowledge regarding empowerment of people. This issue will be discussed in the next chapter.

Assessment and Interventions with Individuals

Much of the knowledge for social work assessment with individuals, such as ego and life cycle assessment, has been described earlier in this chapter. A comprehensive assessment of individuals may include medical and psychiatric evaluations, social work interviews with the client, and contacts with family members and other relevant individuals and institutions, known as *collateral contacts*. As discussed in the previous chapter, such contacts can be done only with the informed consent of the client.

Social workers working with individual clients also need to know how, when and where to refer them for additional assessment, such as their potential for suicide or violence; for needed benefits and services, such as Medicaid or homecare for the elderly; or for specialized interventions, such as domestic violence or eating disorder programs.

Assessment and Interventions with Families

Social work, probably more than any other profession, has always placed a great deal of emphasis on the family unit. Understanding the role and the functioning of families is a critical aspect in helping clients. This is particularly important given the diversity of family patterns found in urban communities. Among the important areas in assessing families are:

- Communication patterns, such as who talks to whom and the manner of their communication
- Family roles and responsibilities and the flexibility in assuming different responsibilities when necessary
- Alliances between different family members
- Supports available to the family
- Family norms and values

Social workers need to understand the interconnection of the family and its social and physical environment, and the impact of trauma in a family through the generations. For example, research studies indicate that profound trauma, such as the Holocaust, impacts not only the survivors, but continues to affect their children and even their grandchildren (Brandler, 2000; Straussner, 2001).

Points to Ponder

Central to family systems theory is the concept that "in family groups, all members influence and are influenced by every other member, creating a system that has properties of its own and that is governed by a set of implicit rules specifying roles, power structure, forms of communication and problem solving. Because each family is a unique system, practitioners must develop a systems framework . . . that will enable them to analyze and to understand the behavior of individuals in relation to the ongoing operations of the family group" (Hepworth, Rooney, & Larsen, 1997, p. 277).

Three useful tools in assessing families are an ecomap, a genogram and a culturagram. These are simple paper and pencil visual aids that present a holistic picture of a family, its members, and their environment.

The *ecomap*, developed in 1975 by Ann Hartman (Hartman & Laird, 1983), consists of a drawing of the family in its social environment. It demonstrates the supports and stresses of each member of the family and their relationships with each other and with other systems, such as extended family members, religious institutions, schools, and social and health systems with which the family interacts.

A *genogram* is a drawing of a family tree, usually over three generations, using circles and squares to identify women and men, respectively. In addition to showing basic information such as sex, age, marital status, and ethnic origins, the genogram can include information on significant life events, such as physical and mental illnesses over the generations, marriages and divorces, levels of education, and other areas important to the particular client.

One benefit of including ecomaps and genograms in assessing families is that clients are the experts on their own families and thus become empowered in the process of identifying individuals and situations that are important to them. Moreover, these tools reflect clients within a larger family and societal context, and not as closed, problematic systems, thereby increasing their sense of acceptance, growth, and empowerment.

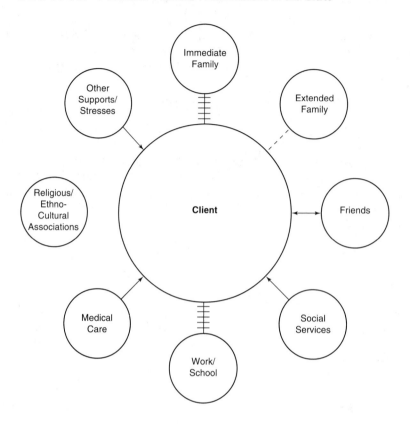

Client can be an individual , couple, or family—each person will have his or her own
environmental resources.

    ◄———————► Reflects Mutual Support

    —++++++++— Reflects Stressful Relationships

    ————————► Reflects One-Way Support

    – – – – – – – Reflects a Tenuous Relationship

FIGURE 9.1 Ecomap

    A more recent tool to assess families is the "culturagram" developed by Elaine
Congress (1994). This tool is particularly useful for social workers in urban communities who are working with immigrants as well as with people from various cultures
(Congress, 2000). It looks at such areas as: reasons for relocation; legal status; length
of time in the community; language spoken at home and in the community; beliefs
about health, disease and treatment; celebration of holidays and special events; impact
of crisis events; values regarding family, education and work; and contact with cultural
and religious institutions.

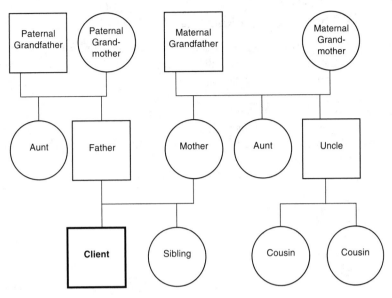

FIGURE 9.2   Basic Outline for a Genogram

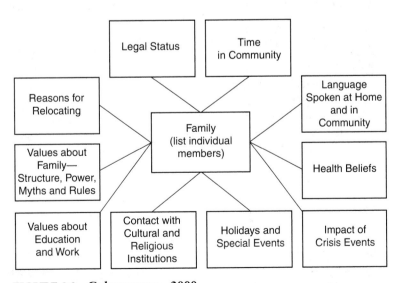

FIGURE 9.3   Culturagram—2000.
Reprinted with permission of Elaine Congress, DSW.

Assessment and Interventions with Groups

Social workers use group work as a method for intervention in virtually every setting, and group-work training is a fundamental part of social work education and practice. Among the many types of groups are:

- Recreational, such as a dance group for senior citizens
- Socialization, such as a cooking group for individuals with severe mental illness
- Skills training, such as an assertiveness-training group for women who have been battered
- Educational, such as a group for new immigrants focused on how to go about looking for a job
- Therapy or counseling, such as a multi-family group for substance abusing adolescents and their parents
- Task groups, such as a community group that is mobilized to establish a garden in an empty lot

Assessment of groups varies, depending on the nature of the group and its goals. For example, the goals of a socialization group for moderately-retarded adults living in a group home will differ from that of a psychoeducation group for men diagnosed with prostate cancer, or of a group of concerned citizens trying to improve their neighborhood. Nonetheless, each group has certain common dynamics that need to be assessed. These include:

- Roles of various group members
- Group cohesion
- Stages of group development, including beginning, middle or work phase, and ending or termination

When running a group, a social worker needs to know how to address both the needs of individual group members and the group as a whole. Social workers also need to have self-awareness regarding their own functioning in groups, and be willing to share authority with the group members.

In addition, social workers need to be knowledgeable about the functioning of numerous self-help groups, such as Alcoholics Anonymous or Parents Anonymous, that may not have a professional leader, but which may be used to great advantage by their clients.

Assessment and Interventions with Communities

There has been a growing awareness of the importance of community life, particularly in urban areas (Delgado, 2000). Nonetheless, the use of the term "community" is not always clear. As pointed out by Germain (1991), "community is an ambiguous concept. . . . For community social workers, the community is the client unit served. For other social workers, the community is the environment in which individuals and families live. . . . It is in the community that many of the society's social, economic, and political processes and events impinge on residents" (p. 38).

The focus in assessment of communities varies depending on the goal one wishes to achieve. For example, Delgado (2000) focuses on a "community capacity enhancement" (p. 28), which emphasizes the strengths, or *assets*, of communities that are important when working in an urban context. He identifies four types of "community assets"—murals, gardens, community-initiated playgrounds, and sculptures. From this perspective, an urban community worker would look at the existence of these assets in a community, and help facilitate their development. Other goals for community social workers may include the development of safer neighborhoods, helping a community apply for public or private funding to start a charter school, or to advocate for the establishment of a neighborhood branch of a city bank or a public library.

Social workers who work with community groups need to be able to identify and develop indigenous leadership. According to Si Kahn (1995), a well-known community activist (as well as a successful folk singer), the most important task of community organizers today is to reach and organize people in ways that change their relationship to the power structure affecting them. For an interesting example of a comprehensive community revitalization effort, see the initiative developed by the Community Service Society of New York in Appendix II.

Points to Ponder

Community practice can be a bridge between client and policy practice: it moves us from micro to macro when the goals change from the immediate interests of a specific community, to seeking change for the broader society. This shift from client to policy practice is termed moving from *case to cause*.

Knowledge for Agency Practice

Most social workers are employed in social agencies or organizations, and participate in the complex process of implementation, or delivery of services. For some social workers, a career ladder may involve moving from being a direct practitioner to

Points to Ponder

"Direct services workers who enter the ranks of management bring with them essential professional values and ethics and important knowledge of the realities of human service work, from which the organization can benefit . . ." (Lewis, et al. 2001, p. 322).

supervisor, administrator, and even an agency executive—with each level requiring a specific set of knowledge and skills.

Some social workers obtain specialized training in supervision and administration of agencies as part of their social work education, and others go on to obtain a degree in business or public administration. Many, however, learn administrative and supervisory skills through on-the-job training. Social workers who are responsible for supervising social work students at an agency often take a special seminar for field instructors offered at schools of social work.

Understanding the Nature of Social Agencies

Not only supervisors and administrators, but all social workers, need some understanding of the internal dynamics of a social service organization and to be able to assess the organization's ability to meet the needs of both clients and staff.

Agency practice today presents many challenges. These include keeping up with the rapid changes in technology and their application to the management of social agencies; changing requirements of managed care; changing client populations and needs; and ongoing changes in social welfare policies that impact funding and the provision of services.

Among the many areas of knowledge needed to practice in agencies are the following:

- The structure of social organizations, particularly bureaucratic organizations
- The nature of organizational change processes
- The methods of assessment of existing agency services, or program evaluation
- Development and implementation of new services
- Evaluation of agency policies and their impact on staff and clients, and development and implementation of new policies
- Administration and management of social service agencies, including the ability to meet existing government regulations, hire and supervise staff, and organize staff development programs
- Effective functioning of a board of directors
- Funding processes, including fund raising, knowledge of grant writing, and financial reporting
- Professional networking, including inter-organizational collaboration and building coalitions by working closely with other agencies in the community
- Dissemination of information about services to the community, potential clients and potential referral sources of clients

Understanding Life Cycle Stages of Organizations

As pointed out by Netting, Kettner & McMurtry (1998), "agencies must be providing needed and relevant services or they will go out of business" (p. 212). Therefore, agencies must constantly renew themselves. Various organizational life cycle stages can be conceptualized as follows:

- *Formation or Entrepreneurial Stage*—in this stage the newly formed organization or agency has little formal structure. The organization is open to innovations in staffing, program development, and use of technology and other resources. Leadership and managerial processes tend to be informal, but a team spirit and enthusiasm for the mission of the agency has to exist if the organization is to overcome the stresses that come with new beginnings.
- *Maturation or Formalization Stage*—during this stage resources are firmly established and leadership becomes more formalized. The establishment of a formal bureaucracy with an emphasis on standardized procedures may limit further innovation and creativity. Original staff may leave since their enthusiasm and identification with the original mission may no longer be supported by the organization.
- *Decline or Stagnation Stage*—this may be the outcome of an organization that lacks appropriate leadership, or is not flexible in its adjustment to changing clientele, funding sources, or policies.
- *Ending or Renewal Stage*—a declining organization will either cease to exist or will undergo a stage of renewal in which changes to its mission, programs, and operations may be required. Moreover, in order for the renewal to occur, previous leadership and staff members may need to be changed.

Application of Crisis Theory to Agency Practice

As noted previously, just as individuals, families, and communities respond to crises, agencies also respond to both anticipated and unanticipated crises. Unanticipated crises may arise from sudden threats to funding, unexpected loss of executives or key administrators due to illness, retirement, or death, or a violent attack on the agency, such as might occur at a family planning clinic. Under such circumstances, agencies are challenged to find innovative ways of surviving and rebuilding their programs.

Knowledge for Policy Practice

As pointed out in Chapter 5, since the time of Jane Addams and her contemporaries, social workers have recognized that social welfare policies play a crucial role in the lives of people and communities. In order to fulfill the social work mission of social justice, social workers need to be able to:

- Analyze the impact of current and proposed social welfare policies on clients and agencies
- Understand political change processes
- Become knowledgeable about political and legal advocacy
- Participate in the political process, including voting

Policy Analysis and Policy Changes

As part of policy practice, social workers analyze the impact of various policies on various groups in society, and propose well-thought-out policy alternatives. Policy practice requires knowledge of:

- Collection and analysis of data, or information, related to the impact of policies on individuals, population groups, and communities
- Presentation of different policy options
- Writing policy statements

Once a new or modified policy is proposed, the next step is to know how to advocate for its implementation.

Application of Crisis Theory to Policy Practice

In times of crisis in the society, there may be drastic changes in the direction of social welfare policies. It is during times of crisis that society, like individuals and agencies, is more open to new ideas to meet the existing conditions—ideas that previously may have been considered to be unacceptable. This may lead to the expansion, retraction, or the establishment of new social welfare policies. For example, as seen in previous chapters, the English Poor Laws came about in response to severe social and economic upheaval, the Social Security Act was passed during the crisis of the Great Depression, and the social reform legislation of the 1960s took place during the turmoil of that decade (Piven & Cloward, 1971).

Knowledge of Political and Legal Advocacy

As pointed out by Ezell (2001), social advocates "must know when advocacy is a useful approach to bring about change and when another intervention will work better. They need to know how to analyze problems, issues, and situations so they can select effective advocacy strategies; and they must be able to plan, coordinate, and implement these strategies" (p. 1). Policy advocacy focuses on either *legislative* or *legal advocacy*.

Legislative Advocacy

Legislative, or political, advocacy may be focused on city, state, or federal levels of government. Social workers need to become familiar with the functioning of the appropriate legislative body that they want to influence, and its procedures for legislative change, including the introduction of new legislation and strategies for lobbying for particular bills. They also need to have some knowledge of the key players and the informal power sources that may impact a particular bill. In addition, they need to know how to monitor the passage of bills to make sure that they are not only passed, but also funded.

Political advocacy often requires the use of social advocacy to mobilize public opinion to influence the political process. It requires knowledge regarding the role of political action committees (PACs), political coalition building, the use of mass media (including writing letters to the editor and op-ed articles), and the use of technology, such as the Internet, for advocacy purposes.

Legal Advocacy

Many policies impacting the provision of social welfare benefits and services are the result of court rulings, and not just the result of laws. Therefore, social workers also need some knowledge regarding legal advocacy.

Social workers have testified as expert witnesses in a variety of cases. Moreover, NASW has frequently filed friend-of-the-court, or *amicus curiae* briefs in support of the rights of certain individuals or groups of people whose cases have come up to state or federal supreme courts, when the outcome had national implications. Among the cases were those related to protection of rights for gay parents, for people with developmental disabilities, and for substance-abusing mothers whose rights have been threatened by the criminal justice system (NASW Joins Court Battles, 1997; "Arrests for Drug Use . . . , 2000).

Points to Ponder

"Most helping professionals are familiar with landmark U.S. Supreme Court cases that established specific client rights in a variety of fields. Litigation and court rulings have established or enforced a right to equal educational opportunity, prisoners' right to decent living conditions, the right to treatment and the right to refuse treatment in mental health settings, the insistence that many types of clients be placed in the least restrictive alternative for their needs, and the right to due process for juveniles accused of crimes, just to name a few" (Ezell, 2001, p. 100).

Political Social Work

The newest arena for policy practice has been termed *political social work*, which requires knowledge related to running for political office or accepting a political appointment. Hundreds of social workers have used their social work experience and knowledge of human behavior, community organization, administration, and social welfare policies to run and be elected to various city, state, and federal offices. During 1997, forty-seven social workers were elected to political office in different cities in the United States (NASW, 1997), and as indicated in Chapter 1, six social workers were elected to the United States Congress during the 2000 elections.

Knowledge of Research and Evaluation for Social Work Practice

The use of social work research, including studies of outcomes of social work interventions and of program evaluations, has become an increasingly important component

Points to Ponder

"Politics is the public side of social work. It is nothing more than the bringing together of people in a public setting to try and solve problems and/or to develop social policy. I think that social workers have excellent skills to build consensus and to solve problems" (Debbie Stabenow, elected to the United States Senate as of 2001, quoted in Haynes & Mickelson, 2000, p. 109).

in the education of social work students and in the required knowledge base of social work practitioners, including client, agency, and policy practitioners (Royse, Thyer, Padgett & Logan, 2001).

Research contributes to the knowledge base of social work practice at every level—client, agency and policy practice. Studies can range from a single case design to looking at census data based on millions of respondents. Research findings are used to:

- Evaluate agency programs, services and policies and the effectiveness of approaches to providing services to clients
- Evaluate the professional knowledge and training needs of staff
- Maintain credibility among clients and professional communities
- Demonstrate accountability to funding sources
- Advocate for changing social policies

There are two types of research commonly used in social work: quantitative and qualitative (Ragg, 2001).

Quantitative Research

Quantitative research uses statistics to assess relationships between and among people or services. It focuses on exploring or comparing differences among client groups or intervention methods. There are five different types of quantitative research:

1. *Epidemiology* focuses on frequency, prevalence, and patterns of different types of social and mental health problems. Epidemiological studies provide the basic knowledge about the scope of various social problems. Such knowledge is essential before we can begin planning effective programs and services to address existing problems or to prevent problems in the future. For example, knowing how many adolescents have been arrested for violent crimes in a particular part of a city is necessary in order to develop targeted programs aimed at preventing adolescent violence.

2. *Outcome research* assesses the effectiveness of new or different intervention techniques or strategies on specific clients. For example, what's the outcome of using a behavioral intervention approach with a hyperactive child, or, in agency prac-

Points to Ponder

Since 1993, the *Institute for the Advancement of Social Work Research*, a freestanding, not-for-profit organization, has been promoting the advancement of scientific knowledge among social workers and advocating for the recognition of the role of social work within the national scientific community <www.cosw.sc.edu/iaswr>.

tice, does providing in-service training in a social agency increase the retention of workers?

3. *Program evaluation* is similar to outcome research, but broader in scope. It is helpful in determining the effectiveness of a new program model, such as the impact of the use of harm reduction with substance abusers on the spread of AIDS, or of the family preservation approach in child welfare services on the number of children in foster care.

4. *Cross-sectional research* aids in understanding the impact of an event or experience when comparing different populations. For example, what is the impact of witnessing domestic violence on preschool children as opposed to adolescents?

5. *Comparative research* allows for comparison of different interventions, or to see if the impact on one group is really different than on another. For example, is it better for teen mothers to be offered individual, group, or family counseling services?

Qualitative Research

Qualitative research focuses on identifying spoken or observed themes to better understand certain situations or dynamics. Often easier to read and follow than quantitative research, it does not involve statistical analysis of data, although some numerical information (for example, the mean or the average age of participants) may be offered. However, findings of qualitative studies may be hard to generalize because they tend to be based on a limited number of subjects. Qualitative research may, however, lead to quantitative studies by raising important questions and themes that need further research. Among the most commonly used qualitative research approaches in social work are:

1. *Grounded theory* is developed by categorizing and comparing themes that emerge from information that is obtained from subjects or a review of literature. In this approach the researcher does not begin with a hypothesis, but rather is guided by the available information, which then leads to the formulation of a proposed explanation or theory that may be tested in the future.

2. *Ethnographies* study specific individuals, groups, or communities in great depth and detail. This research approach helps workers understand a dynamic or a situation that subsequently needs to be researched further to see if it can be generalized to other people or situations.

3. *Participant observation* is an approach in which the researchers act as if they are one of the subjects and observe situations and events from the point of view of the people being studied. Such observations are often followed by reflections on their experience and what they have seen. A classic example of such a study is Elliot Liebow's *Talley's Corner*, an in-depth study of African American men hanging out on a street corner in Washington, DC.

4. *Narrative interviews* involve an unstructured approach to interviewing people about their life stories. The researcher then analyzes the content of the responses and notes the themes that emerge. For example, interviews with men with a history of perpetrating domestic violence can be used to understand their perceptions of their own behaviors.

5. *Focus groups* involve a number of selected individuals responding to a set of questions on a specific topic posed by the researcher. The researcher then tracks the themes and consensus of the group and reports the findings. An example would be inviting groups of women on TANF in different cities to discuss the impact of welfare reform on their lives.

Points to Ponder

Social workers "frequently substitute conventional practice wisdom for empirically derived knowledge. Sometimes that unverified practice wisdom may be misleading and unproductive. The profession is becoming increasingly concerned with the evaluation and validation of practice knowledge through standard research methodologies. This is one of the reasons that schools of social work universally require coursework in research methods" (Dinitto & McNeece, 1997, p. 5).

Protection of Human Subjects

In order to conduct any kind of social research, social workers need to adhere to strict guidelines regarding protection of human subjects. This is required by government and agency regulations, as well as by the NASW Code of Ethics. According to these guidelines, individuals cannot be coerced into participating in research studies, and they must be given full information regarding the nature of the study and any potential negative impact that may result from their participation in it. All individuals being studied must sign informed consent. Moreover, researchers must guarantee to protect the confidentiality of all identifiable information obtained from participants.

Conclusion

As we have seen, the scope of knowledge that social workers need to draw upon is vast. Systems theory provides a framework that encompasses the holistic nature of social work practice. At the same time it allows for the inclusion of new ideas and new knowledge related to working with clients, social agencies and social welfare policies.

Information needed for direct practice with clients, to work with social agencies and to change social welfare policies will be elaborated on in various courses across the social work curriculum, such as courses in human behavior in the social environment, social work practice, social welfare policy, and research. Another important aspect of social work knowledge is human diversity. This knowledge is so important, and so broad, that the entire next chapter is devoted to it.

REFERENCES

Allport, G. (1954). *The nature of prejudice*. Reading, MA: Addison-Wesley.

"Arrests for drug use in pregnancy opposed." (2000, November). *NASW News, 45*, 1.

Bellak, L., Hurvich, M., & Gediman, H. (Eds.). (1973). *Ego functions in schizophrenics, neurotics and normals*. New York: John Wiley & Sons.

Brandler, S. (2000). Practice issues: Understanding aged Holocaust survivors. *Families in Society, 81* (1), 66-75.

Brill, N. I. (1998). *Working with people* (6th ed.). New York: Longman.

Brueggemann, W. G. (2001). *The practice of macro social work* (2d ed.). Pacific Grove, CA: Brooks/Cole.

Carter, B. & McGoldrick, M. (1999). *The changing family life-cycle: Framework for family therapy* (3d ed.). Boston: Allyn & Bacon.

Center for Mental Health Services. (1994). *A new federal focus for the prevention and treatment of mental illness*. Washington, DC: USDHHS Publication # 94–3011.

Compton, B. R. & Galaway, B. (1999). *Social work processes* (5th ed.). Pacific Grove, CA: Brooks/Cole.

Congress, E. (1994). The use of culturagrams to assess and empower culturally diverse families. *Families in Society, 75*, 31–54.

Congress, E. (2000, November 3). The use of culturagram 2000 to assess and empower culturally diverse families. Paper presented at the National NASW Conference. Baltimore, MD.

Delgado, M. (2000). *Community social work practice in an urban context*. New York: Oxford.

Dinitto, D. M. & McNeece, C. A. (1997). *Social work: Issues and opportunities in a challenging profession* (2d ed.). Boston: Allyn & Bacon.

Erikson, E. H. (1950/1963). *Childhood and society*. New York: Norton.

Erikson, E. H. (1959). Identity and the life cycle. *Psychological Issues 1*(1), 50–100.

Erikson, E. H. & Erikson, J. M. (1997). *The life cycle completed: Extended version with new chapters on the ninth stage of Development*. New York: Norton.

Ezell M. (2001). *Advocacy in the human services*. Pacific Grove, CA: Brooks/Cole.

Freud, S. (1923/1961). The ego and the id. In J. Strachey (Ed.), *The standard edition of the complete psychological works of Sigmund Freud*. Vol. 19. London: Hogarth Press.

Germain, C. B. (1991). *Human behavior in the social environment: An ecological view*. New York: Columbia University Press.

Germain, C. B. & Gitterman, A. (1996). *The life model of social work practice* (2d ed.). New York: Columbia University Press.

Goffman, E. (1963/1986) *Stigma: Notes on the management of spoiled identity*. New York: Simon & Schuster.

Golan, N. (1978). *Treatment in crisis situations*. New York: Free Press.

Goldstein, E. (1995). *Ego psychology and social work practice* (2d ed.). New York: Free Press.

Goldstein, H. (1990). The knowledge base of social work practice: Theory, wisdom, analogue or art. *Families in Society, 71*(1), 32–42.

Harris, J. R. (1999). *The nurture assumption: Why children turn out the way they do*. New York: Simon and Schuster

Hartman, A. & Laird, J. (1983). *Family centered social work practice*. New York: Free Press.

Haynes, K. S. & Mickelson, J. S. (2000). *Affecting change* (4th ed.). New York: Longman.

Hepworth, D. H., Rooney, R. H & Larsen, J. A. (1997). *Direct social work practice* (5th ed.). Pacific Grove, CA: Brooks/Cole.

James, R. K. & Gilliland, B. E. (2001). *Crisis intervention strategies* (4th ed.). Belmond, CA: Wadsworth.

Kahn, S. (1995). Community organization. In R. L. Edwards (Ed.), *Encyclopedia of social work* (19th ed., Vol. 1), (569–576). Washington, DC: NASW Press.

Liebow, E. (1967). *Tally's Corner*. Boston, MA: Little, Brown & Co.

Mazza, C. (2000). Meeting the needs of adolescent inner-city fathers. Paper presented at the *Joint*

Conference of the International Federation of Social Workers and the International Association of Schools of Social Work (July 29–August 2, 2000) Montreal, Quebec.

Miller, J. B. (1976). *Toward a new psychology of women.* Boston: Beacon Press

NASW joins court battles: Legal briefs back the rights of a gay father and a student with disabilities (1997, September). *NASW News,* 13.

Netting, F. E., Kettner, P. M., & McMurtry, S. L. (1998). *Social work macro practice* (2d ed.). New York: Longman.

Piven, F. & Cloward, R. (1971). *Regulating the poor.* New York: Vintage.

Prochaska, J., DiClemente, C., & Norcross, J. (1992). In search of how people change: Applications to addictive behaviors. *American Psychologist, 47,* 1102–1114.

Ragg, D. M. (2001). *Building effective helping skills: The foundation of generalist practice.* Boston: Allyn & Bacon.

Royse, D., Thyer, B. A., Padgett, D. K., & Logan, T. K. (2001). *Program evaluation: An introduction* (3d ed.). Belmont, CA: Brooks/Cole.

Straussner, S. L. A. (2001). Jewish alcohol and drug abusers: Existing but invisible. In S. L. A. Straussner (Ed.), *Ethnocultural factors in substance abuse treatment.* New York: Guilford.

Straussner, S. L. A. & Phillips, N. K. (1999). The impact of job loss on professional and managerial employees and their families. *Families in Society 80*(6): 642–648.

U.S. Department of Health and Human Services. (1999). *Mental health: A report of the Surgeon General.* Rockville, MD: U.S. Department of Health and Human Services, Substance Abuse and Mental Health Services Administration, Center for Mental Health Services, National Institutes of Health.

10 Knowledge for Social Work Practice: Diversity of Urban Populations

The Mission District in San Francisco: one of the most diverse areas in the United States today. Photo by Yuriko Tanabe, 2000

One of the hallmarks of urban communities is the diversity of their population. Cities today have residents representing a wide range of racial, ethnic, cultural, and religious backgrounds. They also have large groups of people reflecting diverse socioeconomic status, gender roles, sexual orientation and identification, and individuals with various physical and cognitive abilities and mental disorders. It is the existence of this diversity that makes urban life exciting as well as challenging for social workers.

Differences among people may lead to curiosity about each other. They may also lead to fear and expressions of prejudice, stigmatization, discrimination, and oppression of those who are perceived as being different from the mainstream population. Of course, how "mainstream population" is defined will depend on the particular community.

This chapter discusses:

- Ethnic, racial, cultural, and religious diversity found in urban communities
- Concepts of race, culture, ethnicity, and social class

- Aspects of migration
- Changing gender roles
- Sexual orientation
- The wide range of cognitive, developmental, emotional, and physical disabilities
- The role of social workers in empowering people, and working toward social and economic justice

Racial, Ethnic, Cultural, and Religious Diversity of Urban Communities

As indicated in previous chapters, urban communities have always attracted people from other areas of the country, as well as immigrant populations from many parts of the world. In 1965, the United States immigration laws were revised to open the doors of the United States to greater numbers of people from non-European countries, and to give priority to relatives of earlier immigrants. Consequently, this country has seen the arrival of widely diverse ethnic and cultural groups from various parts of the world—the vast majority of whom settled in urban communities.

Points to Ponder

In 1993, the top ten countries from which the U.S. received legal immigrants were: Mexico, Mainland China, the Philippines, Vietnam, the former Soviet Union, the Dominican Republic, India, Poland, El Salvador, and the United Kingdom. That same year, the largest numbers of refugees came from: the former Soviet Union, Vietnam, Haiti, Laos, Somalia, Iraq, Cuba, Iran, Ethiopia, and Liberia (National Immigration Forum, 1994).

In order to understand the dynamics of diversity, it is important to have a clear understanding of what is meant by such concepts as "race," "culture," and "ethnicity."

The Meanings of Race, Culture, and Ethnicity

The terms race, culture, and ethnicity are frequently used interchangeably despite distinct differences in their meanings.

The Concept of Race

Although awareness of racial differences has existed for ages, the modern notion of "race" is a relatively recent one. The use of the term "race" originated during the 17th century as part of the growing European colonization of the Asian, African, and American continents. "Race" was used in an attempt to classify people on the basis of genetically transmitted physical characteristics, such as hair texture and skin color (Hays, 1996).

Racial Identification

The current classification of people as "White," "Black," "Hispanic," "Native American," or "Asian" obscures the unique ethnic and cultural background of the individual, and the distinct differences in cultural values, beliefs, and lifestyle that he or she may hold. For example, those of Hispanic background, increasingly referred to as Latinos, may be of any race and may represent many different cultures. Similarly, an "Asian" from a Japanese background may have no more in common culturally with an Asian from Pakistan, than an Italian American with a Native American.

Current classification also combines "blacks" from the numerous Caribbean Islands and from various African countries together with African Americans, thereby ignoring the tremendous cultural, linguistic, and religious distinctions, and the different traditions of each group. And the category of "whites" may include people whose families originated from many different European countries, or who may have lived for generations in Canada, Australia, South Africa, or the Middle East before emigrating to the United States.

Points to Ponder

How a person is identified racially is known as "racial ascription." "Racial ascription is generally regarded as cultural rather than biological among social theorists. The particular biological traits that significantly determine racial ascriptions vary from society to society. Skin color, hair texture, class status, and other traits may all interact differentially to determine racial ascription; therefore, ascription is primarily a cultural phenomenon. A white Dominican, for example, may be trigueno (mixed, literally 'wheat colored') in Puerto Rico and black in Georgia" (Castex, 1996, p. 531).

Ascribing one racial identity also ignores the fact that a growing number of people are of mixed racial backgrounds. In recognition of this, an important policy change took place in the United States census in the year 2000 when, for the first time, the

Points to Ponder

With reference to the changes in reporting racial identity introduced in the 2000 census, an article in the *New York Times* (Holmes, 2000) states, "These changes point out an abiding feature of this country's racial history: when it comes to determining what exactly is a racial category, politics, not biology is the deciding factor . . . at different times Jews, Italians, and Irish were considered separate races. But as they gained more economic and political power, the larger society accepted them as white and ethnic. At one point the census categorized some blacks according to how many white ancestors they had. But as state-sanctioned segregation arose, all people of African descent were classified into one race—black. These are all basically political decisions . . . . The census always just reflects changing attitudes" (p. 3).

census allowed the option for people to select more than one racial category in describing their identification.

The Concept of Culture

As stated by Devore & Schlesinger (1999), "Culture is a commonly used concept that is difficult to define. It revolves around the fact that human groups differ in the way they structure their behavior, in their world view, in their perspectives on the rhythms and patterns of life, and in their concept of the essential nature of the human condition" (p. 26). In essence, culture is the sum total of values and life patterns shared by people within a given community. All that we do, value, and believe takes place within a cultural context: The language that we speak, the holidays that we celebrate, the rituals and life passages that we commemorate, how we define illness and health, and even who we define as being part of our family and the roles that we expect them to fulfill, all reflect the culture in which we live (McGoldrick, Giordano, & Pierce, 1996).

A *subculture* can develop among different social groups who establish their own definable values and patterns of behavior within the larger culture. For example, the subculture of an urban gang may include a certain dress code and specific tattoo markings; the subculture of mothers in the city may include daily meeting with other mothers and their young children in a park playground; and the subculture of older adults may include sitting for hours on a bench on a city sidewalk.

Culture also defines the social status of individuals and groups: the values of the mainstream culture determine what groups will be oppressed and who will benefit from socioeconomic and political privileges at any given time. Historically, in the United States, being a white male has been a culturally more *privileged* position than being a white female, or a male or female member of any other racial group. Therefore, it is not surprising that every United States president has been a white male and that the overwhelming number of large corporations are headed by white men.

However, cultures are influenced by existing values and beliefs, and societal values and beliefs change over time. Thus, it is no longer unusual to see women or previously discriminated-against members of various racial, ethnic, and religious groups elected to political office or become heads of large corporations, presidents of universities, or directors of large social service agencies.

The Concept of Ethnicity

The term "ethnicity" comes from the Greek word "ethnos," meaning "people" or "nation," and refers to the notion that *members of an ethnic group share common identity, ideals, aspirations, and a sense of past history*. These commonalities provide an individual with an "ethnic identity"—a major form of group identification. Ethnicity reflects greater stability and endurance over time than does culture. Ethnic values and identification are retained for many generations and may be expressed through religious beliefs and practices, rituals, dress, and foods. In this way, people develop an ethnic culture that reflects their unique background (Straussner, 2001).

It is important to keep in mind that while social workers need to try to understand the ethnocultural background of each individual, not all people identify with or want to stay connected to the ethnic cultures or ethnicities that they were born into.

Points to Ponder

"One of the ironies of our time is that the unique customs, values and traditions of cultural groups have become more important as the world has become smaller and the inhabitants of the planet realize that they live in a global village" (Hayton, 1994, p. 99).

In order to avoid stereotyping their clients, social workers need to understand the client's own unique experience with his or her ethnic culture, the degree to which the individual identifies with his or her ethnicity and culture, and the tension that the client may experience because of his or her conformity to, or divergence from, ethno-cultural norms. Some immigrants and their descendants may feel the need to give up certain aspects of their family's ethnic identification, and it is not unusual for immigrants to change their names to one that is less ethnically identifiable. Thus Piotr becomes known as Peter; Amalia changes her name to Amy; and Phoung becomes Phil. Many people also change their last name.

However, moving away from one's ethnic culture can take place on a deeper level than simply changing a name. People may chose to adopt a new ethnic identification for various reasons. For example, Roseanne, a U.S.-born woman whose parents migrated from southern Italy, adopted the customs and values, and even a basic Spanish vocabulary of her Puerto Rican-born husband and his family. Only her immediate family members knew that she came from an Italian, and not a Puerto Rican, ethnic background. Her adoption of her husband's ethnic culture reflected not only her love of him, but also her deeper, and more positive emotional connection to his caring family than she had to her own chronically depressed mother and abusive father.

Religious Diversity

Compared to people in other countries, and even to previous generations in the United States, individuals in the United States today tend to be more religiously identified than in the past. An estimated 68 percent of the population belongs to a church,

Points to Ponder

About 87 percent of the population in the U.S. consider themselves Christians. Of these, 65 percent belong to mainline Protestant, evangelical, Eastern and other Orthodox churches, and 22 percent are Roman Catholic. Slightly more than two percent of the population, almost 6 million, are Jewish, and Hindus and Buddhists number about 800,000 each (Shorto, 1997). Islam is one of the fastest growing religions in the United States today; in fact there are as many Muslims in the United States as Presbyterians. "Among Muslims, the largest group (30 percent) comes from South Asia; about 25 percent are African-American; only 20 percent are Arabs (and, contrary to popular belief, only about 33 percent of Arab-Americans are Muslim)" (Shorto, 1997, p. 60).

synagogue, or mosque, compared to 50 percent who belonged in 1900 (Shorto, 1997). Spiritual beliefs, as well as organized religions, may play an important role in helping people cope with adversity. Many people turn to religious and spiritual advisors for help in times of trouble in their lives, and social workers need to become knowledge-able about the roles that religion and spirituality play in the lives of their clients.

Diversity among Immigrants in Urban Communities

As noted previously, most immigrants coming to the United States tend to settle in urban areas where opportunities for work are generally most likely to be available. Consequently, aspects of many ethnocultural groups, such as food, music, and religious celebrations, are woven into the everyday life of the cities. This cultural diversity con-tributes to the richness of the urban experience.

Nonetheless, many immigrants experience tension between the familiar and the unfamiliar, between their gains and their losses, and between their dreams and their disappointments. Among the many factors that social workers need to assess when working with immigrant clients are:

- Opportunities and limitations based on migration status in the United States
- Level of personal and professional loss experienced by the client, and new oppor-tunities for personal and professional development

Points to Ponder

In 1990, 93 percent of people in the United States who were born outside the country lived in met-ropolitan areas (National Immigration Forum, 1994).

Migration Status

The opportunities and resources available to people arriving in the United States today are primarily defined by their immigration status. Those who are in the United States legally are known as *documented* immigrants, while those who do not hold legal immi-gration status are known as *undocumented* immigrants. The term "documented" refers to the fact that these immigrants have the legal documents necessary to reside in the United States. They are therefore entitled to many of the benefits of living in this country. For example, documented immigrants can work at a job with government protections, such as compliance with minimum wages and safety standards; receive occupational benefits, such as medical and social security insurances; and may be eligi-ble to attend a public university and apply for government scholarships for university studies. They can eventually apply for United States citizenship, and even run for Congress—but not for the presidency.

Points to Ponder

About 13 percent of people living in the U.S. but born elsewhere are undocumented (National Immigration Forum, 1994, p. 1).

Undocumented immigrants, on the other hand, are those individuals who arrive in the United States without legal documents. Some come into the country by crossing a border illegally or flying in with false documents. However, 40 percent enter the country legally, such as with a tourist, business, or student visa, and then stay beyond the legal time limit of their visa (National Immigration Forum, 1994).

Undocumented immigrants do not have the legal right to hold a job. Therefore, many resort to working "off the books" in order to survive. These jobs may not meet minimum wage levels, and do not offer unemployment insurance, and other benefits such as retirement, disability, or survivors benefits. Consequently, some illegal immigrants work in dangerous conditions, such as asbestos removal, without adequate safety precautions, or sewing garments in the overcrowded factories known as sweatshops that are located in many large cities. As was true of the "undeserving poor" in the past, illegal immigrants who need help today cannot receive public welfare benefits, such as public assistance, food stamps, or public housing. Therefore, many live in severe poverty, hoping that somehow their lives will get better, or at least that their children will have a better future.

Policies regarding eligibility for services for immigrants can be quite complicated. According to current immigration laws, each family member has his or her own immigration status. Therefore, the status of parents and children, or of two siblings may differ depending on their place of birth. For example, a child born in the United States to one or two undocumented immigrants will be considered a citizen of the United States, regardless of the immigration status of either parent, while the older siblings who were not born in the United States are not citizens. Should one or both of the parents get into legal difficulties and be deported, it is possible for the child born in the United States to remain in this country.

Points to Ponder

A 34-year-old native of the Dominican Republic described her situation in a newspaper article: "She stayed in an abusive marriage for nine years because she was afraid of losing custody of her two daughters, who are United States citizens. She and her husband, a legal permanent resident of the United States, met in the Dominican Republic. When they married, she said, he promised that he would file residency petitions for her once they arrived in New York. But he never did. 'He did not want me to become legal because that was his way to control me . . . . He never let me leave the house. He never let me take English classes . . . . It was like being a prisoner' " ("Abused Illegal . . . ," 1999, p. 41).

Undocumented immigrants often live in fear of being discovered by legal authorities. Many are afraid to seek any kind of help for themselves or their children for fear of being reported to authorities, arrested, and possibly deported.

The Impact of Migration

The circumstances surrounding migration to the United States vary greatly. For some, migration represents the fulfillment of long held dreams; others wish they did not have to come. This is particularly true of teenagers whose parents decided to immigrate without taking their wishes into account, or political refugees who escaped or who were expelled from their country of origin against their will. Some immigrants have suffered trauma prior to or during their process of migration to the United States, including imprisonment and torture (Marsella, Friedman & Spain, 1994). These experiences can have a profound impact on the rest of their lives.

Points to Ponder

For most immigrants, the process of migration to a new country is often connected to numerous losses: the loss of one's home and homeland, of community, friends, and loved ones, of familiar food, sounds, and smells (Castex, 1997).

In addition to experiencing various personal losses, some immigrants also suffer the loss of their professional careers. Those who had been educated professionally in their homeland may not be able to practice their profession in the United States because of licensing and educational requirements. Consequently, they may take jobs that provide far less money and status. For example:

- A doctor from Russia drives a taxi
- A lawyer from Haiti works as a security guard
- An elementary school teacher from Poland works as a housekeeper
- A history professor from China delivers food for a restaurant

Many who had professional careers in their home country go back to school in order to study for a different profession in the United States. Some new immigrants are drawn to the social work profession and become important sources of help to other people from their country. These social workers serve as role models for newer immigrants and help to bridge their transition to a different language and culture.

Family Responses to Immigration

While ethnic and cultural values and norms continue to influence the behaviors of immigrants and their descendants, in general, those of the youngest generation are quickest to adopt the values of the new culture—a process known as *acculturation*. Even among newly-immigrated families, it is common to see school-aged children and adolescents act as "typical American kids," while their parents tend to maintain the traditions of their home country (Rotheram-Borus & Wyche, 1994).

These differences in acculturation patterns may lead to conflicts among different generations in a family. Some of the more common issues for families raising children after migrating to the cities are conflicts in expectations of children's behavior, such as compliance with authority figures; the level of participation of children in cultural and religious rituals of the family; dating; and religious or ethnic intermarriages. In extreme cases, failure to resolve these conflicts may lead to children running away from home, and may lead to delinquency, substance abuse, and the intensification of mental health problems for both children and adults (Rogler, Cortes & Malgady, 1991).

Points to Ponder

In talking about the custom of arranged marriages in her community, Fahima, a high school student born in the U.S. of Bangladeshi parents, indicated that she is comfortable having her parents find her a husband. However, some of her friends rebel. "One girl who had a lot of family pressure dropped out of school, went to beauty school and ran away with some guy who worked at a gas station . . . . It was very shameful for the family—they didn't talk to anyone after that—and it made everyone guard their daughters more" ("Between Two Worlds", 1999, p. 17).

In addition to age differences, there are gender differences in the process of adapting to a new culture. While women who continue in their traditional roles as homemakers have less exposure to the new culture than do their working husbands, those women who work outside the home tend to make a more rapid transition to the new culture than do their husbands (Coll, 1992). Such shifts in traditional family roles and the resulting changes in family dynamics can challenge the stability of families.

In some cultures physical punishment is an accepted method of disciplining children. However, in the United States this form of discipline may lead to allegations of child abuse. Some parents experience regulations related to the protection of children from abuse as an imposition on their rights to raise their children as they wish.

Obstacles to Receiving Help

In spite of their needs, newcomers to a city may not be aware of the availability of resources or may not know where to go to ask about them. Moreover, they may experience other obstacles in asking for or receiving help. For example:

- Asking for help with personal or family problems from a nonfamily member, or talking to a social worker of a different gender, may be culturally unacceptable
- Agencies may not have social workers who speak the language of the client
- Undocumented immigrants may fear that seeking help from public hospitals or social agencies may lead to their arrest and deportation

Diversity of Language and Communication Styles

An obvious component of life in multicultural cities is the variety of languages spoken. One can walk down a street and within a matter of minutes several different languages can be heard. In addition, nonverbal communication, such as physical gestures, physical contact, distance between speakers, and eye contact, also differs from culture to culture. For example, in some cultures, looking directly into another person's eyes while speaking to them is seen as a sign of respect, while in other cultures, it is the opposite and may be interpreted as a challenge to the authority of the speaker. Similarly, in some cultures people express comfort and concern by touching another person on the arm or shoulder, while in others this is not accepted.

Even when the language is the same, people of different ethnocultural and social status, and people of different age groups, or with different educational backgrounds, may use language differently. For example, both the verbal expressions and the nonverbal communication used among a group of former gang members in Los Angeles may be foreign to their well-educated group leader who, in spite of the fact that he speaks the same language, lacks the knowledge and experience to work with this population.

Points to Ponder

Worker and client may nominally speak the same language but actually not understand one another. "*Eligibility* sounds one way and has one meaning to the worker; it sounds quite different to and evokes a different set of responses in the client. We say *home study* and *court record* and *therapy* without knowing how these unfamiliar words sound to the client" (Kadushin & Kadushin, 1997, p. 40).

The reluctance of some immigrants to speak English may be a result of a variety of factors. Some, even those who have been living in the United States for many years, may be unable to express themselves clearly in English because of their limited experience with English-speaking people. Others may be reluctant to speak, even though

Points to Ponder

Studies demonstrate the importance of communicating in the clients' native language. For example, research on drug prevention programs found that among Spanish-speaking individuals who were also fluent in English, communicating in Spanish is 56 percent more effective as a prevention approach. As a result of this finding, during the year 2000, the federal government expanded a drug prevention parent-education website to include information not only in English, but also in Spanish, Chinese, Korean, Vietnamese, and Cambodian, in the belief that such information will lead to more effective communication between parents and children about the consequences and dangers of illicit drug use (The Office of National Drug Control Policy, <www.theantidrug.com> accessed June 5, 2000).

they are fluent in the language, because they feel stigmatized by their accent. Many social agencies lack professional staff who can speak the language of the clients, and instead use the client's family members or other staff members as interpreters. This, of course, raises serious concerns about the nature of the helping relationship, as well as concerns about confidentiality of the information given by the individual.

Discrimination Based on Race, Ethnicity, Culture, and Religion

While the growing diversity of ethnic and cultural groups has enriched urban life, discrimination toward various groups of people continues. The impact of this discrimination on the lives of millions of urban residents is profound; it is demeaning and destructive to all.

How people react to others because of their race, ethnicity, culture, or religion is important to our understanding of social attitudes and behaviors, such as prejudice, stereotyping, and discrimination. An illustration of stereotyping can be seen in "racial profiling" where police officers target their attention to particular racial groups.

Points to Ponder

In describing police activities in one integrated community in Brooklyn, New York, a reporter notes: "Almost every black or Hispanic teenager on the street has a story of being stopped and frisked, often several times a month, sometimes in the lobbies of their own apartment buildings . . . they tell stories of being ticketed for spitting, for riding bicycles on the sidewalk . . . . White residents and older people said that they largely escaped this sort of treatment" (Barstow, April 1, 2000, p. B6).

Ethnic, cultural, or religious identity can also be mistakenly assigned by others as a consequence of stereotyping and may lead to discrimination. For example, despite the fact that Steven Stein, whose mother was of Scottish origin and whose paternal grandparents came to the United States from Austria, grew up as an active member of his family's Presbyterian church, he was often thought off as being Jewish because of his name, and vividly remembers being called a "Jew boy" while in school and later in the military.

The Impact of Discrimination on Immigrants

The stresses of immigration are often compounded by the experiences of discrimination and anti-immigration sentiment that confront some immigrants in the United States. These experiences may result in increased feelings of alienation. They can also exacerbate or lead to a variety of social, health, and mental health problems that impact the family and community.

Diversity of Socioeconomic Status in Urban Communities

The cities are noted for the social and economic diversity of their populations. While those with higher incomes can enjoy the innumerable benefits of urban life, those lacking economic resources have more limited opportunities for adequate education, employment, good nutrition, adequate housing, and quality health and mental health care.

As described in previous chapters, many current social and economic policies of the United States are discriminatory against the poor and tend to restrict opportunities for economic independence and social mobility. When opportunities for economic independence through traditional means are scarce, and when people feel unprepared for work, some may turn to illegal activities such as selling drugs in order to make money (Johnson, Williams, Dei, & Sanabria, 1990). This, of course, leads to a myriad of other personal, family, community, and legal problems.

Points to Ponder

"Social class is one of the most potent forces in our society. No other demographic factor has been shown to explain so extensively the differences that exist both within and between groups of people. Indeed, much of what is frequently discussed under the rubric of race or ethnicity may be better explained by social class" (Davis and Proctor, 1989, p. 256).

Diversity of Families

In the cities, social workers are likely to encounter clients whose views of families may vary greatly from their own, and from other clients. Consequently, social workers need to understand how their clients define their families and the role of different members in the family.

What had been seen as the "traditional" family, made up of a heterosexual couple and their biological children, is no longer the norm. In addition to single parent families, families today may be defined by numerous other groupings with differing roles. For example:

- Children may be adopted or live in foster families, either by arrangement through the legal or social service system, or informally; the latter are often kinship arrangements, such as grandparents raising their grandchildren.
- Among Hispanic families, the children's godparents ("compadres" and "commadres"), may have considerable decision-making power regarding their godchildren.
- In African-American families it is not unusual for a nonblood "relative" to be "absorbed into a coherent network of mutual emotional and economic support" and be considered an important part of one's family (Boyd-Franklyn, 1989, p. 43).

- Same-sex partners often raise children together; the children may be the biological offspring of one or both of the partners, or adopted by one or both of them.
- In step-families, children may be raised by one or two of the parents and their spouses.
- In blended families, each spouse may have children from previous relationships, and the couple may also have children together.

For some people, "substitute families" can become very important even though their membership may be temporary, such as:

- Roommates sharing an apartment in the city
- College students living in a dormitory
- A group of homeless individuals living under a highway
- Members of urban street gangs
- Residents of institutions, such as schools, rehabilitation centers, or prisons

These "family" groupings have their own structure, with a variety of different relationships and roles.

Points to Ponder

Social workers need to be aware that seemingly "simple questions about family membership can be posed in ways that shame or alienate the client or encourage deception . . . the questions that families are asked directly and on intake forms either encourage clients to acknowledge openly their families' unique membership and set of relationships, roles, and needs or convey the assumption that client families must be traditionally constituted. Questions should anticipate that children may be biological, step, adopted, or foster children or members of the extended family (nieces or nephews) and that they may have one caregiver (a single mother or father, a grandmother, an aunt, or a godparent), two caregivers, (such as a mother and a father, a mother and a mother, a father and a father, a mother and an aunt, or a grandmother and a grandfather), or two or more parents in separate households with joint custody" (Hess and Jackson, 1995, pp. 134-5).

The Changing Role of Grandparents

One of the most dramatic changes occurring in urban communities is the growing number of middle-aged and elderly people taking care of their grandchildren. Between 1970 and 1997, grandparent-headed households grew from 2.2 million to 3.9 million, comprising 5.5 percent of all households in the United States with children under the age of 18. This increase has been attributed to drug use among the children's parents, AIDS, teen pregnancy, mental and physical illness, crime, child abuse and neglect, and incarceration of parents (Bryson & Casper, 1999).

Although some of these grandparents may be relatively young, many suffer from a variety of health problems. Some have few social and emotional supports and need help from social workers to cope with the daily stresses of their lives (Pruchno, 1999).

Points to Ponder

"In many inner cities, hit hard by multiple social epidemics, health and social services providers estimate that between 30% and 50% of children younger than 18 years of age live in the care of their grandparents" (Pruchno, 1999, p. 209).

Moreover, housing policies can have a profound effect on grandparents caring for their grandchildren in urban areas. As pointed out by Burnett (1997), "grandparent caregivers living in public housing with leases that do not cover grandchildren are at risk for eviction. It may be especially difficult to procure alternative housing in inner-city areas where affordable housing is scarce and waiting lists are long" (p. 496).

Diversity of Gender Roles

Since the growth of the women's movement in the 1960s, there has been a dramatic shift in the definition of roles for both men and women.

Women and Men as Caregivers

In 1976, fewer than 30 percent of children under age six had working mothers. In contrast, by 1998, over 59 percent of children under age six—and over 73 percent of school age children—had working mothers (Lewin, 2000).

With the increase in opportunities for well-paying jobs for women and the entry of mothers into the workforce, it is no longer unusual to see men assume full responsibility for the care of their children—a phenomenon known as "Mr. Mom." According to 1997 U.S. Census Bureau statistics, the estimated number of stay-at-home married dads is between one and two million. In addition, another two million single dads have primary responsibility for their children.

Despite these care-giving men, women continue to assume most of the responsibilities for caring for family members (Kolb, 2000). As a result of the increase in life

Points to Ponder

"Fathers working in service occupations such as police, firefighters, and security personnel were about twice as likely as those in any other occupation to be taking care of their preschoolers" ("Number of Single Dads Growing" <www.thereporter.com/current/horizons/horiz062198.html> accessed 4/26/00).

span, a growing number of women are assuming responsibility for their aging parents, in-laws, and other relatives, even though they are not necessarily living in their homes. A 1997 survey by the National Alliance for Caregiving found that 40 percent of the caregivers studied also had children at home, requiring these women to meet the needs of their young children while at the same time addressing the needs of their elderly parents (Elders' Caregivers, 1998). While conforming to cultural expectations of their role, this growing *sandwich generation* of women finds little time for meeting their own personal, health, and social needs.

Points to Ponder

The number of families in the U.S. that are providing care for elderly relatives has increased three-fold over the last decade, with women providing about 75% of all the caregiving (Elders' Caregivers, 1998).

Discrimination Based on Gender

Discrimination based on gender, while theoretically applying to both men and women, is much more likely to be experienced by women. This can lead to numerous consequences, from lower income to inability to move up in the corporate world, or even to qualify for popular game shows, such as "Who Wants to Be a Millionaire?", which are based on male-oriented skills and knowledge.

Workplace Discrimination

During the past three decades, women have entered the workforce in unprecedented numbers and have broken through many previously existing boundaries, reshaping traditional ideas regarding "women's work." Nonetheless, gender discrimination in the workplace remains. The majority of employed women have jobs with low wages, few opportunities for advancement, and inadequate fringe benefits. According to government data, as of the end of 1999, women earned an average of 75 cents for every $1 that men earned. This disparity is even greater for black and Hispanic women: 64 cents for blacks and 55 cents for Hispanics ("Clinton Urges Congress . . . ," 2000, p. A18).

Although management and executive jobs have been among the fastest growing professional positions during the last two decades, women continue to be underrepresented in these positions. This is particularly so for women of color (Morrison & Von Glinow, 1990). In their attempt to rise in management, many women encounter what is referred to as a *glass ceiling*. The glass ceiling is a concept popularized in the 1980s to describe barriers that are subtle, almost glass-like in visibility, yet, at the same time so strong that they prevent women from moving up in the management hierarchy.

Sexual Harassment

Another form of oppression of women is *sexual harassment*. Despite a few well publicized incidents of sexual harassment of men, as seen in the popular movie "Indecent Proposal," it is a dynamic that is more often experienced by women. Researchers find that anywhere from 40 to 90 percent of working women experience some form of harassment (Stiver, 1994). It can be experienced by all women, from a junior high school student to a college professor.

Sexual harassment is an expression of power and aggression, not of sexuality. At times, like the glass ceiling, the harassment can be so subtle that it may be difficult for a woman to label it and react to it appropriately without feeling that somehow it is her own fault. For example, Lenora Pietrowski, an administrator at a large social agency in Milwaukee, dreaded meeting with her male executive director because he always made some sexual jokes that she did not find funny. She assumed that it was her own limited sense of humor that made her feel so uncomfortable whenever she was with him. It was only when she heard that he was asked to resign because of several complaints made by other female staff members that she realized that it was his behavior and not her sense of humor that was problematic.

Points to Ponder

"Although the term 'sexual harassment' was not coined until the mid-1970s, the phenomenon has characterized the workplace for as long as women have been in it. Yet it is primarily since Anita Hill's allegations against Clarence Thomas during Thomas's U.S. Supreme Court confirmation hearings in 1991 that sexual harassment became legitimized as a very serious concern of women" (Stiver, 1994, p. 444).

Sexual Diversity: Gays, Lesbians, Bisexuals, and Transgendered Individuals in Urban Communities

For many years, discussion of sexual orientation and sexual identity had been limited due to existing moralistic attitudes. It took the 1969 Stonewall riot, resulting from a violent police raid on a gay bar in New York City's Greenwich Village, to bring about a turning point in gay and lesbian consciousness and to gradually open the discussion. However, even now, more than 30 years later, lesbians, gays, bisexuals, and transgendered (LGBT) individuals are often misunderstood and frequently are victims of discrimination.

Discrimination Based on Sexual Orientation

LGBT individuals have been stigmatized in most communities through the ages. Discrimination against gay men and lesbian women is seen as a result of *homophobia*—the fear and hatred of those who are homosexual. In the past, *homosexuality*, a term coined by a Hungarian physician in 1869, had been viewed as a sin, a crime, or a sickness (Van Wormer, Wells, & Boes, 2000). Until 1976, the American Psychiatric Association viewed homosexuality as a mental illness. However, as research studies were carried out, and as gays and lesbians became more visible in society, it became increasingly clear that sexual orientation has nothing to do with a person's mental health.

An increasing number of major companies and city governments have begun to offer health benefits to their employees' same-sex domestic partners, and in 2000, Vermont became the first state to recognize same-sex marriages, giving married same-sex couples the same rights and privileges as married straight couples. However, no other state has followed suit, and LGBT individuals continue to suffer from discrimination within the social, legal, and economic systems. Since LGBT individuals do not have the benefit of any federal civil rights protections, people can be denied housing and employment because of their sexual orientation. Moreover, they are subject to severe discrimination in their relationships as couples. Since there are hundreds of civil rights that accompany marriage, such as insurance benefits, the right to make medical decisions for an ill or disabled partner, rights of survivorship, filing joint tax returns, the right to adopt children, child custody, and many others, homosexual couples continue to be penalized.

Homophobia and overt discrimination continue to play a major destructive role for many LGBT individuals. An extreme form of discrimination is "gay bashing," which involves physical attack because of the person's sexual orientation. This kind of occurrence is not uncommon. A most heinous example was the murder of a college student, Matthew Shepard, outside of Laramie, Wyoming in October 1998.

Discrimination of gays has also been aggravated by the spread of AIDS during the last two decades. Although the rate of HIV infection in the gay community has decreased over the last few years, the experience of discrimination against the gay community continues. Some fundamentalist religious groups even attribute the spread of AIDS among gay men as punishment for homosexuality, despite the fact that globally, the majority of the HIV virus is transmitted through heterosexual contact.

Points to Ponder

"Serving persons who are lesbian and gay . . . requires that organizations and practitioners identify and address social problems that affect them individually and collectively. These include discrimination in employment, in health and other benefits, in educational settings, and in family courts, as well as violence perpetuated against gay and lesbian persons. Addressing such problems requires social workers to advocate with and on behalf of lesbian and gay clients, be vigilant against institutional discrimination against gay and lesbian clients, and be visible in joining with the lesbian and gay community . . ." (Hess and Hess, 1998 p. 35).

Diversity of Mental and Physical Abilities

The nature of disabilities can vary widely and ranges from developmental to physical to mental. It is estimated that approximately 49 million Americans have some form of disability; over five million of them are children under 21 years of age who are diagnosed with developmental disabilities (DeWeaver, 1995).

It is important to realize that definitions of disabilities change over time and reflect the values of the culture in which one lives. For example, although in the past alcoholism had been considered a moral failing or a sin, currently dependence on alcohol is a legally recognized disability. Most professionals view it as a disorder or illness that includes a genetic component. This perspective is further supported by government policies that impact the provision of services and insurance coverage. Since 1991, with the passage of the Americans with Disabilities Act (and the 1994 Developmental Disabilities Assistance and Bill of Rights Act Amendments), people with disabilities have the benefit of expanded civil rights protections.

Some disabilities are so mild that even the affected individual may be unaware of it. Others are so profound that the person's whole life, and that of their family members and even the community, is organized around responding to the disability. For example, Jesse, a popular 15-year-old high school student, was diagnosed with a rare blood disorder requiring numerous transfusions. His friends, neighbors, and the religious organizations in his community organized an extensive blood drive, and helped his single mother by baby-sitting for his younger siblings so that she could spend more time with him in the hospital.

It is important that social workers have some knowledge of the various disabilities and their impact on the individual and his or her family, and also on the community. At times, agency and policy advocacy is essential in order to make sure that all individuals with varying levels of disability receive appropriate services and that their rights are protected.

Points to Ponder

Approximately 37.7 million people, or 15 percent of the population in the United States, are currently physically disabled, and many have more than one disabling condition. Approximately 20 million are under 65 years of age (DeWeaver, 1995).

Developmental Disabilities

Advances in neonatal medicine have enabled the survival of extremely low-birth weight infants who in the past might have died at birth or shortly afterward. Consequently, there are more people with severe developmental disabilities who need lifelong care, and an increasing number of social workers encounter these clients and their families.

Developmental disability is a broad category of conditions that impairs a person's lifelong functioning. It includes a wide range of problems such as: mental retardation, autism, learning disabilities, cerebral palsy, epilepsy, traumatic brain injury, hearing, and orthopedic problems, among others. In order to be recognized for legal purposes, the condition has to be identified before an individual reaches the age of 22.

Points to Ponder

According to the 1990 Developmental Disabilities Assistance and Bill of Rights Act, in order to be classified as developmentally disabled, an individual must show deficits in three of the following seven areas: self-care; language; learning; mobility; self-direction; capacity for independent living; or economic self-sufficiency.

Mental Disorders

Mental disorders are defined as "health conditions that are characterized by alterations in thinking, mood or behavior (or some combination thereof) associated with distress and/or impaired functioning" (U.S. Department of Health and Human Services (USDHHS), 1999, p. 5). Mental disorders impact people of all ages and ethnic and racial backgrounds. They range from attention-deficit/hyperactivity disorders to schizophrenia to depression to Alzheimer's disease and have a profound impact on individuals, families, communities and society.

According to government findings (USDHHS, 1999, p. 20):

- Approximately one in five Americans experiences a mental disorder in the course of a year.
- Approximately fifteen percent of all adults who have a mental disorder also experience a co-occurring substance (alcohol or other drug) use disorder, which complicates treatment.
- Fifteen percent of the adult population used some form of mental health service during a year. Eight percent have a mental disorder; 7 percent have a less severe mental health problem. However, nearly two-thirds of all people with a diagnosable mental disorders do not seek treatment, primarily due to the existing stigma and lack of knowledge regarding the treatability of these disorders.
- Twenty-one percent of children ages 9 to 17 receive mental health services in a year.
- Normal aging is not characterized by mental or cognitive disorders. Although stressful life events, such as declining health and/or the loss of mates, family members, and friends, increase with age, persistent bereavement or serious depression is not "normal" and can be treated.

Of all the health and mental health professionals, it is social workers who are the most likely to provide services to individuals with mental disorders and to their families, and are also most likely to advocate for their needs.

Stigma and Discrimination Due to Disability

Persons with disabilities, whether physical or mental disorders, experience many social and economic obstacles and are frequently subject to social ostracism, ridicule, and job discrimination. According to the Americans with Disabilities Act, "discrimination against individuals with disabilities persists in such critical areas as employment, housing, public accommodations, education, transportation, communication, recreation, institutionalization, health services, voting, and access to public services" (ADA, Public Law 101-306, Section 2).

The stigma associated with mental illness is a major concern for patients, families, and providers of health services. One reason for the stigmatization of the mentally ill is the public perception that they are violent and dangerous. Frequently the stigma gets expressed in the reluctance, or outright opposition of communities to allow for the establishment of group homes for the mentally ill.

Points to Ponder

"Stigma must be overcome. Research that will continue to yield increasingly effective treatments for mental disorders promises to be an effective antidote. When people understand that mental disorders are not the result of moral failings or limited will power, but are legitimate illnesses that are responsive to specific treatments, much of the negative stereotyping may dissipate. . . . As stigma abates, a transformation in public attitudes should occur. People should become eager to seek care. They should become more willing to absorb its cost. And, most importantly, they should become far more receptive to the messages that . . . mental health and mental illness are part of the mainstream of health, and they are a concern for all people" (USDHHS, 1999, p. 9).

The Need for Social Justice and Client Empowerment

The discrimination experienced by various groups in urban communities, and in United States society as a whole, calls for social justice—a major focus of the mission of social work, as reflected in the Code of Ethics discussed in Chapter 8. Among the ways that social workers address social justice are:

- Heightening social awareness of discrimination and its consequences for individuals, families, groups, and communities
- Advocating for policy reforms that provide greater legal protection for oppressed groups
- Developing cultural competency to better understand the experiences of oppressed groups and appropriately address their needs

- Empowering clients to address discrimination by educating them about their rights to protection under the law and about resources in the community

The *empowerment model* is an important component of social work practice, particularly when working with clients who have been oppressed (Gutierrez, 1990). The concept of empowerment-based social work was first described by Barbara Solomon in her 1976 book, *Black Empowerment: Social Work in Oppressed Communities*. Empowerment in social work practice focuses on the clients' strengths rather than pathology. Practicing from this strengths perspective, the social worker recognizes the socio-political, economic, and environmental forces central to the clients' difficulties, and works on the assumption that clients know best how to address their problems (Gutierrez, 1990). Consequently, the primary role of the social worker is not to be an authority figure, but rather an advocate who can help people and communities achieve their own goals.

According to Gibson (1993), there are five characteristics of the empowerment process:

1. Providing clients with essential information and decision-making power
2. Offering clients choices rather than assuming that the social worker knows what is best for them
3. Recognizing the importance of social interaction and helping people build support networks
4. Facilitating clients' ethnic identity and using ethnically sensitive intervention methods
5. Identifying inequities in the system that have a negative impact on the lives of clients, and strategies to address them

Client empowerment and the goal of social justice are central issues when working with all clients, whether individuals, families, groups, or communities. This is an ongoing struggle that requires the involvement of all social workers.

Conclusion

Social workers must learn to walk the fine line between awareness of client diversity and stereotyping of individuals and groups. They must be careful to assess the needs of different communities and of individuals within their social context and use appropriate skills in their interventions. They must make sure that society at large, as well as their communities and social agencies, recognize and value the diversity that comprises the urban populations of the United States today. Most of all, social workers must remain aware of their feelings and reactions to their own and their clients' ethnic and cultural backgrounds; to differences in gender, sexual orientation, and abilities; and develop the skills needed to provide effective services and just social policies. These issues will be explored further in the next chapter.

REFERENCES

Abused illegal residents fear spouses, and law. (1999, April 18). *New York Times*, pp. 37, 41.

Barstow, D. (2000, April 1). Antidrug tactics exact price on a neighborhood, many say. *New York Times*, pp. A1, B6.

Between two worlds. (1999, December 12). *New York Times*, p. 17.

Boyd-Franklyn, N. (1989). *Black families in therapy: A multisystems approach*. New York: Guilford.

Bryson, K. & Casper, L. M. (1999, May). Co-resident grandparents and grandchildren. *Current Population Report*. Washington, DC: Economics and Statistics Administration, pp. 1–10.

Burnette, D. (1997). Grandparents raising grandchildren in the inner city. *Families in Society 3*(3), 489–499.

Castex, G. M. (1996). Providing services to Hispanic/Latino populations: Profiles in diversity. In P. L. Ewalt, E. M. Freeman, S. A. Kirk, D. L. Poole (Eds.), *Multicultural issues in social work* (pp. 523–538). Washington, DC: NASW Press.

Castex, G. M. (1997). Immigrant children in the United States. In N. K. Phillips & S. L. A. Straussner, (Eds.), *Children in the urban environment: Linking social policy and clinical practice* (pp. 43–60). Springfield, IL: Thomas.

Clinton urges Congress to close the wage gap between the sexes. (2000, January 25). *New York Times*, p. A18.

Coll, C. G. (1992). Cultural diversity: Implications for theory and practice. *Work in Progress*. No. 59. Wellesley, MA: Stone Center, Wellesley College.

Davis, L. E. & Proctor, E. K. (1989). *Race, gender & class*. Englewood Cliffs, NJ: Prentice Hall

Devore, W. & Schlesinger, E. (1999). *Ethnic sensitive social work practice* (5th ed.). Boston: Allyn & Bacon.

DeWeaver, K. L. (1995). Developmental disabilities: Definitions and policies. In R. L. Edwards (Ed.), *Encyclopedia of social work* (19th ed., Vol. 1), (712–720). Washington, DC: NASW Press.

Elders' caregivers also are growing in numbers (1998, November). *NASW News*, 11.

Gibson, C. M. (1993). Empowerment theory and practice with adolescents of color in the child welfare system. *Families in Society 74*, 387–396.

Gutierrez, L. (1990). Working with women of color: An empowerment perspective. *Social Work 33*, 149–153.

Hays, P. A. (1996). Addressing the complexity of culture and gender in counseling. *Journal of Counseling and Development, 74*(4), 332–338.

Hayton, R. (1994). European-American perspective: Some considerations. In J. U. Gordon (Ed.), *Managing multiculturalism in substance abuse services* (pp. 99–116). Thousand Oaks, CA: Sage Publications.

Hess, P. M. & Hess, H. J. (1998). Values and ethics in social work practice with lesbian and gay persons. In E. G. Mallon (Ed.), *Foundations of social work practice with lesbian and gay persons* (31–46). New York: Harrington Park Press.

Hess, P. M. & Jackson, H. (1995). Practice with and on behalf of families. In C. Meyer and M. Mattaini (Eds.), *The foundations of social work practice* (126–155). Washington, DC: NASW.

Holmes, S. (2000, March 19). The politics of race and the census. *New York Times*, p. 3.

Johnson, B., Williams, T., Dei, K., & Sanabria, H. (1990). Drug abuse and the inner city: Impact on drug users and the community. In M. Tonry & J. Q. Wilson (Eds.), *Drugs and crime* (pp. 9–67). Crime and Justice Series, Vol. 13, Chicago: University of Chicago Press.

Kadushin, A. & Kadushin, G. (1997). *The social work interview: A guide for human service professionals* (4th ed.). New York: Columbia University Press.

Kolb, P. (2000). Continuing to care: Black and Latina daughters' assistance to their mothers in nursing homes. *Affilia, 15* (4), 502–525.

Lewin, T. (2000, October 24). Now a majority: Families with 2 parents who work. *New York Times*, p. A20.

Longino, C. (1994). Myths of an aging America. *American Demographics, 16*, (8), 36–42.

Lum, D. (1996). *Social work practice and people of color: A process-stage approach* (3d ed.). Pacific Grove, CA: Brooks/Cole.

Marsella, A. J., Friedman, M. J., & Spain, E. H. (1994). Ethnocultural aspects of posttraumatic stress disorder. In J. Oldham, M. B. Riba, & A. Tasman. (Eds.), *Review of psychiatry* (Vol. 12) (pp. 157–181). Washington, DC: American Psychiatric Press.

McGoldrick, M., Giordano, J., & Pierce, J. K. (1996). *Ethnicity and family therapy* (2d ed.). New York: Guilford.

National Immigration Forum. (1994). *Fast facts on today's newcomers*. Washington, DC: Author.

Pruchno, R. (1999). Raising grandchildren: The experiences of black and white grandmothers. *The Gerontologist 39*(2), 209–221.

Rogler, L., Cortes, D., & Malgady, R. (1991). Acculturation and mental health among Hispanics. *American Psychologist, 46* (6):585–597.

Rotheram-Borus, M. J. & Wyche, K. F. (1994). Ethnic differences in identity development in the United

States. In S. Archer (Ed.), *Interventions for adolescent identity development* (pp. 62–83). Thousand Oaks, CA: Sage.

Shorto, R. (1997, December 7). Belief by the numbers. *New York Times Magazine*, 60–61.

Solomon, B. (1976). *Black empowerment: Social work in oppressed communities*. New York: Columbia University Press.

Stiver, I. P. (1994). Women's struggles in the workplace: A relational model. In M. P. Mirkin (Ed.), *Women in context: Toward a feminist reconstruction of psychotherapy*. New York: Guilford.

Straussner, S. L. A. (Ed.). (2001). *Ethnocultural factors in substance abuse treatment*. New York: Guilford.

U.S. Committee for Refugees (1998, December). *Refugee Report*. Washington, DC: National Immigration Forum.

U.S. Department of Health and Human Services. (1999). *Mental health: A report of the Surgeon General*. Rockville, MD: U.S. Department of Health and Human Services, Substance Abuse and Mental Health Services Administration, Center for Mental Health Services, National Institutes of Health.

U.S. Immigration and Naturalization Service. (1997). *Statistical yearbook of the Immigration and Naturalization Service, 1996*. Washington, DC: U.S. Government Printing Office.

U.S. Immigration and Naturalization Service. (1997, January). *Estimates of the unauthorized immigrant population residing in the United States*. Washington, DC: Government Printing Office.

Van Wormer, K., Wells, J., & Boes, M. (2000). *Social work with lesbians, gays and bisexuals: A strengths perspective*. Boston: Allyn & Bacon.

11 Skills for Social Work Practice

A social service agency in Savannah, Georgia, 2000. Photo by Lala Straussner

Social work practice requires not only extensive knowledge about people, agencies, and policies, and the interrelationship among them, but also necessitates the development of a variety of skills for effective client, agency, and policy practice. Primary among the skills social workers need is the ability to form a helping relationship with clients. This chapter focuses on the *social worker–client relationship*, and discusses the skills needed for client, agency, and policy practice, including:

- Performing different social work roles
- Observation, communication, and interviewing skills
- Skills of helping during different stages of intervention
- Skills related to the social work roles in agency practice
- Skills related to the social work roles in policy practice
- Functioning as part of teams
- Engaging in ongoing self-assessment and service evaluation

Skills for Client Practice

While many of the skills that social workers use for client practice are also useful when working in agency or policy practice, the skills discussed in this section focus on the provision of direct services with individuals, families, groups, communities, and organizations.

Establishing a Professional Relationship

The cornerstone of the helping process is the professional relationship between the social worker and the client. As pointed out in Chapter 1, social workers do not have some of the "tools" that may exist among other helping professions, such as blood pressure monitors or psychometric tests. Instead, they must rely on their conscious "use of self," as they develop a professional relationship with their clients. The establishment of a professional relationship also requires self-awareness on the part of the social worker. This ensures that the social worker will keep the work focused on the needs of the client, rather than on his or her own personal needs.

Characteristics of the Helping Relationship

The helping relationship is defined by several characteristics that distinguish it from other relationships that we have, such as with a family member or a friend. These characteristics are:

Purpose

Unlike other relationships, the purpose of the social worker–client relationship is to help the client achieve a generally agreed-upon and desired change. Without a specific and clear purpose, the work with a client will meander and will not have any identifiable outcomes. An important way of concretizing the purpose is through the establishment of a worker-client "contract," which will be elaborated on later in this chapter.

Concern for Clients

Social workers need to care about what happens to their clients, and develop the skills to communicate their concern. However, social workers also need to know how to establish clear boundaries so that their clients' problems do not become their own, thereby causing them to lose their objectivity and ability to help the client. For example, social workers working in child protective services may find that they are no longer able to respond to the needs of a situation because they become enraged every time they see an abused child. On the other hand, if they become too distant emotionally and no longer care about the children—a condition referred to as "burnout"—they also cannot, and should not, continue in the position without dealing with their reactions, either with a supervisor, with colleagues, or by seeking professional help. Finding the proper balance between caring while maintaining an objective, professional distance is an important aspect of social work education and practice.

Acceptance of Clients

A basic value of the social work profession is respect for the dignity and acceptance of people. As pointed out in the discussion of social work values, "to accept" does not always mean agreeing with clients. What it does involve is an acceptance that the client's views and feelings are legitimate reflections of the client's perspective. For example, we know that a father who grew up being abused by his own father is more likely to abuse his children. Understanding this dynamic helps us accept, if not condone, this man and to appreciate that he may still love his children despite his abusive behavior.

Expectations of Clients

Social workers need to convey a realistic hopefulness and encouragement to clients in the process of helping them meet their goals. The current focus on the strengths perspective in social work has highlighted the importance of recognizing and reinforcing peoples' capacities to grow and change (Saleebey, 1997). As the classic study by Rosenthal and Jacobson (1968) showed, children whose teachers expected them to do well, did so, while pupils whose teachers were told to have low expectations had a harder time achieving academically.

Points to Ponder

"The social workers who are most effective in the helping process are those who expect that their clients will change, given appropriate help and support" (Compton & Galaway, 1999, p. 179).

Empathy

Empathy refers to the capacity of social workers to "put themselves into their clients' shoes" and to understand the feelings and experiences of a client. Empathy is different than "sympathy." While sympathy refers to the process of *feeling sorry for* another person, empathy reflects a worker's *feeling with* a client. When a social worker expresses empathy, clients generally feel not only that their situation is understood, but more importantly, that their feelings about the situation are understood and accepted. This process provides a great deal of emotional support for the client.

Expressing empathy can also enable clients to talk, or explore, more about the situation and their feelings about it. For example, if a client is grieving because a parent recently died, the social worker might have a sympathetic response and say, "I'm sorry about your loss." The client might respond "Thank you for your concern" and not talk about it anymore. In the same situation, the social worker could have an *empathic response* and say, "Given what you told me about your relationship with your mother, I know this is a difficult loss for you," thereby connecting with the client's feelings and encouraging the client to talk more about them.

Points to Ponder

"From its inception, social work has recognized the importance of empathy. The frequent references to starting where the client is and the concept of client self-determination reflect an emphasis on understanding, appreciating, and respecting clients' feelings, thoughts and experiences. . . . In most contexts, empathic understanding is probably the single most important quality that you must regularly demonstrate in your work with clients" (Compton and Galaway, 1999, p. 222).

Developing Self-Awareness

Because the sole purpose of the client and social worker meeting together is for the social worker to help the client, the social worker cannot use the contact for his or her own purposes. For example, the social worker might be concerned about something going on in his or her own personal life and would rather talk about this than listen to the client talk and respond to the client's needs. Or, as pointed out in the discussion of values and ethics in Chapter 8, social workers might hold personal opinions or biases that they might wish to express to clients thereby interfering with client self-determination. Therefore, it is crucial that social workers be aware of their own feelings whenever they are engaged in professional work so that they can always protect client self-determination.

In order to maintain self-awareness, social workers need to constantly reflect on their work, talk with supervisors or consultants, discuss their concerns with colleagues, and, as students, engage in classroom discussion and exercises that promote the development of self-awareness.

Points to Ponder

"Often certain characteristics of either the worker or the client or their interaction make it difficult for a positive working relationship to be established and maintained. For example . . . a worker who is not sensitive to a client's cultural background and style of relating may alienate the client. The worker's responsibility is to acknowledge these difficulties and strive to overcome or surmount them" (Goldstein & Noonan, 1999, p. 61)

Social Work Roles and Related Skills

Social workers assume many different roles as part of the provision of micro-level services to clients. Each role requires that social workers develop specific skills. While the roles listed below are presented separately, in reality most social workers assume several roles at any one time.

Counselor or Enabler

In this role, social workers engage in counseling with individuals, families, groups and communities. The social worker helps people articulate their needs, identify and clarify their problems or situations, understand the possible dynamics or issues regarding their present circumstances, explore various alternatives and solutions, and encourage the development of clients' capacities to deal with the situation or problems more effectively (Compton & Galaway, 1999; Straussner, 1990). The skills essential to this role include: biopsychosocial assessment, communication, interviewing, and a wide range of intervention skills, some of which will be elaborated on later.

The counselor/enabler role is exemplified in the following case:

> Victor Perez, a social worker in a community health center, met with 67-year-old Yoko Yamamoto whose husband is suffering with end-stage lung cancer. Mrs. Yamamoto had been caring for her husband at home, but felt that she was no longer able to provide the kind of care that her dying husband needed. She felt guilty about considering putting him in a nursing home and has not been able to sleep worrying about what to do. Mr. Perez validated Mrs. Yamamoto's feelings of ambivalence—while she wanted to care for her husband, she also was feeling overwhelmed and resentful because she did not have any time for herself.
>
> After further assessing the financial and emotional resources available to the family, the social worker enabled her to explore the various available options. The couple's two grown children lived too far away to help, and the weekly visiting nurse service was not enough of a help. Their small city apartment made it difficult to have an aide stay with them; moreover, Mrs. Yamamoto's cultural upbringing made it difficult for her to consider having another person take care of her husband in their home. Finally, with the encouragement and support of the social worker, and after further discussions with her husband and children, Mrs. Yamamoto made a decision to put her husband in a nearby hospice that would allow her to spend time with him every day without having the full responsibility for his care.

Social Broker

The social worker links clients with existing resources that may be supportive to them. The social worker also has the responsibility to follow up on the referrals as well as to identify the lack of appropriate resources and work within the agency and community to develop needed resources.

Inherent in this role are: skills in assessment of clients' needs, skills in obtaining information regarding organizational and community resources, referrals skills, and skills in resource development such as advocacy and networking. For example, Sarina Sythe, a social worker in an urban middle-school, worked hard throughout the school year to link the principal of her school with local businesses and religious institutions that provided volunteers to serve as mentors and role models to children in this school.

Advocate

In this role, social workers help clients obtain services and resources that the clients have been unable to obtain on their own. Patterned after the legal profession, social workers need skills to advocate on behalf of their clients, to provide leadership in collecting relevant data, and, if necessary, to challenge decisions of institutions in order to modify or change current positions or policies. For example, Michaela Case is a social work student with a field placement in a "naturally occurring retirement community" (NORC), an urban housing complex where many of the tenants have grown old and are in need of services. Becoming aware of tenants' complaints about the frequently broken elevator in one of the buildings, Ms. Case decided to advocate with the building owners for its replacement. After collecting information that the elevator had already been repaired five times in the last four months, and organizing the support of the tenants, she was able to convince the owners that it would be less expensive in the long run to replace the elevator instead of constantly repairing it and having many of the tenants unable to leave their apartments for days during each repair.

Mediator

As mediators, social workers manage conflicts between two or more individuals or clients and interpret their needs to each other. Mediation or conflict resolution skills include: assessment of the nature and cause of the conflict, identifying areas of commonality, separating problems from solutions, depersonalizing the situation, and examining alternative solutions. For example, Christopher Stephanapolos is a social worker in a clinic specializing in helping step-families address family problems. A recent client is a family in which there has been a continual conflict between the step-father and the two teenage children from the wife's first marriage. A careful assessment of the situation revealed that the children believed that by listening to their step-father they would be disloyal to their biological father. By identifying the common desire of all family members to have a more pleasant time when they're together, helping the parents to acknowledge the children's feelings of love for their biological father, and by negotiating more flexible curfew times for the children on the weekend in exchange for having them home earlier during the week, the social worker was able to help all the members of this family.

Case Manager

The work of case managers is to monitor the functioning of the client, provide emotional support, and to facilitate access to services by linking clients to needed resources, coordinating various services, and ensuring the continued availability of these services to the client. Case managers combine the functions and skills of brokers, enablers, mediators, and advocates. For example, Dwayne Robinson, a social work student at an outpatient department of a psychiatric hospital, has been assigned as a case manager to Susanne Reed, who has been diagnosed with paranoid schizophrenia and has had a 10-year history of numerous hospitalizations in psychiatric facilities for brief periods of time. In his role as case manager, Dwayne Robinson monitors that Ms. Reed comes to the clinic for her medication shots, attends her job as a receptionist in a city agency, and goes to her weekly support group meetings at the hospital clinic. He also mediates, when necessary, between his client and her mother with whom she lives, and advocates for his client to obtain disability benefits whenever her condition worsens and she becomes unable to work.

Teacher

In this role, social workers provide new information and offer explanations that help clients have a better understanding of their situation and how to handle it. Examples of this role include social workers who offer various psychoeducational lectures, such as providing information to a group of parents on how to best help children with asthma, or teaching smoking cessation skills in a criminal justice setting. Skills needed for this role include: ability to access the latest information on a particular topic via the Internet and professional literature, how to present information to different audiences, and how to lead group discussion.

All of the above roles require the ability not only to establish a professional relationship with people, but also to communicate with diverse clients and agencies.

Skills of Observation, Communication, and Interviewing

In order to become a competent practitioner, social workers need to develop the *skills of observation, communication,* and *interviewing.* These three important skills are closely interconnected in practice.

Observation Skills

Observation skills are crucial for the assessment of clients. What we notice depends on what is important to us: Observing who sits next to whom may be important to a social worker doing family assessment, but not to a social worker providing a stress management workshop, and observing the uncollected garbage in an inner city neighborhood may be critical to a community organizer, but barely noticed by a case manager.

Points to Ponder

"Nonverbal messages are conveyed through the person and the setting. Age, sex, color, speech, personal appearances—physique, posture, body odor, dress, tension, facial expression, behavior, silence or speech, tone of voice, gestures or movements, eye contact, touch, body sounds—all convey messages to the receiver, as does the physical setting—its appearance, aesthetic quality, comfort and privacy (or lack of them), and general climate. The ways in which we convey nonverbal messages about ourselves are endless. Once workers know where to look and what to listen for and to sense in both self and client, their sensitivity and ability to understand will increase" (Brill, 1998, p. 76).

Like all skills, the skill of observation develops with experience. However, due to the subjective nature of our observations, it is important that the interpretation of what we see be verified further through direct communication with the client. For example, noticing that Stella Greener, a new member in a group for women recently diagnosed with AIDS, sits quietly, with her chair slightly outside the circle, during the whole hour-and-a-half of the group, is an important observation that can have a number of different interpretations. Only by appropriately sharing this observation with Stella and the group can the meaning of this behavior become clearer.

Communication Skills

Despite the fact that people are communicating from the moment they are born, professional communication skills are not as simple as they sound, and require extensive training. Such training is an important component of the fieldwork experience and of social work supervision.

There are three ways of communicating that are important to social workers: listening, talking, and writing.

Listening Skills

In order to listen to clients, social workers need to develop the ability to tune in to what the client is feeling, but is not expressing, directly or verbally. Social workers also need to learn to differentiate between the *manifest*, or verbalized, communication, and the *latent*, or the underlying communication. For example, an 8-year-old boy who is sitting with tears in his eyes while telling a social worker that "everything is fine" and that he's not afraid of the classmate who has been bullying him in the playground is obviously experiencing powerful emotions that need to be further explored and understood. To accept as is the verbalized statement that "everything is fine" would be to ignore the child's latent communication—and thus his true feelings. Therefore, a crucial communication skill for social workers is learning how to listen for feelings and how to explore or ask appropriate questions in order to identify these feelings.

Talking Skills

Unlike the informal and spontaneous talking that goes on in social situations, verbal communication by social workers has specific professional goals. The two most common communication goals in client practice are: *information gathering* and *therapeutic change*. They will be discussed later in this chapter.

Writing Skills

As part of their professional responsibilities, social workers must have good writing skills. In most settings, social workers need to write for both agency records and for purposes of advocacy and networking outside the agency, such as:

- Maintain written records of their contacts and communications with clients
- Write progress notes in clients' charts or case records
- Write memos to other people in their agencies
- Write referral and case summary letters to other agencies
- Write advocacy letters regarding a client or a cause

An important component of social work education in many settings is the use of *process recordings*. Social work students write down, word for word, their communication with clients and their reactions to what they observed and what they and their clients said. Although this recording of the whole interview process can be time consuming, it is a valuable learning tool. Process recordings are read by the student's supervisor, who then discusses them with the student.

Interviewing Skills

Much of client practice is done through interviewing people, and calls for the development of good interviewing skills. The skills used during interviewing will vary depending on the number of people interviewed—whether it is one person, a family, a small group, or a large community group; the age of the interviewee—whether it is a child or an adolescent, or an elderly person; the mental or cognitive ability of the client; the ethnocultural background; and the client's ability to understand and communicate in English or another language, including sign language for those who are hearing impaired. Most importantly, the skills used will depend on the goals of the interview: do the goals include obtaining information regarding a client's eligibility for services or benefits, or effecting therapeutic change? Do they include advocacy for change in a community? It is not unusual to have different goals during different stages of working with a particular client, whether an individual, family, group, or community. For example, during the beginning phase of working with a client or potential client, the social worker is more likely to listen or ask questions related to gathering information, while later on, the goal may shift to a different focus. The stages of interviewing, and the skills needed during each, will be elaborated on later in this chapter.

Information Gathering Interview: Intake and Screening

The purpose of an information-gathering interview is to obtain factual and specific information, or data, which is then used to:

■ Decide eligibility for specific services or benefits
■ Determine the nature of the problem and services needed
■ Make a biopsychosocial assessment

Such information is often obtained during special interviews called *intakes* or *screenings*. For example, a social worker working for a child protection agency needs to respond to an allegation of child abuse by asking specific questions in order to screen for, or determine, if a child is being physically abused. This is an example of a screening interview. On the other hand, a social worker working for a home care agency will do an intake interview to assess the eligibility for, and the kinds of services needed by, an elderly stroke victim. To effectively conduct such interviews, the worker needs to be able to quickly establish a trusting relationship, to ask appropriate questions without reflecting a judgmental attitude, and to stay focused on the information needed.

Points to Ponder

Some helpful hints about interviewing:

- In general, it is helpful to ask open-ended questions and avoid "yes-no" answers.
- "Why" questions tend to make people feel put on the spot and should be avoided whenever possible. Alternatives might be, "What was going on when . . ." or "How were you feeling when . . ."
- Reassuring clients prematurely, called "false reassurance," should always be avoided. It is not helpful to clients, and may be misleading to reassure them without first having the necessary information and understanding the clients' feelings. Thus, telling a client who is concerned about being evicted "don't worry about that, everything will be fine" may not help the client take the necessary steps to avoid the eviction, and certainly will not help the client to stop worrying. A more useful approach would be to help the client find out the details of the situation and make a realistic plan.

Therapeutic Change Interview

The goal of a therapeutic change interview is to effect change in the functioning of clients or their environment. Therapeutic communication is focused not only on obtaining factual information but rather on *how and what the client feels, thinks, perceives, and wants*. Because there are a wide variety of approaches used to effect therapeutic change, the kinds of skills needed vary.

Following are examples of how a social worker can apply some frequently-used skills during a therapeutic change interview (Brandler & Roman, 1999; Shulman, 1999):

Skill	Example
Elaborating or exploring	Could you tell me more about . . .
Paraphrasing	What I hear you saying is . . .
Expressing empathy	This is a hard time for all of you.
Reflecting feelings	Sounds like you're feeling . . .
Maintaining focus	You were talking about . . .
Seeking concreteness	Can you give me a specific example?
Generalizing the theme	Many of you in this group seem to be concerned about . . .
Reaching inside of silences	It seems to be very hard for you to talk about what happened.
Owning one's feelings	Can you use "I" instead of saying "they" or "people"?
Partializing the problems	Let's see if we can separate some of the issues that you brought up today.
Prioritizing	Which of your many concerns would you like to address first?

Skills of Helping during the Different Phases of Intervention

Social work interventions can range from a single interview to months and even years of meeting with clients. For example, Josh Krauz, a social worker working in an employee assistance program for firefighters, saw Olga Lopez for one interview to discuss her concern regarding the stress she was feeling as the only female firefighter in the station house. After the interview, in which Ms. Lopez felt that her concerns were validated, she decided to talk to her union representative and asked to be transferred to another unit that had two female firefighters. She did not need the help of a social worker again.

On the other hand, Wendy Ellington, a social worker employed in a long-term therapeutic community for adolescent substance abusers, was responsible for the same five residents during their eighteen-month stay in treatment. She saw them in daily group meetings, in weekly individual meetings, and in monthly family meetings.

Regardless of their length, all social work interventions, whether with individuals, families, groups, or communities, have a common process that includes a beginning phase, a middle or work phase, and an ending or termination phase. Each phase has different goals and requires the development of different skills.

Beginning Phase

This phase of intervention includes a number of different components, some of which may vary if one is working with individuals, families, groups, or communities.

Engagement and Contracting Skills

The two major components that apply to all clients are engagement and contracting (Shulman, 1999).

- *Engagement* requires the ability to establish a productive client–worker relationship. An important aspect of engagement is developing skills in cultural competence when working with clients whose ethnic and cultural backgrounds are different than one's own.
- *Contracting* refers to the skills needed to clearly establish mutual goals and expectations.

Points to Ponder

"Planning and implementing intervention is not a one-sided process but involves the active collaboration of both worker and client. One way of ensuring that the worker and client are proceeding together is for them to make an explicit agreement about the problem to be addressed and the goals, focus, and structure of intervention. This action, called contracting, optimally solidifies the engagement process and is not meant to be legalistic or mechanical. Its intent is to provide a common basis from which to proceed. Its exact nature varies according to the client and the agency, can be general or highly specific and detailed, or can be verbal or formalized in writing" (Goldstein & Noonan, 1999, p. 109).

Engagement and contracting require skills in communication, interviewing, and assessment. Also required is the ability to clearly define the purpose, possibilities, and limitations of the service. The special skills needed to engage and work with resistant clients and clients who are mandated to obtain services will be discussed later in this chapter.

Skills in Dealing with Issues of Worker Power and Authority

Social workers should be aware that many clients view the helping person as being in a position of power and authority. How the social worker and the client handle this is a critical aspect of the beginning phase. To address this issue, the worker needs skills in clarifying the limits of confidentiality, identifying the clients' feeling about and reactions to authority figures, their expectations of the social worker, and their fears and hopes about the services that are offered.

Points to Ponder

"All new relationships, particularly those with people in authority, begin somewhat tentatively. Clients perceive workers as symbols of authority with power to influence their lives. Clients often bring with them a fund of past experiences with professionals or stereotypes of helping professionals passed on by friends or family. Thus, the first sessions are partly efforts to explore the realities of the situation" (Shulman, 1999, p. 232).

Middle or Working Phase

During this phase, the worker needs to use empathic and elaborating skills to help clients "tell their story" and work toward the contracted goal, or, if needed, to redefine the goal. The worker needs to help clients not become derailed from their initial goal of seeing the social worker. When working with small groups or communities, it is important to help the members depend less on the worker, while instead listening to, valuing, and supporting each other.

Points to Ponder

In describing the middle phase of group work, Brandler and Roman (1999) state: "In the middle phase, the worker assumes a less directive role than in the beginning or termination phase. Still, it is an active role, one that requires the worker to play a less pivotal part while developing group leadership and autonomy. In some sense, the worker must now relinquish control and help the group embrace it . . . workers model how to engage in, grow from, and survive conflict . . . . The middle phase requires specific worker skills such as clarifying communication; mediating; confronting; identifying commonalities to build deeper levels of cohesiveness, mutuality, and bonding; and identifying and respecting difference to build independence and individuality" (pp. 45–46).

Ending or Termination Phase

The termination of the client–worker relationship can take place under a variety of circumstances, which may be planned or unplanned. It may be due to the satisfactory achievement of the stated goals, such as a couple whose marriage has improved after seeing a social worker for 12 weeks. It may come about because the client is no longer eligible for services, even though the goals may not have been fully achieved, such as a client who must leave a victims' support group because the managed care insurance company will not approve additional services. Termination can also result from a worker leaving the agency or taking on different duties in the same agency, or when clients decide that they no longer want the services of a social worker and just stop coming. Regardless of the cause, ending an established relationship is difficult and elicits emotional reactions, both from clients and social workers. While challenging, dealing directly with the process of termination can also be an empowering and growth producing process for both clients and social workers.

It is the social worker's task to help clients address this phase in a helpful way. Among the skills needed are: the ability to raise the impending termination of services in a timely manner so that it is experienced as a process rather than an abrupt disruption; being able to identify the progress achieved by the client; and being able to plan and implement the next steps, which may include referral to another agency or transfer to another social worker in the same agency (Shulman, 1999). The process of *referral* may include collaboration and advocacy with other agencies, or with staff members in the same agency.

In addition to evaluating the client's progress, termination requires skills of obtaining an evaluation or feedback of the worker by the client. It also includes skills of follow-up of the client regarding the outcome of the work done.

Points to Ponder

"One of the major tasks of termination is to construct a bridge between treatment and the clients' subsequent problem-solving efforts. In part this may be accomplished through a synthesis of termination evaluation and planning. Clients should be empowered through the termination process to embark upon a self-directed course of action based upon a realistic assessment of their problem solving strengths. The mastery of termination issues supports client self-esteem and reinforces the client's hope that ongoing progress can be achieved. The work of the ending also frees the client to reinvest energy in appropriate life tasks and on-going relationships that support problem solving" (Hess & Hess, 1999, p. 491).

Working with Mandated Clients

Many social workers are employed in settings where they provide services to *mandated clients*. These are clients who are required to see a social worker as the basis for receiving other benefits, or in order to avoid negative consequences. For example, attending a group for batterers led by a social worker might be a requirement for people convicted of beating their partners, or a teenager might be required to see a social worker every week as a term of probation. Since such individuals are seeing the social worker involuntarily, they are more likely to be resistant, or unwilling to accept or use help.

A useful skill for working with involuntary and resistant clients, particularly those with a history of substance abuse, is *supportive confrontation*. Due to the denial inherent in substance abuse and in many antisocial activities, the traditional supportive counseling roles assumed by social workers may not be effective (Levinson & Straussner, 1978). In using supportive confrontation techniques, the social worker may involve family members or other people important to the individuals to confront the client with the problems resulting from their behavior, and to encourage acceptance of further interventions or treatment. The effective use of this approach requires an understanding of: psychological defense mechanisms; the impact of substance abuse on individuals and on family systems; the use of power and authority; and an understanding of the impact of peer pressure (Straussner, 1993).

Points to Ponder

"An argument has existed in the field about whether it is possible to work effectively with mandated clients. Some believe that the use of authority to require engagement so profoundly distorts the helping relationship that it can only be an illusion of work. In some cases, it is clearly true that no matter what the worker says or does, the client refuses to accept the service. In some situations, the client may not yet be ready, and in other cases, the client may never be ready. This is one of the reasons children must be removed permanently from some abusive homes, men need to go to prison for battering their partners, and some heroin addicts end their lives overdosing on the street. The worker can only do her or his best to maximize the possibility that the client can use the help, leaving the final decision to the client. For some categories of clients, however, the requirement that forces them to seek help serves as the beginning of a process of change" (Shulman, 1999, p. 111).

Issues Related to Self-Disclosure

At times, social workers may want to use themselves in a conscious and purposeful way to model a certain behavior, attitude, or to share a personal experience that may be helpful for a client. Whether or not to *self-disclose* is a difficult decision and should be made carefully under the close guidance of a supervisor. It requires a high level of self-awareness, and the ability to separate personal needs from the needs of the clients.

In certain situations, self-disclosure might be useful. For example, Andy Nova, a social worker in a college counseling center, is working with a group of students who are struggling with coming-out to their parents regarding their homosexuality. After careful consideration, he decided that it may be helpful to the group members if he shared his own experience of coming-out, and revealed both the positive and negative reactions that he received from various family members and peers.

Points to Ponder

"Use of self-disclosure should be sparing so that it does not overwhelm the interviewee. Interviewers should offer it discriminately, delicately, with some sensitivity to the client's readiness for such information, (and) with a conscious idea as to what is likely to be helpful" (Kadushin & Kadushin, 1997, p. 198).

Selected self-disclosure can be very effective in helping clients who, like the members of Andy Nova's group, may lack helpful role models, or those who may not have been exposed to different ways of thinking and behaving (Goldstein, 1994). However, it is important to remember that social workers are ethically forbidden from imposing their values and opinions on clients. Therefore, any self-disclosure should be limited to information that can be helpful to the client, and must not be offered in order to meet the needs of the worker.

Roles and Skills for Agency Practice

As part of their agency practice, social workers assume a number of different roles and need to develop specific skills to fulfill them. While all social workers working in agencies and organizations contribute to the functioning of the agency, it is helpful to look at the roles and skills of social workers whose major responsibility is to provide direct services to clients separately from those whose major responsibilities are to administer the agency.

Understanding Organizational Power Structure

All social workers need a clear understanding of their status in the power structure of the organization in which they work. Such knowledge is particularly important when working in host settings, such as hospitals, schools, or criminal justice institutions, whose primary mission is other than the delivery of social or human services. In such settings the role of social work may not be clearly understood by other professionals, and may even conflict with the mission of the organization. For example, the role of the criminal justice system is to punish offenders, not to help them understand their behavior. Therefore, social workers need to be clear about their roles, and able to educate other professionals and show the need for, and the value of, social work interventions.

Organizational Assessment and Change Skills

Helping organizations grow by adapting to the changing environment is an important aspect of agency practice. Social workers need to develop skills in organizational assessment and organizational change processes in order to better meet the needs of both clients and staff. As indicated in Chapter 9, organizations have a life cycle and need to change to reflect the ever-changing internal and external conditions and new knowledge that becomes available. Social workers need skills in assessing an organization's life cycle, its readiness for change, its leadership, and its ability to provide effective services to clients. They also need to know how to implement organizational change that can benefit both staff and clients.

Roles of Social Workers in Agency Practice

While the roles of social workers vis-à-vis their clients have been described earlier, it is also important to understand that social workers have certain roles and responsibilities, and need to use professional relationship skills in dealing with supervisors, administrators, other staff members, and their peers in the agency.

Role of Supervisee

Many social workers are closely supervised. This is particularly true for social work students. While some supervision is focused on administrative aspects of working in an agency, all social work students, and even some experienced social workers providing direct client services, are assigned a supervisor to help them address the many practice issues related to working with clients. Consequently, social workers, and social work students, need to be open to discussion about their work with their supervisors. They also need to know how to ask and how to receive appropriate professional help from supervisors.

Role of Colleague

The most important source of support for many social workers is their peers, and the establishment of collaborative and collegial relationships with other social workers, as well as professionals from other disciplines, is a crucial part of working in an agency or organization.

Points to Ponder

"Being an effective colleague means limiting competition with others and minimizing one-upmanship in favor of maximizing problem-solving. . . . To be a good colleague, one must understand and be sensitive to the values and skills of other professions as well as the demands of their roles and tasks" (Weissman, Epstein, & Savage, 1983, pp. 110, 112).

Social workers also need to know how to work with an agency's support staff such as secretaries, receptionists, and custodians. Although their role is not always clearly visible, support staff have a very important role in the functioning of an agency and they impact the provision of services to clients. A client's first impressions of the agency may be formed from their initial contact with the receptionist or with the elevator operator.

Points to Ponder

The importance of support staff cannot be overstated. Consequently, support staff need information about the purpose and function of the agency, and need to identify with the goals of the agency. Moreover, they should receive ongoing recognition of their importance to the successful functioning of the agency.

Roles of Agency Supervisor and Administrator

Among the most important roles and skills of social workers who are responsible for the establishment, development, and functioning of social agencies or programs are:

- **Executive Director**—In this position the social worker is fully responsible for the functioning of an agency. The executive director guides the fulfillment of the agency's mission and becomes its spokesperson to the community and funding sources. The executive director needs to be able to deal with the board of directors, with actual and potential financial and political supporters, with regulatory bodies, and with staff members who administer the organization. Among the skills needed for this position are communication, leadership, team building, and professional networking skills.

- **Agency/Program Administrator or Manager**—Depending on the size of the organization, this role may involve some of the responsibilities of an executive director and/or the supervisor, which are discussed below. The administrator is usually responsible for the development, implementation, and monitoring of effective services and programs within the agency, hiring and evaluating of staff, and monitoring funding and financial reporting.

   In order to fulfill this role, the social worker needs to have good managerial skills, as well as skills in communication, decision making, financial accountability, collaboration, mediation, negotiation, and leadership.

- **Supervisor**—Supervision of staff is one of the most important functions in social agencies. The role of the supervisor is to increase the skills of staff and monitor the quality of the services delivered to clients. The supervisor may also function as a mediator between his or her supervisees and other staff members in the organization, or in other agencies. The supervisor often assumes the role of mentor to new staff members, helping to socialize them to the profession. The skills required for this role include teaching, negotiating, mediating, advocacy, and monitoring of quality of service delivery.

- **Program Planner and Developer**—In this role, the social worker plans, implements, and assesses new programs. Among the skills essential in fulfilling this function are the ability to do a formal or informal needs assessment, and skills in organizational change strategies, program development, collaboration, and advocacy.

- **Policy Developer**—This role calls for a social worker to propose or develop new policies in relation to the delivery of services or the functioning of the organization or

Points to Ponder

"Because they originally adhered to an apprenticeship approach to skill development, social agencies have continued to depend heavily on supervision for monitoring and evaluating the work of practitioners and for helping them upgrade their competence. . . . The effective social work supervisor . . . is able to combine both the supervisor and consultant roles in helping staff perform the services of the agency. The quality of supervision is one of the most important factors for the new social worker to look for when seeking a social work job" (Morales & Schafer, 1995, p. 147).

staff members. For example, members of the National Association of Social Workers propose a policy in relation to dealing with breach of professional ethics by social workers. This policy is then adopted by NASW and serves to provide guidelines for social workers in all settings.

■ **Consultant/Evaluator**—Many agencies employ social workers as outside consultants to help develop or evaluate programs, policies, or procedures. For example, a social worker may be hired to help develop a new computerized management system to streamline the paper work, or help an agency prepare for reaccreditation by a government or a professional accrediting body, such as the Joint Commission on Accreditation of Health Care Organizations (JCAHO).

■ **Public Relations/Agency Marketer**—This is a relatively new role for social workers that has expanded rapidly with the development of private sector programs, especially those that are for-profit. This role requires good communication, marketing, and networking skills.

■ **Trainer**—In this role, the social worker functions as a teacher, helping organizational staff members learn new administrative procedures, or new approaches for dealing with clients or issues. For example, staff in an agency that has received a grant to establish a community organization component may need training in how to do a community needs assessment in order to meet the requirements of the grant. Skills needed for this role include communication, training, and group leadership.

■ **Researcher/Data Manager**—Collects and analyzes data for research or for decision-making purposes. Skills needed are understanding of research methodology, and the ability to conceptualize and organize large amounts of data.

■ **Advocate**—Agency advocacy focuses on promoting changes in agency programs and service delivery that will impact many clients, as well as other staff. For example, Thomas Joel, a forensic social worker in a correctional facility for men, felt that the deteriorating condition of the visiting room made it unpleasant and even dangerous for the children of prisoners to visit their fathers, and thus fewer families with young children were coming to visit than in the past. After collecting letters from family members and identifying professional literature showing that the rates of recidivism increased for prisoners who did not maintain contact with their families, Thomas Joel was able to get the prison authorities to repair the visiting room and even allow some drawings the children made during their visits to be displayed on the walls.

Roles and Skills for Policy Practice

As indicated in previous chapters, policy practice focuses on the formulation or development, identification, analysis, and advocacy for those public policies, programs, and services that directly or indirectly affect social welfare. Social workers engaged in policy practice assume a variety of interesting and challenging roles.

Policy Analyst

In this role, the social worker examines existing or proposed policies and analyzes their impact on different populations and on the delivery of services to clients. An example may be an analysis of the implications of the aging of the population on the need for social work services in the future. Skills needed include: logical thinking, use of research data, ability to synthesize information, and verbal and written communications skills.

Policy Developer

Policy developers work on formulating new policies that, if adopted, will influence or impact the delivery of social work and social welfare services. Policy development requires knowledge of policy analysis. An example of a policy developer is a social worker who is involved in the writing of a state policy addressing the decriminalization of marijuana use for medical purposes. Policy development requires collaboration with other individuals. In addition, it requires understanding of policy formulation and political processes, good conceptual abilities, advocacy, and writing skills.

Policy Advocate

The adoption of any social welfare policy requires advocacy. According to Ezell (2001), public advocacy takes "persistence, tenacity, and patience" because it usually takes three legislative sessions to get a bill passed (p. 182). Critical advocacy skills include: written and verbal communications; ability to gather appropriate data in support of the advocacy; networking and coalition building; assertiveness; persuasiveness; ability to negotiate, compromise, and deal with conflict; and the use of mass media.

Lobbyist

A lobbyist is hired by one or more large groups or organizations, including NASW, to advocate for specific policies that impact clients or the social work profession. Unlike policy advocates, lobbyists are paid for their advocacy by their employing organization.

In addition to having all the advocacy skills described above, a lobbyist needs to have good public relations skills.

Political Coalition Builder

The goal of a coalition builder is to bring together various groups and organizations with a specific interest in order to influence policy. The importance of personal relationships in this role has been noted, as well as skills in facilitation and negotiation (Mizrahi & Rosenthal, 2001).

Expert Witness

The direct contact that social workers have with people and communities experiencing problems helps makes them aware of issues and solutions that may not be considered by others in the political or judicial arena. Being an expert witness allows social workers to share their knowledge and advocate for a particular policy. For example, a social worker may be called to present to a city planning agency about the impact that the lack of preschool programs has on the ability of mothers to stay in welfare-to-work programs. Among the skills needed are: communication, data collection, and data organization.

Legislative Aide/Advisor

A growing number of social workers serve as expert advisors on social welfare issues to policymakers at all levels of government, or to administrators in public and private sectors. To fulfill this role requires the knowledge of social welfare policies, skills in research and analysis of data, and ability to communicate verbally and in writing.

Social Warner

This role, first proposed by Yossi Korazim (1977), is seen as similar to the role of the "military radar" in which "it is up to the social worker to report and to warn of the development of, or the worsening of, social phenomena which he witnesses" (p. 4), and consequently to influence social policymakers. Such warning may include "letter-writing, the formulation of position papers, research, persuasion, organizing study-days, and protests" (p. 4) and requires all the skills discussed in the previous roles as well as skills in public speaking.

Politician

Becoming a politician allows a social worker to have far-reaching influences on the development and implementation of social policy and the ability to assist many individuals at once. Political skills involve many of the same skills used in client practice, particularly listening and public speaking, skills in negotiating, persuading, linking, brokering, and advocacy. According to Haynes and Mickelson (2000), the only skill-development needed may be to "transfer these skills from case (individual) to class (constituent). . . ." (p. 178).

Points to Ponder

"If a student is interested in eventually running for elected office, my advice would be to work in the political sector first. There are a growing number of elected officials whose constituent services are run by social workers. These are perfect places for social work students to have a field placement or to use as an entry-level position to enter the political arena. Such practice as doing constituent work, public policy work, or working in a government agency can be a real strength when you run for office some day" (Ruth Messinger, MSW, Manhattan Borough President, quoted in Haynes & Mickelson, 2000, p. 193).

Skills for Functioning as Part of Professional Teams and Coalitions

As part of their agency and policy practice, social workers often need to work as members of teams and coalitions. "A team is a group of people, each of whom possesses particular expertise and each of whom is responsible for individual decisions and actions; team members share a common purpose, and meet together to pool knowledge, ideas, and meanings from which interaction plans are made, actions taken, and future plans influenced" (Brill, 1998, p. 193).

Participating in Teams

As part of their work in agencies, social workers frequently function as team members with other social workers, as well as with members of other disciplines, whether in their own agency or with professionals of other agencies. At times, clients become important members of the team.

While the composition of teams can vary, professional teams usually are comprised of either other social workers in what has been termed intradisciplinary teams, or of members of different professions, referred to as inter- or multidisciplinary teams.

- *Intradisciplinary teams* include members of the same profession working in the same or different settings. For example, social workers from a foster care agency, a pediatric clinic in a hospital, and an early-intervention preschool program meet together with a mother caring for a four-year-old foster child who is HIV-positive to discuss handling of medical, educational, childcare, and behavioral problems of the child.
- *Inter- or multidisciplinary teams* include members of different professions who work together and coordinate their services on behalf of one or a group of clients in the same or different settings. For example, in a school for profoundly retarded adults, the social worker, teachers in the day program, nurse, psychologist, psychiatrist, and house parents meet together regularly to discuss the residents and coordinate their activities. Even the bus driver who takes the residents to the day program joins the team when there are behavior difficulties on the bus.

Points to Ponder

In teamwork, we need to recognize the inevitability of conflicts and differences; we must learn to negotiate them, in the best interests of clients and their families" (Compton & Galaway, 1999, p. 441).

Whether working as part of an intradisciplinary or multidisciplinary team "the capacity to operate as a productive member of a team is an important social work practice skill" (Compton & Galaway, 1999, p. 437). Among the skills needed as part of teamwork are: collaboration, professional communication, case presentation, negotiation, and advocacy. In addition, the social worker who functions as a team leader needs to develop specific leadership skills appropriate to that role and be able to mediate among team members with different points of view.

Participating in Coalitions

All social workers may function as part of various coalitions, and some may assume leadership roles in coalition building. According to Humphreys (1979, quoted in Haynes & Micherson, 2000), "a coalition is a loosely woven, ad hoc association of constituent groups, each of whose primary identification is outside the coalition" (p. 112). The purpose of a coalition is to influence politicians and the public to take action on social change on a given issue. A coalition is usually time-limited and issue-focused.

As pointed out by Popple and Leighninger (2001), "Coalitions can focus on agency policies, court cases and legal decisions, city and county ordinances, legislative rules and regulations, rulings by government administrators and state or federal legislation" (p. 326). An example of a coalition is a group of leaders of all major national organizations in the fields of mental health and substance abuse who meet on a regular basis to obtain the latest information and develop strategies regarding advocating for insurance parity laws that would provide the same coverage for mental health and substance abuse treatment as for any other health condition. Skills needed include effective use of mass media and modern technology, including the Internet, E-mail, listserves, and chat groups, along with the ability to compromise, build consensus, and advocate.

Skills in Self-Assessment and Service Evaluation

Social workers need to be able to evaluate their own interventions with clients and see which approaches and which skills are more effective in their work. In line with this, they also need to develop skills that encourage clients to provide feedback as to how they see the worker and the services that have been provided by the agency. Social workers also need to be able to evaluate their ability to function as part of a service delivery team, and, as indicated previously, to accept and incorporate feedback from their supervisors. Moreover, they need to be able to effectively advocate for changes at the agency, community, and societal level to improve client services and the social environment. It is only through the processes and skills of self-evaluation, combined with client, peer, and supervisory feedback, that social workers and social agencies can provide the best services within the context of fair and just social policies.

Conclusion

This chapter has focused on the skills needed for client, agency, and policy practice. As pointed out by Zastrow (1996), "The acquisition of social work skills depends partly on people's innate abilities and partly on learning experiences. Social work educational programs facilitate learning of such skills by presenting theoretical material to students (e.g., material on how to interview) by monitoring and critiquing students who are practicing these skills (e.g., videotaping students in simulated counseling situations), and by extensively supervising students in practicum courses" (p. 618). It is important to remember that there is a great deal of overlap of skills needed for client, agency, and policy practice, and that once the social worker gains these skills, they can be transferred from one form of practice to the other.

REFERENCES

Brandler, S. & Roman, C. (1999). *Group work: Skills and strategies for effective interventions* (2d ed.). New York: Haworth.

Brill, N. (1998). *Working with people: The helping process* (6th ed.). New York: Longman.

Compton, B. R. & Galaway, B. (1999). *Social work processes* (5th ed.). Pacific Grove, CA: Brooks/Cole.

Ezell, M. (2001). *Advocacy in the human services.* Belmont, CA: Wadsworth.

Goldstein, E. (1995). *Ego psychology and social work practice* (2d ed.). New York: Free Press.

Goldstein, E. G. & Noonan, M. (1999). *Short-term treatment and social work practice.* New York: Free Press.

Haynes, K. S. & Mickelson, J. S. (2000). *Affecting change* (4th ed.). New York: Longman.

Hess, H. & Hess, P. M. (1999). Termination in context. In Compton, B. R. & Galaway, B. (Eds.), *Social work processes* (6th ed.), (pp. 489–497). Pacific Grove, CA: Brooks/Cole.

Kadushin, A. & Kadushin, G. (1997). *The social work interview* (4th ed.). New York: Columbia University Press.

Korazim, Y. (1977). The Israeli social worker as a social Warner. Paper presented at the *Asian Regional Seminar on processes and approaches to social policy formulation and planning, with special emphasis on the role of social workers.* New Delhi, India, October.

Levinson, V. & Straussner, S. L. A. (1978). Social workers as 'enablers' in the treatment of alcoholism. *Social Casework, 59,* (1), 4–20.

Mizrahi, T. & Rosenthal, B. B. (2001). Complexities of coalition building: Leaders' successes, strategies, struggles and solutions. *Social Work, 46,* (1), 63–78.

Morales, A. T. & Sheafor, B. W. (1995). *Social work: A profession of many faces* (5th ed.). Boston: Allyn & Bacon.

National Association of Social Workers (NASW). (1997). Social workers serving in elected office. *Political Action for Candidate Endorsement.* Washington, DC: Author.

Popple, P. R. & Leighninger, L. (2001). *Policy-based profession: An introduction to social welfare policy analysis for social workers* (2d ed.). Boston: Allyn & Bacon.

Rosenthal, R. & Jacobson, L. (1968). *Pygmalion in the classroom: Teacher expectation and pupils' intellectual development.* New York: Rinehart & Winston.

Saleebey, D. (Ed.). (1992). *The strengths perspective in social work practice* (2d ed.). New York: Longman.

Shulman, L. (1999). *The skills of helping individuals, families, groups and communities* (4th ed.). Itasca, IL: Peacock.

Straussner, S. L. A. (1990). Occupational social work today: An overview. In S. L. A. Straussner (Ed.). *Occupational social work today* (pp. 1–14). New York: Haworth.

Straussner, S. L. A. (1993). Assessment and treatment of clients with alcohol and other drug abuse problems: An Overview. In S. L. A. Straussner (Ed.). *Clinical work with substance-abusing clients* (pp. 3–30). New York: Guilford.

Weissman, H., Epstein, I., & Savage. A. (1983). *Agency based social work*. Philadelphia: Temple University Press.

Zastrow, C. (1996). *Introduction to social work and social welfare* (6th Ed.). Pacific Grove, CA: Brooks/Cole.

EPILOGUE

Outside the Bronx Courthouse, New York City. Courtesy of Georgeen Comerford, project photographer, and the Bronx Institute Archives, Lehman College Library of the City University of New York

As has been seen in the chapters in this book, social work grew out of the chaos of the cities. Early voluntary agencies developed in the United States in response to numerous social problems, including joblessness, poverty, and overcrowded housing. Later, during the depression of 1929, in response to the economic crisis, we saw another critical change—the entry of the federal government into social welfare. The voluntary and public sectors together formed an elaborate system of social welfare that, over the years, has expanded and retracted. The consequences of retractions of the social welfare system are most apparent in urban communities, where problems such as poverty, domestic and community violence, substance abuse, and homelessness affect millions of people.

Yet we still hear the question, "what does social welfare policy have to do with social work practice?" Students, and even some seasoned social workers, continue to question this connection, and wonder why social workers need to be concerned with policy. Why not just confine the study of social work to developing skills for direct practice? Haynes and Mickelson (2000) have addressed the same issue:

I still hear from some students and from some community practitioners, the question, 'What does policy and political action have to do with what I'll be practicing?' In other words, 'What do private troubles have to do with public issues?'

We must define private troubles as public issues right now . . . Does it make any sense for clinicians to spend hundreds of hours to keep a family together, only to watch public policy rip them apart again? Is it reasonable to work to empower parents to address the issues facing them, and then leave them with outdated and punitive policies that may destroy them? If we are willing to devote everything it takes to keep a family functioning and intact, then we must also be willing to turn our efforts to advocacy in the political arena.

We must simultaneously pull our clients out of the destructive river *and* go upstream to prevent their being pushed in (p. 31).

By thinking about social work practice from the broad perspective of client, agency, and policy practice, students can more readily gain an appreciation for what social work can accomplish. In this conceptualization, client, agency, and policy practice are on a horizontal plane, rather than the vertical, hierarchical level suggested by the terms "micro, mezzo, and macro." Neither client, nor agency, nor policy is larger or smaller than the other. They all are equally important, and social workers need to attend to all of them. They are all happening simultaneously, and each impacts the other at all times.

This perspective also reflects the broad scope of social work activities described by NASW (1996), which includes:

direct practice, community organizing, supervision, consultation, administration, advocacy, social and political action, policy development and implementation, education, and research and evaluation. Social workers seek to enhance the capacity of people to address their own needs. Social workers also seek to promote the responsiveness of organizations, communities, and other social institutions to individuals' needs and social problems (p.1).

When thinking about social work in complex urban settings, with their variety of large bureaucracies and the urgency of coordinating services to clients, the importance of the role that agencies play in the process of the delivery of services becomes clear. Yet, the agency as a system has not received sufficient attention and study, and the role of social workers in agency practice is often misunderstood. For example, one of the authors was talking to a student who was thinking about applying to an undergraduate social work program. The student was uncertain about what to do, and after talking about her goals, she said, "I don't want to be a social worker, I want to run an agency that helps people." To many people, as to this student, the notion of "being a social worker" is limited to client practice. This student was saying that she wanted to be involved with agency practice, a valid and important role for social workers, but one that often is not recognized as such. While one would question how realistic it is to plan to start out a career by running an agency, being an agency administrator surely is a goal to work toward as one moves along the career ladder within the profession.

In addition, as students do field placements and later are employed in social agencies, they can realize that the agency is a place where social workers network to figure out how clients can be better served. The agency also provides opportunities for social workers to discuss the policies that impact their clients, including those that are beneficial as well as those that are detrimental. It is a place where social workers can work together to advocate and work toward change, and feel part of a profession that is effective in bringing about change. This makes it possible for the social worker to not only be concerned with the single client, but to simultaneously be concerned with social action and direct her or his energies to a *cause*, as well as to a *case*.

Social work students also learn that there are many opportunities to work in client, agency, and policy practice simultaneously. For example:

- A social worker providing direct services to clients might also supervise students doing their fieldwork at the agency, and also lobby at the state capital to advocate for a new licensing bill for social work
- A social work administrator in an agency might also carry some direct service cases, as well as being active in PACE, the political arm of NASW, to advocate for health-care reform
- A policy analyst working for an agency could also have a small private practice as a social worker

By keeping client, agency and policy practice in sight at all times, and integrating them in day-to-day practice, we can experience the richness that the social work profession can offer.

REFERENCES

Haynes, K. S. & Mickelson, J. S. (2000). *Affecting change* (4th ed.). New York: Longman.

National Association of Social Workers. (1996). *Code of Ethics*. Washington, DC: Author.

Code of Ethics of the National Association of Social Workers

Approved by the 1996 NASW Delegate Assembly and Revised by the 1999 NASW Delegate Assembly

Preamble

The primary mission of the social work profession is to enhance human well-being and help meet the basic human needs of all people, with particular attention to the needs and empowerment of people who are vulnerable, oppressed, and living in poverty. A historic and defining feature of social work is the profession's focus on individual well-being in a social context and the well-being of society. Fundamental to social work is attention to the environmental forces that create, contribute to, and address problems in living.

Social workers promote social justice and social change with and on behalf of clients. "Clients" is used inclusively to refer to individuals, families, groups, organizations, and communities. Social workers are sensitive to cultural and ethnic diversity and strive to end discrimination, oppression, poverty, and other forms of social injustice. These activities may be in the form of direct practice, community organizing, supervision, consultation, administration, advocacy, social and political action, policy development and implementation, education, and research and evaluation. Social workers seek to enhance the capacity of people to address their own needs. Social workers also seek to promote the responsiveness of organizations, communities, and other social institutions to individuals' needs and social problems.

The mission of the social work profession is rooted in a set of core values. These core values, embraced by social workers throughout the profession's history, are the foundation of social work's unique purpose and perspective:

- service
- social justice
- dignity and worth of the person
- importance of human relationships
- integrity
- competence

This constellation of core values reflects what is unique to the social work profession. Core values, and the principles that flow from them, must be balanced within the context and complexity of the human experience.

Purpose of the NASW Code of Ethics

Professional ethics are at the core of social work. The profession has an obligation to articulate its basic values, ethical principles, and ethical standards. The *NASW Code of Ethics* sets forth these values, principles, and standards to guide social workers' conduct. The Code is relevant to all social workers and social work students, regardless of their professional functions, the settings in which they work, or the populations they serve.

The *NASW Code of Ethics* serves six purposes:

1. The Code identifies core values on which social work's mission is based.
2. The Code summarizes broad ethical principles that reflect the profession's core values and establishes a set of specific ethical standards that should be used to guide social work practice.
3. The Code is designed to help social workers identify relevant considerations when professional obligations conflict or ethical uncertainties arise.
4. The Code provides ethical standards to which the general public can hold the social work profession accountable.
5. The Code socializes practitioners new to the field to social work's mission, values, ethical principles, and ethical standards.
6. The Code articulates standards that the social work profession itself can use to assess whether social workers have engaged in unethical conduct. NASW has formal procedures to adjudicate ethics complaints filed against its members.* In subscribing to this Code, social workers are required to cooperate in its implementation, participate in NASW adjudication proceedings, and abide by any NASW disciplinary rulings or sanctions based on it.

The Code offers a set of values, principles, and standards to guide decision making and conduct when ethical issues arise. It does not provide a set of rules that prescribe how social workers should act in all situations. Specific applications of the Code must take into account the context in which it is being considered and the possibility of conflicts among the Code's values, principles, and standards. Ethical responsibilities flow from all human relationships, from the personal and familial to the social and professional.

Further, the *NASW Code of Ethics* does not specify which values, principles, and standards are most important and ought to outweigh others in instances when they conflict. Reasonable differences of opinion can and do exist among social workers with respect to the ways in which values, ethical principles, and ethical standards should be rank ordered when they conflict. Ethical decision making in a given situation must apply the informed judgment of the individual social worker and should also consider

*For information on NASW adjudication procedures, see *NASW Procedures for the Adjudication of Grievances*.

how the issues would be judged in a peer review process where the ethical standards of the profession would be applied.

Ethical decision making is a process. There are many instances in social work where simple answers are not available to resolve complex ethical issues. Social workers should take into consideration all the values, principles, and standards in this Code that are relevant to any situation in which ethical judgment is warranted. Social workers' decisions and actions should be consistent with the spirit as well as the letter of this Code.

In addition to this Code, there are many other sources of information about ethical thinking that may be useful. Social workers should consider ethical theory and principles generally, social work theory and research, laws, regulations, agency policies, and other relevant codes of ethics, recognizing that among codes of ethics social workers should consider the *NASW Code of Ethics* as their primary source. Social workers also should be aware of the impact on ethical decision making of their clients' and their own personal values and cultural and religious beliefs and practices. They should be aware of any conflicts between personal and professional values and deal with them responsibly. For additional guidance social workers should consult the relevant literature on professional ethics and ethical decision making and seek appropriate consultation when faced with ethical dilemmas. This may involve consultation with an agency-based or social work organization's ethics committee, a regulatory body, knowledgeable colleagues, supervisors, or legal counsel.

Instances may arise when social workers' ethical obligations conflict with agency policies or relevant laws or regulations. When such conflicts occur, social workers must make a responsible effort to resolve the conflict in a manner that is consistent with the values, principles, and standards expressed in this Code. If a reasonable resolution of the conflict does not appear possible, social workers should seek proper consultation before making a decision.

The *NASW Code of Ethics* is to be used by NASW and by individuals, agencies, organizations, and bodies (such as licensing and regulatory boards, professional liability insurance providers, courts of law, agency boards of directors, government agencies, and other professional groups) that choose to adopt it or use it as a frame of reference. Violation of standards in this Code does not automatically imply legal liability or violation of the law. Such determination can only be made in the context of legal and judicial proceedings. Alleged violations of the Code would be subject to a peer review process. Such processes are generally separate from legal or administrative procedures and insulated from legal review or proceedings to allow the profession to counsel and discipline its own members.

A code of ethics cannot guarantee ethical behavior. Moreover, a code of ethics cannot resolve all ethical issues or disputes or capture the richness and complexity involved in striving to make responsible choices within a moral community. Rather, a code of ethics sets forth values, ethical principles, and ethical standards to which professionals aspire and by which their actions can be judged. Social workers' ethical behavior should result from their personal commitment to engage in ethical practice. The *NASW Code of Ethics* reflects the commitment of all social workers to uphold the profession's values and to act ethically. Principles and standards must be applied by individuals of good character who discern moral questions and, in good faith, seek to make reliable ethical judgments.

Ethical Principles

The following broad ethical principles are based on social work's core values of service, social justice, dignity and worth of the person, importance of human relationships, integrity, and competence. These principles set forth ideals to which all social workers should aspire.

Value: Service

Ethical Principle: Social workers' primary goal is to help people in need and to address social problems.

Social workers elevate service to others above self-interest. Social workers draw on their knowledge, values, and skills to help people in need and to address social problems. Social workers are encouraged to volunteer some portion of their professional skills with no expectation of significant financial return (pro bono service).

Value: Social Justice

Ethical Principle: Social workers challenge social injustice.

Social workers pursue social change, particularly with and on behalf of vulnerable and oppressed individuals and groups of people. Social workers' social change efforts are focused primarily on issues of poverty, unemployment, discrimination, and other forms of social injustice. These activities seek to promote sensitivity to and knowledge about oppression and cultural and ethnic diversity. Social workers strive to ensure access to needed information, services, and resources; equality of opportunity; and meaningful participation in decision making for all people.

Value: Dignity and Worth of the Person

Ethical Principle: Social workers respect the inherent dignity and worth of the person.

Social workers treat each person in a caring and respectful fashion, mindful of individual differences and cultural and ethnic diversity. Social workers promote clients' socially responsible self-determination. Social workers seek to enhance clients' capacity and opportunity to change and to address their own needs. Social workers are cognizant of their dual responsibility to clients and to the broader society. They seek to resolve conflicts between clients' interests and the broader society's interests in a socially responsible manner consistent with the values, ethical principles, and ethical standards of the profession.

Value: Importance of Human Relationships

Ethical Principle: Social workers recognize the central importance of human relationships.

Social workers understand that relationships between and among people are an important vehicle for change. Social workers engage people as partners in the helping process. Social workers seek to strengthen relationships among people in a purposeful effort to promote, restore, maintain, and enhance the well-being of individuals, families, social groups, organizations, and communities.

Value: Integrity

Ethical Principle: Social workers behave in a trustworthy manner.

Social workers are continually aware of the profession's mission, values, ethical principles, and ethical standards and practice in a manner consistent with them. Social workers act honestly and responsibly and promote ethical practices on the part of the organizations with which they are affiliated.

Value: Competence

Ethical Principle: Social workers practice within their areas of competence and develop and enhance their professional expertise.

Social workers continually strive to increase their professional knowledge and skills and to apply them in practice. Social workers should aspire to contribute to the knowledge base of the profession.

Ethical Standards

The following ethical standards are relevant to the professional activities of all social workers. These standards concern (1) social workers' ethical responsibilities to clients, (2) social workers' ethical responsibilities to colleagues, (3) social workers' ethical responsibilities in practice settings, (4) social workers' ethical responsibilities as professionals, (5) social workers' ethical responsibilities to the social work profession, and (6) social workers' ethical responsibilities to the broader society.

Some of the standards that follow are enforceable guidelines for professional conduct, and some are aspirational. The extent to which each standard is enforceable is a matter of professional judgment to be exercised by those responsible for reviewing alleged violations of ethical standards.

1. Social Workers' Ethical Responsibilities to Clients

1.01 Commitment to Clients

Social workers' primary responsibility is to promote the well-being of clients. In general, clients' interests are primary. However, social workers' responsibility to the larger society or specific legal obligations may on limited occasions supersede the loyalty owed clients, and clients should be so advised. (Examples include when a social worker is required by law to report that a client has abused a child or has threatened to harm self or others.)

1.02 Self-Determination

Social workers respect and promote the right of clients to self-determination and assist clients in their efforts to identify and clarify their goals. Social workers may limit clients' right to self-determination when, in the social workers' professional judgment, clients' actions or potential actions pose a serious, foreseeable, and imminent risk to themselves or others.

1.03 Informed Consent

(a) Social workers should provide services to clients only in the context of a professional relationship based, when appropriate, on valid informed consent. Social workers should use clear and understandable language to inform clients of the purpose of the services, risks related to the services, limits to services because of the requirements of a third-party payer, relevant costs, reasonable alternatives, clients' right to refuse or withdraw consent, and the time frame covered by the consent. Social workers should provide clients with an opportunity to ask questions.

(b) In instances when clients are not literate or have difficulty understanding the primary language used in the practice setting, social workers should take steps to ensure clients' comprehension. This may include providing clients with a detailed verbal explanation or arranging for a qualified interpreter or translator whenever possible.

(c) In instances when clients lack the capacity to provide informed consent, social workers should protect clients' interests by seeking permission from an appropriate third party, informing clients consistent with the clients' level of understanding. In such instances social workers should seek to ensure that the third party acts in a manner consistent with clients' wishes and interests. Social workers should take reasonable steps to enhance such clients' ability to give informed consent.

(d) In instances when clients are receiving services involuntarily, social workers should provide information about the nature and extent of services and about the extent of clients' right to refuse service.

(e) Social workers who provide services via electronic media (such as computer, telephone, radio, and television) should inform recipients of the limitations and risks associated with such services.

(f) Social workers should obtain clients' informed consent before audiotaping or videotaping clients or permitting observation of services to clients by a third party.

1.04 Competence

(a) Social workers should provide services and represent themselves as competent only within the boundaries of their education, training, license, certification, consultation received, supervised experience, or other relevant professional experience.

(b) Social workers should provide services in substantive areas or use intervention techniques or approaches that are new to them only after engaging in appropriate study, training, consultation, and supervision from people who are competent in those interventions or techniques.

(c) When generally recognized standards do not exist with respect to an emerging area of practice, social workers should exercise careful judgment and take responsible steps (including appropriate education, research, training, consultation, and supervision) to ensure the competence of their work and to protect clients from harm.

1.05 Cultural Competence and Social Diversity

(a) Social workers should understand culture and its function in human behavior and society, recognizing the strengths that exist in all cultures.

(b) Social workers should have a knowledge base of their clients' cultures and be able to demonstrate competence in the provision of services that are sensitive to clients' cultures and to differences among people and cultural groups.

(c) Social workers should obtain education about and seek to understand the nature of social diversity and oppression with respect to race, ethnicity, national origin, color, sex, sexual orientation, age, marital status, political belief, religion, and mental or physical disability.

1.06 Conflicts of Interest

(a) Social workers should be alert to and avoid conflicts of interest that interfere with the exercise of professional discretion and impartial judgment. Social workers should inform clients when a real or potential conflict of interest arises and take reasonable steps to resolve the issue in a manner that makes the clients' interests primary and protects clients' interests to the greatest extent possible. In some cases, protecting clients' interests may require termination of the professional relationship with proper referral of the client.

(b) Social workers should not take unfair advantage of any professional relationship or exploit others to further their personal, religious, political, or business interests.

(c) Social workers should not engage in dual or multiple relationships with clients or former clients in which there is a risk of exploitation or potential harm to the client. In instances when dual or multiple relationships are unavoidable, social workers should take steps to protect clients and are responsible for setting clear, appropriate, and culturally sensitive boundaries. (Dual or multiple relationships occur when social workers relate to clients in more than one relationship, whether professional, social, or business. Dual or multiple relationships can occur simultaneously or consecutively.)

(d) When social workers provide services to two or more people who have a relationship with each other (for example, couples, family members), social workers should clarify with all parties which individuals will be considered clients and the nature of social workers' professional obligations to the various individuals who are receiving services. Social workers who anticipate a conflict of interest among the individuals receiving services or who anticipate having to perform in potentially conflicting roles (for example, when a social worker is asked to testify in a child custody dispute or divorce proceedings involving clients) should clarify their role with the parties involved and take appropriate action to minimize any conflict of interest.

1.07 Privacy and Confidentiality

(a) Social workers should respect clients' right to privacy. Social workers should not solicit private information from clients unless it is essential to providing services or conducting social work evaluation or research. Once private information is shared, standards of confidentiality apply.

(b) Social workers may disclose confidential information when appropriate with valid consent from a client or a person legally authorized to consent on behalf of a client.

(c) Social workers should protect the confidentiality of all information obtained in the course of professional service, except for compelling professional reasons. The general expectation that social workers will keep information confidential does not apply when disclosure is necessary to prevent serious, foreseeable, and imminent harm to a client or other identifiable person. In all instances, social workers should disclose the least amount of confidential information necessary to achieve the desired purpose; only information that is directly relevant to the purpose for which the disclosure is made should be revealed.

(d) Social workers should inform clients, to the extent possible, about the disclosure of confidential information and the potential consequences, when feasible before the disclosure is made. This applies whether social workers disclose confidential information on the basis of a legal requirement or client consent.

(e) Social workers should discuss with clients and other interested parties the nature of confidentiality and limitations of clients' right to confidentiality. Social workers should review with clients circumstances where confidential information may be requested and where disclosure of confidential information may be legally required. This discussion should occur as soon as possible in the social worker–client relationship and as needed throughout the course of the relationship.

(f) When social workers provide counseling services to families, couples, or groups, social workers should seek agreement among the parties involved concerning each individual's right to confidentiality and obligation to preserve the confidentiality of information shared by others. Social workers should inform participants in family, couples, or group counseling that social workers cannot guarantee that all participants will honor such agreements.

(g) Social workers should inform clients involved in family, couples, marital, or group counseling of the social worker's, employer's, and agency's policy concerning the social worker's disclosure of confidential information among the parties involved in the counseling.

(h) Social workers should not disclose confidential information to third-party payers unless clients have authorized such disclosure.

(i) Social workers should not discuss confidential information in any setting unless privacy can be ensured. Social workers should not discuss confidential information in public or semipublic areas such as hallways, waiting rooms, elevators, and restaurants.

(j) Social workers should protect the confidentiality of clients during legal proceedings to the extent permitted by law. When a court of law or other legally authorized body orders social workers to disclose confidential or privileged information without a client's consent and such disclosure could cause harm to the client, social workers should request that the court withdraw the order or limit the order as narrowly as possible or maintain the records under seal, unavailable for public inspection.

(k) Social workers should protect the confidentiality of clients when responding to requests from members of the media.

(l) Social workers should protect the confidentiality of clients' written and electronic records and other sensitive information. Social workers should take reasonable steps to ensure that clients' records are stored in a secure location and that clients' records are not available to others who are not authorized to have access.

(m) Social workers should take precautions to ensure and maintain the confidentiality of information transmitted to other parties through the use of computers, electronic mail, facsimile machines, telephones and telephone answering machines, and other electronic or computer technology. Disclosure of identifying information should be avoided whenever possible.

(n) Social workers should transfer or dispose of clients' records in a manner that protects clients' confidentiality and is consistent with state statutes governing records and social work licensure.

(o) Social workers should take reasonable precautions to protect client confidentiality in the event of the social worker's termination of practice, incapacitation, or death.

(p) Social workers should not disclose identifying information when discussing clients for teaching or training purposes unless the client has consented to disclosure of confidential information.

(q) Social workers should not disclose identifying information when discussing clients with consultants unless the client has consented to disclosure of confidential information or there is a compelling need for such disclosure.

(r) Social workers should protect the confidentiality of deceased clients consistent with the preceding standards.

1.08 Access to Records

(a) Social workers should provide clients with reasonable access to records concerning the clients. Social workers who are concerned that clients' access to their records could cause serious misunderstanding or harm to the client should provide assistance in interpreting the records and consultation with the client regarding the records. Social workers should limit clients' access to their records, or portions of their records, only in exceptional circumstances when there is compelling evidence that such access would cause serious harm to the client. Both clients' requests and the rationale for withholding some or all of the record should be documented in clients' files.

(b) When providing clients with access to their records, social workers should take steps to protect the confidentiality of other individuals identified or discussed in such records.

1.09 Sexual Relationships

(a) Social workers should under no circumstances engage in sexual activities or sexual contact with current clients, whether such contact is consensual or forced.

(b) Social workers should not engage in sexual activities or sexual contact with clients' relatives or other individuals with whom clients maintain a close personal relationship when there is a risk of exploitation or potential harm to the client. Sexual activity or sexual contact with clients' relatives or other individuals with whom clients maintain a personal relationship has the potential to be harmful to the client and may make it difficult for the social worker and client to maintain appropriate professional boundaries. Social workers—not their clients, their clients' relatives, or other individuals with whom the client maintains a personal relationship—assume the full burden for setting clear, appropriate, and culturally sensitive boundaries.

(c) Social workers should not engage in sexual activities or sexual contact with former clients because of the potential for harm to the client. If social workers engage in conduct contrary to this prohibition or claim that an exception to this prohibition is warranted because of extraordinary circumstances, it is social workers—not their clients—who assume the full burden of demonstrating that the former client has not been exploited, coerced, or manipulated, intentionally or unintentionally.

(d) Social workers should not provide clinical services to individuals with whom they have had a prior sexual relationship. Providing clinical services to a former sexual partner has the potential to be harmful to the individual and is likely to make it difficult for the social worker and individual to maintain appropriate professional boundaries.

1.10 Physical Contact

Social workers should not engage in physical contact with clients when there is a possibility of psychological harm to the client as a result of the contact (such as cradling or caressing clients). Social workers who engage in appropriate physical contact with clients are responsible for setting clear, appropriate, and culturally sensitive boundaries that govern such physical contact.

1.11 Sexual Harassment

Social workers should not sexually harass clients. Sexual harassment includes sexual advances, sexual solicitation, requests for sexual favors, and other verbal or physical conduct of a sexual nature.

1.12 Derogatory Language

Social workers should not use derogatory language in their written or verbal communications to or about clients. Social workers should use accurate and respectful language in all communications to and about clients.

1.13 Payment for Services

(a) When setting fees, social workers should ensure that the fees are fair, reasonable, and commensurate with the services performed. Consideration should be given to clients' ability to pay.

(b) Social workers should avoid accepting goods or services from clients as payment for professional services. Bartering arrangements, particularly involving services, create the potential for conflicts of interest, exploitation, and inappropriate boundaries in social workers' relationships with clients. Social workers should explore and may participate in bartering only in very limited circumstances when it can be demonstrated that such arrangements are an accepted practice among professionals in the local community, considered to be essential for the provision of services, negotiated without coercion, and entered into at the client's initiative and with the client's informed consent. Social workers who accept goods or services from clients as payment for professional services assume the full burden of demonstrating that this arrangement will not be detrimental to the client or the professional relationship.

(c) Social workers should not solicit a private fee or other remuneration for providing services to clients who are entitled to such available services through the social workers' employer or agency.

1.14 Clients Who Lack Decision-Making Capacity

When social workers act on behalf of clients who lack the capacity to make informed decisions, social workers should take reasonable steps to safeguard the interests and rights of those clients.

1.15 Interruption of Services

Social workers should make reasonable efforts to ensure continuity of services in the event that services are interrupted by factors such as unavailability, relocation, illness, disability, or death.

1.16 Termination of Services

(a) Social workers should terminate services to clients and professional relationships with them when such services and relationships are no longer required or no longer serve the clients' needs or interests.

(b) Social workers should take reasonable steps to avoid abandoning clients who are still in need of services. Social workers should withdraw services precipitously only under unusual circumstances, giving careful consideration to all factors in the situation and taking care to minimize possible adverse effects. Social workers should assist in making appropriate arrangements for continuation of services when necessary.

(c) Social workers in fee-for-service settings may terminate services to clients who are not paying an overdue balance if the financial contractual arrangements have been made clear to the client, if the client does not pose an imminent danger to self or others, and if the clinical and other consequences of the current nonpayment have been addressed and discussed with the client.

(d) Social workers should not terminate services to pursue a social, financial, or sexual relationship with a client.

(e) Social workers who anticipate the termination or interruption of services to clients should notify clients promptly and seek the transfer, referral, or continuation of services in relation to the clients' needs and preferences.

(f) Social workers who are leaving an employment setting should inform clients of appropriate options for the continuation of services and of the benefits and risks of the options.

2. Social Workers' Ethical Responsibilities to Colleagues

2.01 Respect

(a) Social workers should treat colleagues with respect and should represent accurately and fairly the qualifications, views, and obligations of colleagues.

(b) Social workers should avoid unwarranted negative criticism of colleagues in communications with clients or with other professionals. Unwarranted negative criticism may include demeaning comments that refer to colleagues' level of competence or to individuals' attributes such as race, ethnicity, national origin, color, sex, sexual orientation, age, marital status, political belief, religion, and mental or physical disability.

(c) Social workers should cooperate with social work colleagues and with colleagues of other professions when such cooperation serves the well-being of clients.

2.02 Confidentiality

Social workers should respect confidential information shared by colleagues in the course of their professional relationships and transactions. Social workers should ensure that such colleagues understand social workers' obligation to respect confidentiality and any exceptions related to it.

2.03 Interdisciplinary Collaboration

(a) Social workers who are members of an interdisciplinary team should participate in and contribute to decisions that affect the well-being of clients by drawing on the perspectives, values, and experiences of the social work profession. Professional and ethical obligations of the interdisciplinary team as a whole and of its individual members should be clearly established.

(b) Social workers for whom a team decision raises ethical concerns should attempt to resolve the disagreement through appropriate channels. If the disagreement cannot be resolved, social workers should pursue other avenues to address their concerns consistent with client well-being.

2.04 Disputes Involving Colleagues

(a) Social workers should not take advantage of a dispute between a colleague and an employer to obtain a position or otherwise advance the social workers' own interests.

(b) Social workers should not exploit clients in disputes with colleagues or engage clients in any inappropriate discussion of conflicts between social workers and their colleagues.

2.05 Consultation

(a) Social workers should seek the advice and counsel of colleagues whenever such consultation is in the best interests of clients.

(b) Social workers should keep themselves informed about colleagues' areas of expertise and competencies. Social workers should seek consultation only from colleagues who have demonstrated knowledge, expertise, and competence related to the subject of the consultation.

(c) When consulting with colleagues about clients, social workers should disclose the least amount of information necessary to achieve the purposes of the consultation.

2.06 Referral for Services

(a) Social workers should refer clients to other professionals when the other professionals' specialized knowledge or expertise is needed to serve clients fully or when social workers believe that they are not being effective or making reasonable progress with clients and that additional service is required.

(b) Social workers who refer clients to other professionals should take appropriate steps to facilitate an orderly transfer of responsibility. Social workers who refer clients to other professionals should disclose, with clients' consent, all pertinent information to the new service providers.

(c) Social workers are prohibited from giving or receiving payment for a referral when no professional service is provided by the referring social worker.

2.07 Sexual Relationships

(a) Social workers who function as supervisors or educators should not engage in sexual activities or contact with supervisees, students, trainees, or other colleagues over whom they exercise professional authority.

(b) Social workers should avoid engaging in sexual relationships with colleagues when there is potential for a conflict of interest. Social workers who become involved in, or anticipate becoming involved in, a sexual relationship with a colleague have a duty to transfer professional responsibilities, when necessary, to avoid a conflict of interest.

2.08 Sexual Harassment

Social workers should not sexually harass supervisees, students, trainees, or colleagues. Sexual harassment includes sexual advances, sexual solicitation, requests for sexual favors, and other verbal or physical conduct of a sexual nature.

2.09 Impairment of Colleagues

(a) Social workers who have direct knowledge of a social work colleague's impairment that is due to personal problems, psychosocial distress, substance abuse, or mental health difficulties and that interferes with practice effectiveness should consult with that colleague when feasible and assist the colleague in taking remedial action.

(b) Social workers who believe that a social work colleague's impairment interferes with practice effectiveness and that the colleague has not taken adequate steps to address the impairment should take action through appropriate channels established by employers, agencies, NASW, licensing and regulatory bodies, and other professional organizations.

2.10 Incompetence of Colleagues

(a) Social workers who have direct knowledge of a social work colleague's incompetence should consult with that colleague when feasible and assist the colleague in taking remedial action.

(b) Social workers who believe that a social work colleague is incompetent and has not taken adequate steps to address the incompetence should take action through appropriate channels established by employers, agencies, NASW, licensing and regulatory bodies, and other professional organizations.

2.11 Unethical Conduct of Colleagues

(a) Social workers should take adequate measures to discourage, prevent, expose, and correct the unethical conduct of colleagues.

(b) Social workers should be knowledgeable about established policies and procedures for handling concerns about colleagues' unethical behavior. Social workers should be familiar with national, state, and local procedures for handling ethics complaints. These include policies and procedures created by NASW, licensing and regulatory bodies, employers, agencies, and other professional organizations.

(c) Social workers who believe that a colleague has acted unethically should seek resolution by discussing their concerns with the colleague when feasible and when such discussion is likely to be productive.

(d) When necessary, social workers who believe that a colleague has acted unethically should take action through appropriate formal channels (such as contacting a state licensing board or regulatory body, an NASW committee on inquiry, or other professional ethics committees).

(e) Social workers should defend and assist colleagues who are unjustly charged with unethical conduct.

3. Social Workers' Ethical Responsibilities in Practice Settings

3.01 Supervision and Consultation

(a) Social workers who provide supervision or consultation should have the necessary knowledge and skill to supervise or consult appropriately and should do so only within their areas of knowledge and competence.

(b) Social workers who provide supervision or consultation are responsible for setting clear, appropriate, and culturally sensitive boundaries.

(c) Social workers should not engage in any dual or multiple relationships with supervisees in which there is a risk of exploitation of or potential harm to the supervisee.

(d) Social workers who provide supervision should evaluate supervisees' performance in a manner that is fair and respectful.

3.02 Education and Training

(a) Social workers who function as educators, field instructors for students, or trainers should provide instruction only within their areas of knowledge and competence and should provide instruction based on the most current information and knowledge available in the profession.

(b) Social workers who function as educators or field instructors for students should evaluate students' performance in a manner that is fair and respectful.

(c) Social workers who function as educators or field instructors for students should take reasonable steps to ensure that clients are routinely informed when services are being provided by students.

(d) Social workers who function as educators or field instructors for students should not engage in any dual or multiple relationships with students in which there is a risk of exploitation or potential harm to the student. Social work educators and field instructors are responsible for setting clear, appropriate, and culturally sensitive boundaries.

3.03 Performance Evaluation

Social workers who have responsibility for evaluating the performance of others should fulfill such responsibility in a fair and considerate manner and on the basis of clearly stated criteria.

3.04 Client Records

(a) Social workers should take reasonable steps to ensure that documentation in records is accurate and reflects the services provided.

(b) Social workers should include sufficient and timely documentation in records to facilitate the delivery of services and to ensure continuity of services provided to clients in the future.

(c) Social workers' documentation should protect clients' privacy to the extent that is possible and appropriate and should include only information that is directly relevant to the delivery of services.

(d) Social workers should store records following the termination of services to ensure reasonable future access. Records should be maintained for the number of years required by state statutes or relevant contracts.

3.05 Billing

Social workers should establish and maintain billing practices that accurately reflect the nature and extent of services provided and that identify who provided the service in the practice setting.

3.06 Client Transfer

(a) When an individual who is receiving services from another agency or colleague contacts a social worker for services, the social worker should carefully consider the client's needs before agreeing to provide services. To minimize possible confusion and conflict, social workers should discuss with potential clients the nature of the clients' current relationship with other service providers and the implications, including possible benefits or risks, of entering into a relationship with a new service provider.

(b) If a new client has been served by another agency or colleague, social workers should discuss with the client whether consultation with the previous service provider is in the client's best interest.

3.07 Administration

(a) Social work administrators should advocate within and outside their agencies for adequate resources to meet clients' needs.

(b) Social workers should advocate for resource allocation procedures that are open and fair. When not all clients' needs can be met, an allocation procedure should be developed that is nondiscriminatory and based on appropriate and consistently applied principles.

(c) Social workers who are administrators should take reasonable steps to ensure that adequate agency or organizational resources are available to provide appropriate staff supervision.

(d) Social work administrators should take reasonable steps to ensure that the working environment for which they are responsible is consistent with and encourages compliance with the *NASW Code of Ethics*. Social work administrators should take reasonable steps to eliminate any conditions in their organizations that violate, interfere with, or discourage compliance with the Code.

3.08 Continuing Education and Staff Development

Social work administrators and supervisors should take reasonable steps to provide or arrange for continuing education and staff development for all staff for whom they are responsible. Continuing education and staff development should address current knowledge and emerging developments related to social work practice and ethics.

3.09 Commitments to Employers

(a) Social workers generally should adhere to commitments made to employers and employing organizations.

(b) Social workers should work to improve employing agencies' policies and procedures and the efficiency and effectiveness of their services.

(c) Social workers should take reasonable steps to ensure that employers are aware of social workers' ethical obligations as set forth in the *NASW Code of Ethics* and of the implications of those obligations for social work practice.

(d) Social workers should not allow an employing organization's policies, procedures, regulations, or administrative orders to interfere with their ethical practice of social work. Social workers should take reasonable steps to ensure that their employing organizations' practices are consistent with the *NASW Code of Ethics*.

(e) Social workers should act to prevent and eliminate discrimination in the employing organization's work assignments and in its employment policies and practices.

(f) Social workers should accept employment or arrange student field placements only in organizations that exercise fair personnel practices.

(g) Social workers should be diligent stewards of the resources of their employing organizations, wisely conserving funds where appropriate and never misappropriating funds or using them for unintended purposes.

3.10 Labor–Management Disputes

(a) Social workers may engage in organized action, including the formation of and participation in labor unions, to improve services to clients and working conditions.

(b) The actions of social workers who are involved in labor–management disputes, job actions, or labor strikes should be guided by the profession's values, ethical principles, and ethical standards. Reasonable differences of opinion exist among social workers concerning their primary obligation as professionals during an actual or threatened labor strike or job action. Social workers should carefully examine relevant issues and their possible impact on clients before deciding on a course of action.

4. Social Workers' Ethical Responsibilities as Professionals

4.01 Competence

(a) Social workers should accept responsibility or employment only on the basis of existing competence or the intention to acquire the necessary competence.

(b) Social workers should strive to become and remain proficient in professional practice and the performance of professional functions. Social workers should critically examine and keep current with emerging knowledge relevant to social work. Social workers should routinely review the professional literature and participate in continuing education relevant to social work practice and social work ethics.

(c) Social workers should base practice on recognized knowledge, including empirically based knowledge, relevant to social work and social work ethics.

4.02 Discrimination

Social workers should not practice, condone, facilitate, or collaborate with any form of discrimination on the basis of race, ethnicity, national origin, color, sex, sexual orientation, age, marital status, political belief, religion, or mental or physical disability.

4.03 Private Conduct

Social workers should not permit their private conduct to interfere with their ability to fulfill their professional responsibilities.

4.04 Dishonesty, Fraud, and Deception

Social workers should not participate in, condone, or be associated with dishonesty, fraud, or deception.

4.05 Impairment

(a) Social workers should not allow their own personal problems, psychosocial distress, legal problems, substance abuse, or mental health difficulties to interfere with their professional judgment and performance or to jeopardize the best interests of people for whom they have a professional responsibility.

(b) Social workers whose personal problems, psychosocial distress, legal problems, substance abuse, or mental health difficulties interfere with their professional judgment and performance should immediately seek consultation and take appropriate remedial action by seeking professional help, making adjustments in workload, terminating practice, or taking any other steps necessary to protect clients and others.

4.06 Misrepresentation

(a) Social workers should make clear distinctions between statements made and actions engaged in as a private individual and as a representative of the social work profession, a professional social work organization, or the social worker's employing agency.

(b) Social workers who speak on behalf of professional social work organizations should accurately represent the official and authorized positions of the organizations.

(c) Social workers should ensure that their representations to clients, agencies, and the public of professional qualifications, credentials, education, competence, affiliations, services provided, or results to be achieved are accurate. Social workers should claim only those relevant professional credentials they actually possess and take steps to correct any inaccuracies or misrepresentations of their credentials by others.

4.07 Solicitations

(a) Social workers should not engage in uninvited solicitation of potential clients who, because of their circumstances, are vulnerable to undue influence, manipulation, or coercion.

(b) Social workers should not engage in solicitation of testimonial endorsements (including solicitation of consent to use a client's prior statement as a testimonial endorsement) from current clients or from other people who, because of their particular circumstances, are vulnerable to undue influence.

4.08 Acknowledging Credit

(a) Social workers should take responsibility and credit, including authorship credit, only for work they have actually performed and to which they have contributed.

(b) Social workers should honestly acknowledge the work of and the contributions made by others.

5. Social Workers' Ethical Responsibilities to the Social Work Profession

5.01 Integrity of the Profession

(a) Social workers should work toward the maintenance and promotion of high standards of practice.

(b) Social workers should uphold and advance the values, ethics, knowledge, and mission of the profession. Social workers should protect, enhance, and improve the integrity of the profession through appropriate study and research, active discussion, and responsible criticism of the profession.

(c) Social workers should contribute time and professional expertise to activities that promote respect for the value, integrity, and competence of the social work profession. These activities may include teaching, research, consultation, service, legislative testimony, presentations in the community, and participation in their professional organizations.

(d) Social workers should contribute to the knowledge base of social work and share with colleagues their knowledge related to practice, research, and ethics. Social workers should seek to contribute to the profession's literature and to share their knowledge at professional meetings and conferences.

(e) Social workers should act to prevent the unauthorized and unqualified practice of social work.

5.02 Evaluation and Research

(a) Social workers should monitor and evaluate policies, the implementation of programs, and practice interventions.

(b) Social workers should promote and facilitate evaluation and research to contribute to the development of knowledge.

(c) Social workers should critically examine and keep current with emerging knowledge relevant to social work and fully use evaluation and research evidence in their professional practice.

(d) Social workers engaged in evaluation or research should carefully consider possible consequences and should follow guidelines developed for the protection of evaluation and research participants. Appropriate institutional review boards should be consulted.

(e) Social workers engaged in evaluation or research should obtain voluntary and written informed consent from participants, when appropriate, without any implied or actual deprivation or penalty for refusal to participate; without undue inducement to participate; and with due regard for participants' well-being, privacy, and dignity. Informed consent should include information about the nature, extent, and duration of the participation requested and disclosure of the risks and benefits of participation in the research.

(f) When evaluation or research participants are incapable of giving informed consent, social workers should provide an appropriate explanation to the participants, obtain the participants' assent to the extent they are able, and obtain written consent from an appropriate proxy.

(g) Social workers should never design or conduct evaluation or research that does not use consent procedures, such as certain forms of naturalistic observation and archival research, unless rigorous and responsible review of the research has found it to be justified because of its prospective scientific, educational, or applied value and unless equally effective alternative procedures that do not involve waiver of consent are not feasible.

(h) Social workers should inform participants of their right to withdraw from evaluation and research at any time without penalty.

(i) Social workers should take appropriate steps to ensure that participants in evaluation and research have access to appropriate supportive services.

(j) Social workers engaged in evaluation or research should protect participants from unwarranted physical or mental distress, harm, danger, or deprivation.

(k) Social workers engaged in the evaluation of services should discuss collected information only for professional purposes and only with people professionally concerned with this information.

(l) Social workers engaged in evaluation or research should ensure the anonymity or confidentiality of participants and of the data obtained from them. Social workers should inform participants of any limits of confidentiality, the measures that will be taken to ensure confidentiality, and when any records containing research data will be destroyed.

(m) Social workers who report evaluation and research results should protect participants' confidentiality by omitting identifying information unless proper consent has been obtained authorizing disclosure.

(n) Social workers should report evaluation and research findings accurately. They should not fabricate or falsify results and should take steps to correct any errors later found in published data using standard publication methods.

(o) Social workers engaged in evaluation or research should be alert to and avoid conflicts of interest and dual relationships with participants, should inform participants when a real or potential conflict of interest arises, and should take steps to resolve the issue in a manner that makes participants' interests primary.

(p) Social workers should educate themselves, their students, and their colleagues about responsible research practices.

6. Social Workers' Ethical Responsibilities to the Broader Society

6.01 Social Welfare

Social workers should promote the general welfare of society, from local to global levels, and the development of people, their communities, and their environments. Social workers should advocate for living conditions conducive to the fulfillment of basic human needs and should promote social, economic, political, and cultural values and institutions that are compatible with the realization of social justice.

6.02 Public Participation

Social workers should facilitate informed participation by the public in shaping social policies and institutions.

6.03 Public Emergencies

Social workers should provide appropriate professional services in public emergencies to the greatest extent possible.

6.04 Social and Political Action

(a) Social workers should engage in social and political action that seeks to ensure that all people have equal access to the resources, employment, services, and opportunities they require to meet their basic human needs and to develop fully. Social workers should be aware of the impact of the political arena on practice and should advocate for changes in policy and legislation to improve social conditions in order to meet basic human needs and promote social justice.

(b) Social workers should act to expand choice and opportunity for all people, with special regard for vulnerable, disadvantaged, oppressed, and exploited people and groups.

(c) Social workers should promote conditions that encourage respect for cultural and social diversity within the United States and globally. Social workers should promote policies and practices that demonstrate respect for difference, support the expansion of cultural knowledge and resources, advocate for programs and institutions that demonstrate cultural competence, and promote policies that safeguard the rights of and confirm equity and social justice for all people.

(d) Social workers should act to prevent and eliminate domination of, exploitation of, and discrimination against any person, group, or class on the basis of race, ethnicity, national origin, color, sex, sexual orientation, age, marital status, political belief, religion, or mental or physical disability.

APPENDIX II

Community Building: Community Service Society of New York

Community Service Society of New York, a private, nonprofit social service organization dedicated to fostering a better life for poor residents of the country's gateway city. Since it began over 150 years ago, CSS has been a leader in the fight against poverty, focusing its efforts on income maintenance, health care, affordable housing and education.

Community Building

In January 1997, the Community Service Society of New York launched a comprehensive community revitalization initiative in Bedford-Stuyvesant, a Brooklyn neighborhood.

Following the examples of comprehensive community building around the country, as well as CSS's own experience as an organizer in housing and political development in New York City, CSS conceived an initiative rooted in "bottom-up" organizing—gathering issues, strategies and decision-making processes from the people who will be directly affected by the effort: neighborhood residents. The core of the CSS plan is to convene a body of grassroots organizations and individual neighborhood leaders as a committee to work toward a common vision of renewal, with CSS staff serving as facilitator. As of December 1997, Long Life Information and Referral Network (Long Life) and Black Veterans for Social Justice (Black Vets) have joined the collaboration.

Concepts and Lessons in Comprehensive Community Building

CSS's model seeks to revitalize neighborhoods by addressing the multiple and interconnected factors that contribute to poverty. The characteristics of comprehensive community organizing that are at the heart of the CSS initiative include:

- *Community-based*, meaning efforts are located in neighborhoods and local residents play a central role in planning, implementing and governing the project.

- Collaborative, with shared resources and responsibility, and shared decision making. Initiatives are guided by a broad-based *partnership* of stakeholders, including individual residents and private, public, and nonprofit actors.
- Acknowledge differences of age, race, gender, and culture and establish *principles of mutual respect and understanding.*
- Focus on existing assets in the community rather than on needs. In building on current resources, initiatives attempt to *incorporate existing organizations* and programs. New programs are developed only if a gap exists.
- Aim to *develop leaders* and *civic capacity* in the community to realize sustained development. Stress the training and development of community leaders and organizations who can continue the revitalization of the neighborhood long after the formal initiative is over.
- Address the issues of poverty in a *holistic*, comprehensive way that cuts across disciplines and agencies. Economic, social, and political issues are inextricably entwined.
- Emphasize the *integration of sophisticated technology, communications*, and *data/policy analysis* in the initiatives. Some feel that the lack of these supports were a major reason that earlier antipoverty efforts did not succeed.

Geographic Focus of the Initiative

During the start-up year, CSS efforts have focused on two building complexes situated on the Gates Avenue corridor, a string of high-density, low-rise, low-income housing. The two blocks of buildings that comprise Medgar Evers Houses is home to 315 families while Gates Avenue Houses spans one block and shelters 160 families. Both buildings were owned by private landlords who were neglecting basic maintenance and security needs. Both owners were benefiting from massive subsidies from HUD.

The Gates Avenue corridor is located in Bedford-Stuyvesant, the largest African-American community in New York City. Eighty-five percent of Bedford-Stuyvesant's residents are African-American; and 15 percent are Latino. Thirty-nine percent of the area's families live below the poverty level; and unemployment is 16 percent.

Setting a Platform of Trust and Achievement: Tenant Organizing

The first year of this initiative (January–December 1997) concentrated on establishing partnerships and a visible presence in the neighborhood, including the undertaking of an ambitious tenant organizing/housing improvement project that will serve as the nucleus for the broader-based community revitalization effort. To launch the project, CSS joined with Long Life Information and Referral Network, a community-based agency providing social services to the developmentally disabled. Northeast Brooklyn Housing Development Corporation also participated in the tenant organizing project in the last year; while East Brooklyn Legal Services represented tenants in legal actions against the delinquent landlords.

In organizing a large group of tenants to work for change in their own homes, and possibly take on the responsibility of home ownership and management in the future, CSS was initiating more than just a housing revitalization project. Our purposes were several:

- To empower and mobilize a significant population in this neighborhood and tangibly improve conditions in buildings that dominate the area in terms of size and the social problems that exist there.
- To demonstrate in a relatively short time the positive results that can be achieved when residents come together to strive toward common goals. The substantial improvement in these enormous building complexes would represent highly visible "wins" to inspire and motivate comprehensive community renewal that, by its very definition, can take years before tangible outcomes are in sight.
- To identify and establish relationships with grassroots partners and individual leaders who would be able to take on active roles in the comprehensive initiative.
- To gain the trust and support of hundreds of area residents.

Milestones in Year One

- Established two tenants associations, the Gates Avenue Tenants Association and the Medgar Evers Tenants Association, both with democratically-elected executive committees, floor captains, and committees in charge of special events, house rules and security, screening, and repairs and maintenance.
- Organizers from CSS, Long Life, and Northeast Brooklyn facilitated legal strategies by East Brooklyn Legal Services that resulted in HUD kicking out the slumlord owners and appointing a receiver for both buildings. The organizers continue to work with tenants to foster a professional and accountable relationship with the receiver, Arco Management, that ensures tenants' voices are heard.
- Much needed repairs have begun and increased security has made the buildings safer.
- A leadership training series for the tenants was implemented. Workshops covered topics such as running meetings, building consensus, negotiating, and critical thinking.
- Recognizing that celebrations and traditions help weave the fabric of a community, residents gathered for Umoja (Unity) Family Day in December 1997. In tandem with Women's History Month in March 1997, CSS and partners hosted an awards ceremony, "Women Steppin' Forward," to honor selected leadership of Gates Avenue Houses, the majority of whom are women. In September, an outdoor festival provided food, entertainment, and opportunities to meet and socialize with neighbors.
- With the assistance of CSS Department of Social Services, ancillary services were provided to the residents: 25 children were able to attend summer camp; 54 children and 9 parents attended Kwanzaa and Christmas celebrations in Manhattan.
- Concerned Tenants for Youth Development united tenants from Gates Avenue and Medgar Evers Houses, as well as members of nearby block associations. Together, they have begun to connect the youth of the Gates Avenue corridor to existing opportunities in youth programs in the area (such as the Jackie Robinson Youth Program, the Bedford-Stuyvesant Culture and Education Program). Recently, as a result of the efforts of Concerned Tenants for Youth Development, 100 Black Men agreed to provide scholarships for their SAT preparatory program for young people from the neighborhood.

What's Ahead

In the coming year,

- Organizers will work with the tenants to determine which ownership structure best fits their needs and desires and prepare them for the ownership transfer process.
- CSS will recruit at least 3 more partners for the community collaboration. The collaboration will begin to meet and develop a common vision, as well as determine its structure, operating guidelines, and future areas of collaboration. In addition, CSS will continue to work with the tenant associations with the intention of them becoming partners in the larger neighborhood-wide collaboration.
- The community partners will discuss the formation of an Advisory Council to enlist the guidance and support of prominent people and institutions and the establishment of a Technical Advisory Committee to explore economic development, job training, and job creation possibilities.

CASE INDEX

NAME INDEX

SUBJECT INDEX